The Intellectual Climate
of
the Early University

The Intellectual Climate

of

the Early University

Essays in Honor of Otto Gründler

edited by

Nancy Van Deusen

Studies in Medieval Culture, XXXIX
Medieval Institute Publications

WESTERN MICHIGAN UNIVERSITY

Kalamazoo, Michigan — 1997

Library of Congress Cataloging-in-Publication Data

The intellectual climate of the early university : essays in honor of
   Otto Gründler / edited by Nancy van Deusen.
         p.   cm. -- (SMC ; 39)
     Includes bibiliographical references.
     ISBN 1-879288-83-4 (casebound : alk. paper). -- ISBN 1-879288-84-2
   (pbk.   : alk. paper)
     1. Education, Medieval--Europe.   2. Universities and colleges-
   -Europe--History.   3. Europe--Intellectual life.   4. Theology-
   -History--Middle Ages, 600-1500.   5. Learning and scholarship-
   -Europe--History--Medieval, 500-1500.   I. Gründler, Otto. II. Van
   Deusen, Nancy (Nancy Elizabeth)   III. Series: Studies in medieval
   culture ; 39.
   CB351.S83 vol. 39
   [LA177]
   940. 1 s--dc21
   [378.4'09'02]   97-12890
                                                                    CIP

Printed in The United States of America

Cover design by Linda K. Judy

Contents

Preface

*I*n the introduction to their edition of Robert Grosseteste's *Hexaemeron*, Richard C. Dales and Servus Gieben summarize the situation of the early university as Grosseteste found and left it, pointing to the tremendous intellectual changes that took place in Grosseteste's lifetime (ca 1175–1253):

> When Grosseteste was born, there were not yet any universities in Europe; the translating activity from Greek and Arabic into Latin was well under way, but had as yet made virtually no impact on European thought, and Theology was far from being a systematic discipline. By the time he died in 1253, the great universities were at the height of their vigor; Greek and Arabic writings had been incorporated into the mainstream of European thought; and Theology was a highly organized scientific discipline.[1]

In spite of a good deal of research and writing concerning it, this amazing period of intellectual transformation—the intellectual climate of the early university—remains in many respects enigmatic. What, for example, was the initial concept that provided a structure for the university, and how did that concept originate? What was the nature of the bond that united the parts of the early university into a whole, and whence came this unique idea of many "modes" of expression of knowledge that were loosely, but actually, joined into a flexible, nevertheless real unity? These questions and the vehement discussions that have attempted to resolve the apparent paradoxes they contain ought not, I believe, be relegated to an old curiosity shop of dscarded preoccupations. Rather, they have relevance for the univerisity today. Precisely this conviction prompted the inception of this volume.

For example, many cf the issues that confronted the early university are issues that an academic professional immediately recognizes, even today. What, for example, *is* the "life of the mind?" What should one learn? What is learning "good for"? What is a discipline, and is it possible for disciplines to reinforce one another? Can some university disciplines be identified as givens, as forming an unquestionably self-evident basis for university study? Or are all university disciplines up for discussion, subject to negotiation, with their respective values and continued inclusion within the academic curriculum dependent almost entirely upon a relatively transient academic market appeal or upon powerful disciplinary cliques to lobby for their inclusion? Is the loudest voice heeded; the still, quiet, voice banished to irrelevance?

How do disciplines align themselves in terms of reciprocity, or of prior/posterior progression? Finally, what, in fact, *is* a university after all? A finishing school? A sports club? A corporation? A group of professional guilds? A paradigm for the culture that supports it? Ideally, a physical, visible, comprehensible expression of what may be most abstract and fragile—intellectual vitality, and the cultivation of idealistic, spiritual, and intellectual values? What is the university's role in government, and how does this ideal, if somewhat ambiguous, "life of the mind," with values that are in essence spiritual, relate to, even translate into, rulership and power in any age or society?

The going, in the thirteenth century, was not easy. Real struggles abounded then—and continue today. A sense of urgency prevailed in the "intellectual climate of the early university," an urgency with which committed academics today can wholeheartedly identify. All of these questions were immensely important as well to an emerging thirteenth-century academic profession, and the members of that profession received real answers to their questions. It is humbling to discover that both their questions and the answers they received are useful not just as historical memorabilia but also for the light they can shed on universities and their needs and aspirations today.

Universities, then and now, are monuments to *cultivation*—monuments to the fact that complex, hidden things and issues do, in fact, exist, to be slowly exposed through a lifetime of patient, daily effort. This is the seat of the power of the university and the crux of its message as an institution as it actively forms a polarity to exigency and daily necessity—a contrast to what is obviously, hastily, conveniently perceived. A university exists to make known what can only be revealed by consistent, dedicated effort. Ultimately, a university exists in order to understand the things that are hidden from ordinary, casual view. This is a message that is subtly reinforced by all of the articles in this volume.

It is especially appropriate that this volume should be published in honor of Otto Gründler. University statesman, dedicated to the idea of the university, tireless in his encouragement of the work and careers of countless academic professionals, Professor Gründler's has been a lifelong cultivation of the ideal of an effective university environment. It is with gratitude that the editor and authors of this volume present this collection of essays to him.

Many of the essays were presented as papers either within the context of a conference entitled "Intellectual Climate of the Early University," sponsored by the Center for Medieval Studies, California State University, Northridge during Fall, 1988, or in a session on the same topic at the annual International Conference in Medieval Studies, organized by Otto Gründler, and held at Western Michigan University, May 1989. Grateful acknowledgment is made for funds from the California State University that made this conference possible.

Nancy Van Deusen
Los Angeles, 1996

Note

1. *Robert Grosseteste. Hexaemeron*, ed. Richard C. Dales and Servus Gieben, O.F.M. Cap (London: Oxford University Press for the British Academy, 1982), p. xi.

The Sentence Collection and the Education of Professional Theologians in the Twelfth Century

Marcia Colish

*I*n the third volume of his study of the Christian tradition, Jaroslav Pelikan surprised many readers, at least at first, by giving pride of place to the twelfth century rather than the thirteenth.[1] While on one level this move was a revisionistic attack on the lingering vestiges of the "Thirteenth, Greatest of Centuries" mentality, Pelikan made a good case for his choice in terms of the actual doctrinal developments of the period. His accent, though, fell on the substance of Christian thought—what the church believed and taught. He left to the side the issue of methodology. My own concern here is the emergence of school theology in the twelfth century. I would thus like to turn attention to the question of theological method, the method created by the early scholastics that continued to inform the university teaching of the high Middle Ages. In looking for an economical way to illustrate how the early scholastics taught theology and the intellectual techniques they tried to foster in their students, I swiftly landed on the twelfth-century sentence collection as a means to that end.

The sentence collection was a standard genre of theological literature during this period, especially during the first half of the twelfth century. Yet, despite its pedagogical centrality, it has suffered a sad fate at the hands of modern scholars. It was depreciated by an earlier generation of medievalists who viewed the full-blown *summae* and *quaestiones disputatae* of the late thirteenth century as the ideal that earlier writers were groaning and travailing to attain, and in terms of which their own efforts could be judged.[2] More recently, the sentence collection has been

1

marginalized by a different group of scholars, anxious to prove that it was in monastic theology, above all the writings of the Cistercians, that the real theological renewal of the twelfth century took place.[3] Whether informed by one or another of these tendentious attitudes, most scholars surveying the twelfth-century theological scene have given the sentence collections a bad press. They depict these works as mediocre, unoriginal *florilegia* and dismiss their authors as mere compilers who advanced their discipline not one bit.

One of the things I propose to argue in this paper is that this assessment of the twelfth-century sentence collectors is unjust. For, once we take the trouble to crack the hermeneutic code of the sentence collection and learn how to read it, we will be able to see that the theologians who used this genre were, indeed, advancing the state of theology in both substance and method and were actually producing the century's most innovative tool for the education of professional theologians. In the body of this paper I would like to accent two of the ways in which the sentence collectors did just that. One aspect of these texts is the training they imparted on how to think theologically, how to appraise, analyze, and criticize the *donneé* of the Christian tradition, and how to use it in dealing with the theological problems of the day, both the hardy perennials and the topics being newly agitated. A second aspect of the sentence collection that I want to consider is its use in constructing a curriculum of theology, a syllabus that addressed the questions of which topics to include, the order in which to present them, and the overall rationale informing these decisions. This second aspect of the subject will thus enable us to see how the sentence collection was used to promote the development of Christian theology as a systematic intellectual enterprise.

I would like to take up the second of these topics first—the sentence collection as a means of developing a systematic and inclusive overview of the theological enterprise. Before going on, it is important to note that the twelfth century invented systematic theology.[4] Systematic theology simply did not exist in the western world before that time. To be sure, a great deal of theology of various other kinds had been written by the church fathers and their successors. But none of these writers had produced a full-scale theological system, with a place for everything and everything in its place. The fact that twelfth-century theologians perceived a need for systematic theology and responded to that need is, on one level, a reflection of their participation in a twelfth-century renaissance that was concerned with the upgrading and professionalizing of all the learned disciplines. As with the other masters in the twelfth-century schools, the theologians were seeking to turn their subject into a professional discipline, by working out an overall rationale for what to teach and how to teach it. On another level, we should also recognize the fact that the scholastics did not hold a monopoly on systematic theology. It was also being written by twelfth-century monastic theologians with quite different aims in mind.

Both in order to demonstrate that last point and to present a contrast that will sharpen our appreciation of what the scholastic theologians were up to, I would like to bring forward two such monastic authors of systematic theology. Both were Germans; both were Benedictines; both wrote in the early twelfth century; and each was as different from the other as both were from their scholastic opposite numbers.[5] The first of these authors I want to discuss is Rupert of Deutz, whose *On the Holy Trinity and Its Works* was written between 1112 and 1116. Rupert is known primarily for his heavy involvement in the political and ecclesiastical fall-out of the Gregorian reform movement in Germany. He devoted much attention to the polemics it occasioned. Yet, in his *On the Holy Trinity* he produced a theological system, one of the earliest of the twelfth century. This work displays many parallels with contemporary and later sentence collections. Rupert covered many of the same topics as they do, and he dealt with them in much the same order, starting with God, then moving to the creation, and then treating the fall of man and its consequences. Further, Rupert's handling of Trinitarian and Christological matters shows both his up-to-date command of the language of Aristotle and Boethius and his familiarity with the technical features of the current debates over the views of Roscellinus of Compiègne. His preference for a literal account of creation displays his responsiveness to the new interest in cosmology fashionable in some cathedral schools at this time. As well, in discussing marriage, Rupert forecast Hugh of St. Victor's later critique of the anti-Pelagian Augustine on this subject by insisting that sexual relations in marriage are not merely a remedy for sin and are not always at least venially sinful, since marriage is a sacrament instituted in Eden before the Fall.

In these and other ways, Rupert's work looks to be on the same wave length as that of the systematic theologians in the cathedral schools west of the Rhine. But, a closer inspection of *On the Holy Trinity* shows this *summa* to be decidedly monastic in character, both in its intended audience and in the mode of theological reflection it demands and promotes. The model Rupert adopted is that of salvation history. In his view, the triune God can best be known in this life, short of mysticism, not primarily through the natural world or through the analogies of the Trinity in the human soul but through the work of divine creation, redemption, and renovation recounted in Holy Scripture. Rupert took the standard relational terms for describing the Trinitarian person *in se*—unbegotten, begotten, and proceeding—and applied them to the work of each Trinitarian person *ad extra*, as revealed in Scripture. This tactic was designed to support the idea that meditation on God, as he reveals himself in Scripture, will lead the mind to a knowledge of the eternal, unmanifested Trinity in itself. Thus, Rupert's entire enterprise yokes systematic theology to the kind of meditative, reflective *lectio divina* specific to the monastic calling, although with a stress on fundamental doctrine more than on ethical edification.

Another monastic author of systematic theology who will prove highly useful for comparative purposes is Honorius Augustodunensis. Like Rupert, he was deeply involved in monastic reform. In particular, he wanted to defend the right of the Benedictines to minister to the laity and, not incidentally, to receive tithes from their parishioners, against contemporary critics who objected both to the tithes and to the low level of theological training among these monastic pastors.[6] The response of Honorius to this objection was forthright and practical. In the first year or two of the twelfth century,[7] he wrote the *Elucidarium*, a work of systematic theology aimed at instructing his *confrères* in the pastoral ministry, enhancing their theological knowledge, and equipping them to meet the perceived needs of their lay congregations.[8] While Honorius's immediate audience was thus a monastic one, his ultimate goal was to instruct the laity. He did not write to stimulate monastic meditation or to encourage theological speculation. He touched firmly, and lightly, on basic doctrines and emphasized instead their practical consequences in ethics, the sacramental life, and the life to come, in a summary overview presentation sparked by vivid imagery, designed to hold an audience whose theological attention span was likely to be short and whose interest in the subject was anything but professional.

At the same time, the schema laid out by the *Elucidarium* is extremely inclusive, coherent, and sophisticated, rivalling and surpassing in this respect the schemata of many of the scholastic systematizers of the next half-century. Honorius began with God and then took up the creation, angels, man, the Fall, the need for redemption, the incarnation and earthly life of Christ, and the earthly survival and extension of Christ's saving work in the church, viewed as his *corpus mysticum*. This ecclesiology provides the framework for the remaining topics Honorius treated, which include the moral and sacramental life of the church and the permanent assignment of its members, following the last judgment and the resurrection of the body, to Heaven or Hell, each described at length and in glorious technicolor. This remarkably cogent and well thought-out schema is, however, combined with an utterly simplistic and catechetical presentation of the material it contains. Honorius was not out to alert his readers to the controversies of the day. Nor did he seek to apprise them of the fact that the authorities sometimes disagree or give them any advice about what to do about such disagreements. Honorius himself was prodigiously learned and in command of some of the most recent theological contributions of his day. But he did not flaunt his knowledge. Since he aimed not at provoking inquiry but at laying questions to rest, he simply stated clearly and firmly the best answers he could find to those questions, without indicating which authorities he used for this purpose and why he preferred their conclusions. As Valerie Flint has aptly noted, in the *Elucidarium* the author's intention was "to reduce the most complex to the most simple, to substitute the answers for the learning process, and so supposedly to render that process unnecessary by the deft finding of answers."[9]

With these two monastic *comparanda* in mind, I would now like to turn to the enterprise of systematic theology as practiced by the sentence collectors, aimed at their intended audience of professional theologians-in-the-making, first from the standpoint of systematic curriculum building and then from the standpoint of how to think theologically. In each case I will draw on a number of schools and masters of theology dating from ca. 1120 to ca. 1160. In what follows, the names in the news may surprise you. But, the fact of the matter is that the most successful and influential of these school theologians are not necessarily the ones accented in the general surveys and given the most media hype in the scholarly literature.

Let me illustrate that last point immediately by beginning with the school of Gilbert of Poitiers, whose trial at Rheims in 1148 as a philosophical and theological radical was the intellectual *cause célèbre* of the mid-twelfth century. Well before Gilbert's ideas had attained their fullest notoriety, he and his disciples had developed a general course in systematic theology, which can be found in two Porretan sentence collections dating to the early 1140s.[10] Here is how the Porretans envisioned the enterprise of systematic theology. They divided their sentence collections into fourteen books. In the first book they treated the problem of theological language in general, followed, in books 2 and 3, by the Trinity and Christology, as specific applications of that problem. The bulk of their work, books 4 through 11, is devoted to the sacraments. Now, the two most prevalent ways of organizing sacramental theology in this period were to discuss the sacraments either in the order of their institution or in the order of their reception. Another prominent scheme was to distinguish sacraments received by all Christians from those, such as marriage and holy orders, received only by some Christians. The Porretans departed from these models and proposed a four-part model of their own, which they then, however, immediately abandoned. Sacraments, they stated, can be divided into rites of initiation, rites of strengthening, rites of return, and rites of perfection. This scheme suggests that the logical place to begin their exposition would be with baptism. But they led off with the Eucharist, even though they defined it as a rite of strengthening. Also, they omitted holy orders, even though they repeatedly mentioned the clergy as administrators of the other sacraments. And, while they regarded marriage as a sacrament, they could not decide to which of these four categories it belongs. In book 10, while discussing penance, they belatedly took up the question of original sin, vice, and virtue, thus presenting the fall of man before his creation and well after the incarnation of Christ, ordained to remedy it. Creation itself was almost an afterthought for the Porretans. We find it, along with a brief reprise on original sin and an even briefer allusion to last things, in book 13, sandwiched inexplicably in between two books dealing with the liturgy of Advent and Lent, respectively.

That this Porretan schema failed to take root is not surprising. The work of an even more radical hot-shot, Peter Abelard, left an even scantier legacy to the cause of systematic theology, even though he has been hailed, in innumerable textbooks, as the father of scholasticism. Abelard's basic weakness as a guide here is that he left no complete work of systematic theology of his own. He was one of those academics constitutionally incapable of finishing anything he started. He essayed three *theologiae*, each of which exists in several fragmentary versions. All announce an agenda and none follows through. Indeed, the sorting out and dating of these *disiecta membra* has become something of a growth industry in recent Abelard scholarship.[11] Taken collectively, the Abelardian fragments state the author's intention to subdivide Christian theology into three parts—faith, charity, and sacraments. In real life, what we have is what Abelard thought, at various points in his career, about the Trinity, Christology, ethical acts as reducible to ethical intentionalities, and the small selection of sacraments in which he was interested. Although Abelard's acknowledged long suit was logic, his theology is sometimes deficient in just that virtue. For example, he gave as his general definition of sacrament the standard Augustinian view that a sacrament is a visible sign of invisible grace. He regarded marriage as a sacrament. But, he stated that he could find nothing in the relations of spouses that signifies grace.[12]

Abelard's followers took as their cue the master's tripartite division of the subject matter. But, rather than trying to fill the gaps he left, thus developing his ideas into a full-scale *summa*, they saw as their task the defense of the positions that had gotten Abelard into trouble, and even the repetition of some of his least lucid and most regrettable formulae and examples.[13] The organizational skills of some of the Abelardians were questionable. The author of the *Ysagoge in theologiam*, for instance, started with man, continued with Christology and the redemption, ethics and the sacraments, and placed angels and God at the end.[14] All the Abelardians omitted major topics that were heavily debated at the time, omissions that are sometimes stunning. Thus, the authors of the two Abelardian *Sententiae Parisiensis* left out penance, a sacrament that no other contemporary theologian ignored;[15] and Hermannus omitted, of all things, original sin.[16] The apparent reason for these strategic omissions on the part of Abelard's disciples was their evident inability to find arguments against Abelard's critics on those points. As a technique of theological education, however, this tactic left, and was perceived to leave, a great deal to be desired in twelfth-century scholastic circles.

Far more influential than the Abelardians and the Porretans was the systematic theology of two other twelfth-century scholastics, Hugh of St. Victor and Peter Lombard. The Lombard comes at the end of my target period. His work attained a classic balance, avoiding many of the problems found in the sentence collections of many of his predecessors and contemporaries. As we all know, his schema became the dominant one, setting its mark on centuries of school and university education. I will consider why this was the case in a moment. But first I would like to discuss Hugh's *On the Sacraments*, on which Peter's *Four Books of Sentences* are notably dependent. Looked at together, these two works stand out immediately as improvements over the Porretan and Abelardian experiments in systematic theology. Not only are they more inclusive and better organized but also they announce a general theme, designed to provide a cogent rationale for the topics covered. In Hugh's case, as is well known, the big theme is the idea of sacrament, which gives the work its title.[17] Hugh's coverage resembles that of Honorius's *Elucidarium*, with the addition of a proof of God's existence. Hugh's organization of these contents is based on his distinction between God's work of institution and his work of restitution. Hugh regarded as sacramental all the modes by which God reveals himself to man and all the modes by which God redeems man. Each of the two books of *On the Sacraments* is devoted, in principle, to one of these two processes. I say "in principle" because the schema developed by Hugh in practice turns out to be less lucid and more redundant than would have been the case had he adhered more rigorously to his announced model. A few illustrations of this point will have to suffice. Although the controlling concept of Hugh's work is the idea of sacrament, he waited until book 1, chapter 9—almost halfway through the work—to give us his definition of the term, even though he had been using it, and in diverse senses, from the beginning. At the start of book 2, he raised for the first time the meaning of the key terms *person*, *substance*, and *nature* with reference to God, giving here a reprise of his teachings on the Trinity and Christology, which he had treated at length early in book 1, although without the benefit of these lexical clarifications. Hugh also introduced his proof of God's existence after he had been discussing God as three and one for some time. In his treatment of the sacraments in the narrow sense, he inserted a consideration of simony in between the Eucharist and marriage. One sometimes does find simony placed under the sacramental umbrella by twelfth-century theologians. But, when this is the case, it typically follows holy orders, as a perversion of that sacrament. Hugh's reasons for placing simony where he does are apparent to him alone.

While acknowledging his debt to Hugh, Peter Lombard offered his own thematic rationale, at the same time as he tightened up Hugh's organization and eliminated the omissions, redundancies, and departures from logic that mar the work of other sentence collectors of his time.[18] His own schema is both logically and theologically coherent. There are only two organizational problems that he failed to solve. He treated Purgatory twice, as a pendant to penance and in his discussion of last things. And, he located ethics in three parts of the *Sentences*, defining virtue in relation to the intentions of the ethical subject in book 1, vices in connection with the fall of man in book 2, and virtues in connection with Christ's human life in book 3. These difficulties aside, his schema is both inclusive and streamlined, while giving due attention to major theological concerns. He began with the divine nature and the Trinity, devoting one of his four books to the subject of God in and of himself, before addressing God as he reveals himself to man. Next comes the creation. Peter started with the angels and then discussed the material world and man, combining a hexaemeral account of creation with an emphasis on man that leads smoothly into the Fall, the vices, grace and free will, and the effects and transmission of original sin. Fully one quarter of Peter's *Sentences* is then devoted to the Incarnation and the Redemption, which sets the stage for the virtues and a general analysis of the nature of ethical acts. After a crisp definition of sacraments in general, which he confined to the salvific rites of the church, he treated all seven of the rites ventilated by contemporaries in this connection, and put his stamp of approval on the septiform principle. He concluded with last things, in a manner fuller than that of the Porretans but far less fulsome and fanciful than that of Honorius. Indeed, a comparison between Peter and Honorius here is very much to the point. With respect to their schemata, Peter devoted huge amounts of space to the very speculative doctrines that Honorius was most anxious to settle with a lapidary, once-over-lightly solution. If it is not found all in one place, Peter's handling of ethics is theoretical and abstract, with none of the specific examples of different callings in the Christian life and their temptations that Honorius inserted to assist readers who were not seen as capable of applying the general principles on their own. As well, Peter pared down his treatment of the next life to its connection with man's ethical and sacramental practice in this life. He confined himself to what can be found in Scripture and the more sober authorities, instead of catering, as Honorius did, to millennial speculation and to the worries and the wild-eyed curiosity of the non-specialist reader.

As for the thematic orientation that Peter added to his *Sentences*, it is a familiar Augustinian concept, but one that he applied in a new way. From Augustine's *On Christian Doctrine* Peter borrowed the distinctions between signs and things, use and enjoyment.[19] With Augustine he agreed that God is the supreme *res*, who alone warrants enjoyment as a good in himself. The created universe, the virtues, and the sacraments are *signa*, to be used in the enjoyment of God. For their part, human beings are to be enjoyed as well as used. They are beings who deserve to be treated as moral ends; and the created universe is ordered to their needs. At the same time, they should enjoy and serve each other with ultimate reference to God and their own salvation. Peter's reassignment of his Augustinian theme to a new task has the effect of reappropriating something known, but with a fresh eye and a fresh insight into the uses to which it may be put. This observation may well serve as our point of transition to the second major dimension of the sentence collection as an educational device, to which I would now like to turn, viz., the sentence collectors' handling of authorities as a means of teaching students how to reason theologically.

In moving to this aspect of the sentence collection, it must be stressed that these works are not mere anthologies of patristic citations.[20] This fact can be appreciated most easily if we read the sentence collections of the period side by side. When we do so, we can see that the theologians did not always cite, or omit, the same authorities. Nor did they always draw the same ammunition from the authors to whom they appealed. And ammunition it is. For, these theologians had positions of their own to defend. Sometimes they were out to find the best possible way of explaining a doctrine that was part of the Christian consensus but that contemporaries were having difficulty understanding or clarifying. Sometimes they were out to promote their own personal interpretation of controversial doctrines, in the teeth of competing arguments. Either way, the biggest reason for their appeal to authorities was to marshal support from them for their own campaigns. In so doing, they were also trying to teach their students, by example, how to do likewise. A second important way in which the scholastic sentence collectors sought to impart the techniques of theological reasoning is by putting authorities to the test, subjecting them to analysis and criticism, and deciding how weighty or valid they are, and whether or not they can be relativized or disregarded as obsolete or irrelevant. A third pedagogical goal also surfaces in these theologians' handling of their authorities. They wanted to hold up the authorities they considered as models of theological reasoning, exploring with their students how those thinkers have moved from their arguments to their conclusions, analyzing as well the intentions that inform the positions at which they arrive. The author's point of departure, and his intellectual process, are as important in decid-

ing what the student is to think about his position as his final destin-
ation. These three methodological concerns sometimes overlap. They are
all found, in practice, in the work of scholastic theologians well before
Peter Abelard summarized them, in principle, in his *Sic et non*. I would
now like to illustrate all three of them, with examples drawn from
assorted schools and masters, examples that touch on both dogmatic and
sacramental theology.

First, let us consider the use of authorities—both those cited and
those omitted—to marshal support for a theologian's own position. A
fine case in point is the debate over the nature of marriage. The
Abelardians took a strongly negative and concessive view of marriage.
They treated it as a regrettable if necessary accommodation to the fact
of human carnality and as a remedy for sin, period. They posed the question, "Should the wise man marry?" and answered it with a resounding
"No!" In support of this position they cited the most ascetic of the
church fathers on marriage, Gregory the Great and, above all, Jerome.
To the extent that they felt impelled to cite Augustine, they drew only
on his most anti-Pelagian works, in which his most restrictive views on
marriage are found.[21] Conversely, the Victorines[22]—and before them, the
Porretans,[23] and after them, Robert Pullen[24] and Peter Lombard[25]—
praised marriage as the only sacrament instituted before the Fall, noting
as well Christ's approval of it in that he performed his first miracle at
the marriage of Cana. They used these biblical data to refute the ideas
that marriage is merely a remedy for sin and that the sexual relations of
spouses, whatever their intentions, are at least venially sinful. Instead,
they argued that human sexuality and the propagation of the human race
by means of it are good and part of God's original plan. In so doing,
they appealed to the anti-Manichean Augustine, seeking by implication
to tar their opponents, not to mention the anti-Pelagian Augustine on sex,
with the brush of Origenism. They presented marriage as a union of
hearts and minds, and not just as a union of bodies. Thereby, they also
enlarged the scope of issues pertinent to the consideration of marriage
as a sacrament.

Another example under this first heading, but one drawn from
dogmatic theology, is Peter Lombard's use of Augustine and John

Damascene to attack the weak points in Abelard's doctrine of the Trinity. Abelard taught that the names *Power*, *Wisdom*, and *Goodness* could be attributed to the three persons of the Trinity, as proper names distinguishing their personal traits, in contrast with terms such as *eternity*, which apply to the deity in general.[26] Abelard appealed largely to the Bible in support of his theory, multiplying citations in which the text refers to the three Trinitarian persons by his preferred names. This position made Abelard's critics acutely uncomfortable, and with good reason. For, they noted, if we apply to the Father, Son, and Holy Spirit the terms *power*, *wisdom*, and *goodness* in Abelard's manner, then it is impossible to make sense out of all the other biblical passages in which these terms are used to refer to more than one of the Trinitarian persons, or to a person other than the one to whom Abelard assigned the names, or to God in general. Contemporaries such as Hugh of St. Victor and Gilbert of Poitiers were unable to pinpoint just how Abelard had gone wrong and how to refute him. Hugh agreed that the terms *power*, *wisdom*, and *goodness* applied both to the individual persons of the Trinity and to God in general. But he did not succeed in explaining clearly the semantics of how this would work.[27] Gilbert charged Abelard with tritheism for his effort to confine the three attributes exclusively to the three Trinitarian persons. In turn, he himself stressed the unity of God so heavily as to state that the persons of the Trinity could be distinguished from each other only numerically,[28] a position that raised doubts about his own orthodoxy.

Peter Lombard's response was to invoke the Trinitarian theologies of Augustine and Damascene.[29] He chose these authorities for this purpose because, on this point, they were the most speculative and prototypical exponents of Latin and Greek theology, respectively. By comparing these two theologians he was able to show clearly and convincingly where Abelard had gone wrong. Abelard, he noted, had confused the Greek and Latin approaches to the Trinity. The Greeks, as typified by Damascene, were primarily interested in explaining how we can understand the economic Trinity, that is, the Trinitarian persons as they manifest themselves to man. The Latins, as typified by Augustine, were concerned instead with how we can understand the relations of the

Trinitarian persons among themselves, quite apart from anything they may choose to manifest of themselves to man. With this distinction clearly before his students, Peter went on to show that Abelard's doctrine of the Trinity was inadequate to explain the Trinity in either of these modes. Abelard had been correct in distinguishing between terms that apply properly to God *in se* and those that apply properly to the Trinitarian persons individually. But the nouns *power*, *wisdom*, and *goodness* are not proper names as applied to the persons of the unmanifested Trinity in their own internal family relations. For they do not display the relationships that specify what is unique to each of the Trinitarian persons vis-à-vis the other two. Nor do these terms apply properly and exclusively to the way that one, and only one, of the Trinitarian persons manifests himself to man, since they denote attributes common to the divine essence that they share.

The Lombard's positive suggestion for slicing through this whole Gordian knot was to reimport Augustine's famous Trinitarian analogy into the discussion. Man's mental faculties of memory, intellect, and will, he noted, do indeed provide a good model for understanding the Trinitarian persons vis-à-vis each other, without confusing their distinctive functions, which work in and through each other, with the unity of the single subsistent being of which they are functions. This Augustinian analogy, which had been omitted by Abelard and rejected by Gilbert, enabled Peter to finesse the inconclusive volleying back and forth of biblical citations and to rest his case on the insights of the most highly respected Trinitarian theologians to ornament the Christian tradition thus far. His strategy proved to be a success.

I would next like to turn to the question of how twelfth-century sentence collectors put their authorities to the test, in justifying an emerging consensus or in defending their own willingness to depart from tradition. I will offer three examples under this heading, all drawn from the sacrament of baptism. Baptism affords some good cases in point here, since changing attitudes toward this sacrament in the twelfth century were making earlier views of it untenable in some quarters. Most theologians continued to support the principle, put in place in the fifth century by Pope Leo I, that new Christians should be received in baptism only on Easter and Pentecost Sunday, unless they were in danger of death. But the members of the school of Laon rejected this policy, for reasons of pastoral need. Their argument is a fine example of the application of historical criticism to the problem. The Laon masters pointed out that Leo's rule may have made eminent good sense in his own day, when most of the Christians received in baptism were adults and when their communal reception into the church during the great feasts of the resurrection liturgy was an important reinforcement of their group solidarity and an important witness to the largely pagan society in which they lived. But it completely ignores the needs of infants, who now make up the vast majority of baptizands, whose health is very fragile, and who cannot articulate the fact if they are in danger of death. And so, having explained that the situation in the *ecclesia primitiva* was far different from the situation in the here and now, they rejected Leo's authority, on these grounds, as irrelevant and as no longer binding.[30]

While they were taking an unconventional position in the case just mentioned, there was another issue relating to infant baptism on which the school of Laon spoke for an emerging consensus, the feeling that Augustine had been far too harsh in condemning unbaptized infants to Hell. Here, the teaching of the theologians was informed not by an appreciation of the differences between the patristic period and their own times but by the growing emphasis on personalism and intentionalism in the religious life and by the desire to emphasize God's mercy, notes that are real hallmarks of twelfth-century theology. Anselm of Laon clearly voiced his dissatisfaction with the traditional doctrine. As he observed, infants who die unbaptized are not themselves aware of the need for baptism and are not responsible for their failure to receive it. Lacking the knowledge and intentionality required for moral guilt, they will not be penalized by God for this omission. Any punishment to be meted out will go to their negligent parents, not to them.[31] Aside from the reasons given here, Anselm suggested another disquieting idea that contributed to his misgivings, in speaking of the feast of the Holy Innocents. These infants, although unbaptized, are firmly believed to have been received into Heaven and are rightly venerated as saints.[32] William of Champeaux, while he offered no reasons, asserted that the correctness of Augustine's position is not certain.[33] Later in the century, the largely Victorine author of the *Summa Sententiarum* brought these points together. After citing Augustine's teaching on the damnation of unbaptized infants, he stated that it may be dismissed. Offering the case of the Holy Innocents as the objection with which he anchors his argument, he declared the subject to be an open one, "de quo nihil definitus habemus."[34] Going still farther, a Porretan master took this lack of patristic conclusiveness for granted and argued that infants killed before they can be baptized, on the model of the Holy Innocents, are certainly saved.[35]

Some theologians were eager to make an even more positive case against Augustine. Sympathetic to the Victorine position, the early Porretans joined the Abelardian author of the *Ysagoge in theologiam* in taking a cue from Abelard's *Sic et non*, where he noted that the anti-Pelagian Augustine disagrees with the anti-Donatist Augustine on baptism.[36] This suggestion provided our theologians with their argument, and it is a dexterous one. They cited Augustine on predestination against Augustine on infant baptism.[37] This is indeed an elegant strategy, for Augustine's positions on both of these subjects date to his later career, so one cannot claim that the latter view is intrinsically more "mature" than the former. As our theologians chose to read Augustine on predestination, this doctrine means that we can place no limits on God's saving grace. God will save whomever he has predestined to save, whether baptized or not.

Let me offer a third example, also on baptism, still under the same heading, one that combines the countercitation of authority and historical criticism with what we today would call source criticism. A topic debated in the mid-twelfth century was whether the ancient rule of baptism by triple immersion established by Leo I should be retained or replaced with baptism by single immersion. Some scholastics, like Peter Lombard, supported the retention of the ancient custom because of the symbolic link between the three immersions that inaugurate the candidate's spiritual rebirth and the three days Christ's body lay in the tomb before his resurrection.[38] Lombard derived his dossier of patristic sources on this point from the *Summa Sententiarum*, although he disagreed with its author, who, while indicating a preference for triple immersion, gave priority to the importance of following local ecclesiastical custom.[39] The Porretans, on the other hand, rejected the Leonine tradition, on grounds of pastoral utility. They were not interested either in decorum or in symbolism. Both the tender age of the baptizands nowadays and the cold northern climate suggest the desirability of a single immersion that would minimize the chances of their catching a chill. This is the agenda which the Porretans wanted to defend. Their technique in doing so was noteworthy. They drove home this argument from reason and history with a double-barrelled argument from authority, invoking a maxim of Gregory the Great, which their contemporary opponents had cited in defense of their own countervailing positions, combining it with an authority prior to that of Leo as well. How, they asked, did the idea of triple immersion get started in the first place, given the fact that the earliest authority to rule on the subject, Cyprian, ordained single immersion? The culprit, as they saw it, was Augustine. In citing Cyprian, Augustine garbled the text he was quoting and changed the number of immersions to three. As for Leo, he merely rubber-stamped Augustine, without querying the correctness of his research, thus perpetuating his corruption of Cyprian willy-nilly.

Now, Gregory, in developing his opinion, offered two advantages useful in the overturning of Leo's ruling. First, he reconstructed the history of the doctrine and practice of baptism, enabling us to see how a policy based on a corrupt text had become canonical. Second, and in virtue of that first contribution, the Gregorian maxim "diversa consuetudo ecclesie in una fide non obest"[40] could now be invoked to legitimize the sweeping change advocated by the Porretans on the grounds of common sense and contemporary relevance. We are far removed here from the mind-numbing technique of countercitation of one patristic proof-text against another or one pope against another, on a level where it is impossible to state, in the abstract, that one is intrinsically more authoritative than the other. Rather, for the Porretans, Gregory was useful because he could be harnessed efficaciously to the undermining of a tradition that compounds a textual corruption. The fact that Cyprian had antiquity on his side was an advantage, but it was less critical to the methodology that the Porretans wanted to convey than the larger point that an authority can be dismissed if it is based on erroneously reported sources.

My final example will be used to illustrate the third and last way in which the sentence collectors taught their students to reason theologically, by showing them how to analyze and criticize the intentions and argumentation that inform the conclusions of their authorities. With this example we shall return to the subject of marriage. One of the standard questions raised with respect to marriage in the twelfth century was whether a prior adulterous affair should be regarded as an impediment to marriage if the lovers found themselves free to marry each other subsequently. On this point, Leo I said that the previous adultery was an impediment to marriage, while Augustine said that it was not. These same two authorities are the ones invariably cited by the twelfth-century authors who take up this question, however they came down on it. In handling this issue, our sentence collectors were primarily concerned with showing their students how to evaluate the reasoning of Leo and Augustine. The members of the school of Laon agreed with Leo because they found Leo's analysis eminently sound. Leo had imposed the ban because he had feared that the lovers, if permitted to marry, would be tempted to plot the murder of the obstructive spouse or spouses, an outcome he wanted to discourage. Our authors, who added that inheritance rights might get confused in that eventuality as well, found Leo's reasoning compelling.[41] For his part, one of the Porretan masters felt a need to lay out Augustine's reasoning as well as Leo's. As he pointed out, Augustine's whole concern here was the repentance of the adulterers, their sincere desire to amend their way of life and to rectify their past sin by regularizing their relationship when events make this possible.[42] Unfortunately, we are left in suspense at this point, because there is a lacuna in the text, and the remainder of our author's analysis is missing. So we do not know whether he regarded the Leonine and Augustinian positions as equally persuasive, whether he chose between them, and, if so, on what grounds.

This is not the case with Peter Lombard. He, too, reviewed the arguments of Leo and Augustine, and not just their conclusions. Basically, he favored Augustine, preferring his emphasis on penance, forgiveness, and reparation over Leo's more legalistic and punitive approach. But Peter was also interested in the question of whether these two authorities are entirely incompatible. He concluded that there is an instance in which their views would coincide. If, indeed, the lovers have committed murder, they should not be allowed to profit from their crime. In any event, Christians cannot sincerely prepare to receive the sacrament of marriage, understood in this case as a penitential reparation, with such a crime on their consciences. In this situation, Peter thought Augustine would join Leo in forbidding the marriage, the ruling he would make himself. But, when such a condition does not obtain, the spiritual healing of the couple is the primary consideration to stress and is the reason to follow Augustine.[43]

As we have seen, the positions of the Laon masters and Peter Lombard on the problem just aired reflect the fact that, as moral and sacramental theologians, these thinkers had differing opinions and priorities. The evidence that they, and our other sentence collectors, have presented in this essay makes it clear that these men were not mere compilers who just recapitulated patristic authorities. Rather, they emerge as theologians with definite, independent, and sometimes partisan views. At times they invoked authorities for the purpose of showing how and why they should be rejected. When they cited their authorities positively, they did so not just because the authorities are authorities but also because the authorities agree with the writer's own ideas; they provide a means of refuting the writer's contemporary opponents; or they offer a way of resolving a current problem. These theologians were active at a time when theology was in flux and there were rival schools and masters. In the very act of teaching their students how to defend their own positions, they empowered those students to take an independent view of their own masters. Although the literary form of the sentence collection was later supplanted by other genres of theological literature, this training in method flowed right on into the wider stream of high medieval theology, affecting the teaching of other scholastic disciplines as well. At the same time, the system-building propensities of the best of the sentence collectors, their desire to see the enterprise of theology as a schematic whole, was a feature of their work that had immense staying power. This is particularly true of the systematic sentence collection of Peter Lombard, which remained durable yet flexible enough to accommodate the vastly expanded range of materials and questions that characterized scholastic speculation in the later medieval centuries. In both of these respects, then, I think we can say that the sentence collectors of the twelfth century made a contribution to the education of theologians in the medieval universities to come that was truly seminal.

Notes

This paper is a revised version of one delivered at the conference "The Intellectual Climate of the Early University," at California State University, Northridge, 20 October 1988.

1. Jaroslav Pelikan, *The Growth of Medieval Theology (600–1300)*, vol. 3 of *The Christian Tradition: A History of the Development of Doctrine*, 5 vols. (Chicago: University of Chicago Press, 1978).

2. This dispraise and misunderstanding of the sentence collection was formulated early in the century by Otto Baltzer, *Die Sentenzen des Petrus Lombardus: Ihre Quellen und ihre dogmengeschichtliche Bedeutung* (Leipzig: Dieterich, 1902), passim and esp. pp. 1–14. Notable authorities on medieval thought with the same outlook include Martin Grabmann, *Die Geschichte der scholastischen Methode*, 2 vols. (Berlin: Akademische Druck- u. Verlagsanstalt, 1957 [repr. of Freiburg im Breisgau, 1911 ed.]), 2: 404–07; Joseph de Ghellinck, *L'Essor de la littérature latine au XIIe siècle*, 2 vols. (Brussels: L'Edition Universelle, 1946), 1: 70–73; Joseph de Ghellinck, *Le Mouvement théologique du XIIe siècle*, 2nd. ed. (Bruges: De Tempel, 1948), pp. 202–49; and Artur Michael Landgraf, *Introduction à l'histoire de la littérature de la scolastique naissante*, ed. Albert M. Landry, trans. Louis-B. Geiger (Montreal: Institut d'Études Médiévales, 1973), pp. 53, 132. This tradition has been followed more recently by authors writing on Peter Lombard such as Enrico Nobile, "Appunti sulla teologia dei *Quattro libri delle Sentenze* di Pier Lombardo," *Pier Lombardo* 4 (1960), 49–59, and Philippe Delhaye, *Pierre Lombard, sa vie, ses oeuvres, sa morale* (Montreal: Institut d'Études Médiévales, 1961), passim and esp. p. 27. And it has been perpetuated still more recently by Pelikan, *The Growth of Medieval Theology*, p. 270, and Gillian R. Evans, *The Language and Logic of the Bible: The Road to Reformation* (Cambridge: Cambridge University Press, 1985), pp. 102–04.

3. This line of argument has been taken repeatedly by Jean Leclercq. See his *The Love of Learning and the Desire for God: A Study of Monastic Culture*, 2nd. ed. rev., trans. Catherine Misrahi (New York: Fordham University Press, 1974), passim and esp. pp. 1–7, and more recently and pointedly in "The Renewal of Theology," in *Renaissance and Renewal in the Twelfth Century*, ed. Robert L. Benson and Giles Constable (Cambridge, Mass.: Harvard University Press, 1982), pp. 68–87. A recent critique of Leclercq, Brian P. Gaybba, *Aspects of the Mediaeval History of Theology: Twelfth to Fourteenth Centuries* (Pretoria: University of South Africa, 1988), pp. 7–65, urges the substitution of "experiential" and "notional" for Leclercq's "monastic" and "scholastic" categories, but concurs with him in writing the sentence collectors out of the story.

4. Helpful introductions to this point are found in Henri Cloes, *La systématisation théologique pendant la prèmière moitié du XIIe siècle* (Louvain: Publications Universitaires, 1958), pp. 277–329; and Coloman Viola, "Manières personnelles et impersonnelles d'aborder un problème: Saint Augustin et le XIIe siècle. Contribution à l'histoire de la 'quaestio'," in *Les Genres littéraires dans les sources théologiques et philosophiques médiévales: Définition, critique et exploitation* (Louvain-la-Neuve: Institut d'Études Médiévales, Université Catholique de Louvain, 1982), pp. 25–30. Viola's paper is helpful in showing the connection between the posing of *quaestiones* and intellectual system-building in this period.

5. For a fuller consideration of this comparison see Marcia L. Colish, "Systematic Theology and Theological Renewal in the Twelfth Century," *Journal of Medieval and Renaissance Studies* 18 (1988), 138–42. On Rupert see John Van Engen, *Rupert of Deutz* (Berkeley: University of California Press, 1983), esp. pp. 74–94. *De Sancta Trinitate* has been edited by Rhabanus Haacke in *Corpus Christianorum, Continuatio Mediaevalis* (hereafter cited as CCCM), 21–24.

6. On this debate see M. Peuchmaurd, "Le prêtre ministre de la parole dans la théologie du XIIe siècle: Canonistes, moines, et chanoines," *Recherches de théologie ancienne et médiévale* 29 (1962), 52–76.

7. On Honorius's biography and the dating of this work see Valerie I. J. Flint, "Honorius Augustodunensis, *Imago mundi*," *Archives d'histoire doctrinale et littéraire du moyen âge* 49 (1982), 7–8; "The Career of Honorius Augustodunensis: Some Fresh Evidence," *Revue bénédictine* (hereafter cited as *R. bén*) 82 (1972), 63–86 ; and "The Chronology of the Works of Honorius Augustodunensis," *R. bén.* 82 (1972), 215–42. See also Marie-Odile Garrigues, "Quelques recherches sur l'oeuvre d'Honorius Augustodunensis," *Revue d'histoire ecclésiastique* 70 (1975), 388–425; and Eva Matthews Sanford, "Honorius *Presbyter* and *Scholasticus*," *Speculum* 23 (1948), 397–404. Flint's dating of the *Elucidarium* is supported by Robert D. Crouse, "Honorius Augustodunensis: Disciple of

22   Marcia Colish

Anselm?" in *Analecta Anselmiana*, ed. Helmut Kohlenberger (Frankfurt: Minerva, 1975), 4 part 2: 131–39; he challenges the view that Honorius studied with Anselm of Canterbury, although he admits that it is otherwise difficult to account for his up-to-date knowledge of *Cur Deus homo*. Janice L. Schultz, "Honorius Augustodunensis," *Dictionary of the Middle Ages*, ed. Joseph R. Strayer, vol. 6 (New York: Charles Scribner's Sons, 1985), pp. 285–86, reports this difference of opinion without taking sides.

8. Honorius, *Elucidarium*, ed. Yves Lefèvre as *L'Elucidarium et les Lucidaires: Contribution par l'histoire d'un texte à l'histoire des croyances religieuses en France au moyen âge* (Paris: E. de Boccard, 1954). On the context in which this work was written see Valerie I. J. Flint, "The 'Elucidarius' of Honorius Augustodunensis and Reform in Late Eleventh-Century England," *R. bén.* 85 (1975), 179–89; and "The Place and Purpose of the Works of Honorius Augustodunensis," *R. bén.* 87 (1977), 97–118. See also Josef A. Endres, *Honorius Augustodunensis: Beitrag zur Geschichte des geistigen Lebens in 12. Jahrhundert* (Munich: Jos. Kösel, 1906), pp. 16–21.

9. Valerie I. J. Flint, "Heinricus of Augsburg and Honorius Augustodunensis: Are They the Same Person?" *R. bén.* 92 (1982), 150–51.

10. Nikolaus M. Häring, ed., "Die *Sententiae magistri Gisleberti Pictavensis episcopi* I," *Archives d'histoire doctrinale et littérarre du moyen âge* (hereafter cited as *AHDLMA*) 45 (1978), 83–180 ; and Die *Sententiae magistri Gisleberti Pictavensis episcopi* II: Die Version der Florentinischer Handschrift," *AHDLMA* 46 (1979), 45–105.

11. See, in particular, the most recent assessment of the previous literature and the datings given by Constant J. Mews, "On Dating the Writings of Peter Abelard," *AHDLMA* 52 (1985), 73–134; "Peter Abelard's (*Theologia Christiana*) and (*Theologia 'Scholarium'*) Re-examined," *Recherches de théologie ancienne et médiévale* (hereafter cited as *RTAM*) 52 (1985), 109–58 ; and the preface to the volume of Peter Abelard, *Opera theologica*, CCCM, 13, pp. 20–23, which he has edited.

12. On this point see Richard E. Weingart, *The Logic of Divine Love: A Critical Analysis of the Soteriology of Peter Abailard* (Oxford: Clarendon Press, 1970), pp. 195–96; and "Peter Abailard's Contribution to Medieval Sacramentology," *RTAM* 34 (1967), 172–73. This teaching is reprised by [Hermannus], *Sententiae magistri Petri Abelardi* 28, 31, ed. Sandro Buzzetti (Florence: La Nuova Italia, 1983), pp. 120, 135; he states that marriage confers no *donum* or gift of grace.

13. These developments are recounted thoroughly by David E. Luscombe, *The School of Peter Abelard: The Influence of Abelard's Thought in the Early Scholastic Period* (London: Cambridge University Press, 1969).

14. *Ysagoge in theologiam*, ed. Artur Michael Landgraf in *Écrits théologiques de l'école d'Abélard: Textes inédits* (Louvain: Spicilegium Sacrum Lovaniense, 1934).

15. *Les Sententiae Parisiensis* I, ed. Artur Michael Landgraf in *Écrits théologiques de l'école d'Abélard*; and *Sententiae Parisiensis* II, ed. Johannes Trimborn as *Die Sententiae "Quoniam missio" aus der Abelardschule* (Cologne: Photostelle der Universität zu Köln, 1962).

16. [Hermannus], *Sententiae magistri Petri Abelardi*.

17. Hugh of St. Victor, *De sacramentis fide christianae*, *Patrologia cursus completus . . . series latina* (hereafter cited as *PL*), ed. Jacques-Paul Migne, 217 vols. (Paris, 1878–90), 176 .

18. Peter Lombard, *Sententiae in IV libris distinctae*, 2 vols., 3rd ed. rev., ed. Ignatius C. Brady (Grottaferrata: Editiones Collegii S. Bonaventurae ad Claras Aquas, 1981).

19. Peter Lombard, *Sententiae* 1. d. 1. c. 1–2, 1: 55–56.

20. This point has been rightly emphasized for Peter Abelard by Beryl Smalley, "*Prima clavis sapientiae*: Augustine and Abelard," in her *Studies in Medieval Thought and Learning from Abelard to Wyclif* (London: Hambledon Press, 1981), pp. 2, 8; and for Peter Lombard by Ermenegildo Bertola, "Le 'Sententiae' e le 'Summae' tra il XII e il XIII secolo," *Pier Lombardo* 2 (1958), 25–41.

21. The member of this school who provides the fullest discussion of marriage is [Hermannus], *Sententiae magistri Petri Abelardi* 28, 31, pp. 120, 135–39. See also Landgraf, *Sententiae Parisiensis* I, pp. 44–46; and Landgraf, *Ysagoge in theologiam*, pp. 196–99. On the use of Jerome and Theophrastus to support the "aut liberi aut libri" position by the Abelardians see Philippe Delhaye, "Le Dossier anti-matrimoniale de l'*Adversus Jovinianum* et son influence sur quelques écrits latines du XIIé siècle," *Mediaeval Studies* 13 (1951), 65–86.

22. Hugh of St. Victor, *Epistola de beatae Mariae virginitate* 1, *PL* 176.859D–860A, 864A–876C; *De sacramentis* 1.8.13, 2.11.1–19, *PL* 176.314C–318A, 476D–520C. The best full-scale study of Hugh on marriage is Henri A. J. Allard, *Die eheliche Lebens- und Liebesgemeinschaft nach Hugo von St.-Viktor* (Rome: Analecta Dehoniana, 1963). The best study of its genesis in Hugh's Mariology is Corrado Gneo, "La dottrina del matrimonio nel 'De B. Mariae virginitate' di Ugo di S. Vittore," *Divinitas* 17 (1973), 374–94. See also W. E. Gössmann, "Die Bedeutung der Liebe in der Eheauffassung Hugos von St. Viktor und Wolframs von Eschenbach," *Münchener theologische*

Zeitschrift 5 (1954), 205–08, 213; Wendelin Knoch, *Die Einsetzung der Sakramente durch Christus: Eine Untersuchung zur Sakramententheologie der Frühscholastik von Anselm von Laon bis zu Wilhelm von Auxerre*, Beiträge zur Geschichte der Philosophie und Theologie des Mittelalters, n.F. 24 (Münster: Aschendorff, 1983), pp. 110–13; Ludwig Ott, *Untersuchungen zur theologischen Briefliteratur der Frühscholastik* (Münster: Aschendorff, 1937), pp. 404–15; and Christian Shütz, *Deus absconditus, Deus manifestus: Die Lehre Hugos von St. Viktor über die Offenbarung Gottes* (Rome: Herder, 1967), pp. 121–24. Hugh's position is followed by the author of the *Summa Sententiarum* 7.15, *PL* 176.153D–158C. On this passage see Knoch, *Die Einsetzung*, p. 120.

23. *Sententiae magistri Gisleberti* II 11.2–9, pp. 86–88.

24. Robert Pullen, *Sententiarum libri octo* 6.4, 7.28–30, *PL* 186.867B, 945C–949C. For Robert on marriage see Francis Courtney, *Cardinal Robert Pullen: An English Theologian of the Twelfth Century* (Rome: Universitatis Gregorianae, 1954), pp. 251–52, 254.

25. Peter Lombard, *Sententiae* 4. d. 27–31, 2: 416–51. Peter's discussion is the fullest of any of the thinkers in this group. These aspects of Peter's view of marriage have been treated the most thoroughly by Hans Zeimentz, *Ehe nach der Lehre der Frühscholastik: Eine moralgeschichtliche Untersuchung zur Anthropologie und Theologie der Ehe in der Schule Anselms von Laon und Wilhelms von Champeaux, bei Hugo von St. Viktor, Walter von Mortagne und Petrus Lombardus* (Düsseldorf: Patmos-Verlag, 1973), pp. 136–40, 226–28, 237–45. See also Penny S. Gold, "The Marriage of Mary and Joseph in the Twelfth-Century Ideology of Marriage," in *Sexual Practices and the Medieval Church*, ed. Vern L. Bullough and James Brundage (Buffalo: Prometheus Books, 1982), pp. 102–17; P. Seamus Heaney, *The Development of the Sacramentality of Marriage from Anselm of Laon to Thomas Aquinas* (Washington, D.C.: Catholic University of America Press, 1963), pp. 28–31, 154–56; and Knoch, *Die Einsetzung*, pp. 239–41. For the Augustinian background informing Peter and his predecessors on this topic see Michael Müller, *Die Lehre des hl. Augustinus von der Paradiesehe und ihre Auswirkung in der Sexualethik des 12. und 13. Jahrhunderts bis Thomas von Aquin* (Regensburg: Friedrich Pustet, 1954), pp. 19–23, 56–57, 60–103.

26. Peter Abelard, *Theologia "Summa boni"* 1.2.5, 3.1.1–51, ed. Constant J. Mews, CCCM, 13: 88, 157–79; *Theologia Christiana* 1.1–4, 1.7–35, 3.112, 4.47–50, 4.118–119, 4.154–156, 4.161–5.3, ed. Eligius M. Buytaert, CCCM, 12: 72–87, 236, 286–87, 324–25, 342–43, 346–47; and *Theologia "Scholarium"* 1.30–93, 2.135–136, ed. Constant J. Mews, CCCM, 13: 330–56, 475. The best analysis is by Eligius M. Buytaert, "Abelard's Trinitarian Doctrine," in *Peter Abelard. Proceedings of the International Conference, Louvain, May 10–12, 1971*, ed. Eligius M. Buytaert (Leuven: Leuven University Press, 1974), pp. 127–52.

27. Hugh of St. Victor, *De sacramentis* 1.2.5–12, 1.3.26–31, *PL* 176.208A–211A, 227C–234C. The best analysis is by Johann Hofmeier, *Die Trinitätslehre des Hugo von St. Viktor dargestellt im Zusammenhang mit den trinitarischen Strömungen seiner Zeit* (Munich: Max Hueber, 1963), pp. 188–91, 193–95, 197–268. See also Edmund J. Fortman, *The Triune God: A Historical Study of the Doctrine of the Trinity* (Philadelphia: Westminster Press, 1972), p. 190; Jakob Kilgenstein, *Die Gotteslehre des Hugo von St. Viktor* (Würzburg: Andreas Göbel, 1897), p. 127; and Jørgen Pedersen, "La recherche de la sagesse d'après Hugues de Saint-Victor," *Classica et mediaevalia* 16 (1955), 91–133. All these authors note the inconclusiveness of Hugh's critique of Abelard.

28. Gilbert of Poitiers, *In Boethius de Trinitate* 1.3.53–54, 1.5.39, 2.2.72–80; and *In Boethius contra Eutychen et Nestorium* 3.65–74, ed. Nikolaus M. Häring in *The Commentaries on Boethius* (Toronto: Pontifical Institute of Mediaeval Studies, 1966), pp. 113, 147, 178–80, 285–87.

29. Peter Lombard, *Sententiae* 1. d. 3. c. 1.5, d. 8. c. 4–c. 8.1–3, d. 19. c. 2, d. 22. c. 5, d. 24. c. 6–d. 25. c. 3.4, d. 26. c. 3, d. 26. c. 8, d. 27. c. 2.3, d. 30. c.1.1–7, d. 33, c. 1.1–10, d. 34. c. 1.1–9, d. 34. c. 4.2, 1: 70, 98–101, 101–103, 160, 179–80, 189, 195, 203, 204–05, 220–22, 240–43, 245–46, 246–50, 253. On this whole question see Ermenegildo Bertola, "Il problema di Dio in Pier Lombardo," *Rivista di filosofia neoscolastica* 48 (1956): 135–50; Marcia L. Colish, "Gilbert, the Early Porretans, and Peter Lombard: Semantics and Theology," in *Gilbert de Poitiers et ses contemporains: Aux origines de la logica modernorum*, ed. Jean Jolivet and Alain de Libera (Naples: Bibliopolis, 1987), pp. 244–46; and Marcia Colish, "Systematic Theology," *Journal of Medieval and Renaissance Studies* 18 (1988), 153–54.

30. *Sentences of the School of Laon*, no. 371, ed. Odon Lottin, *Psychologie et morale aux XIIe et XIIIe siècles*, 6 vols. (Louvain: Abbaye de Mont César, 1948–59), 5: 275–76; and *Sententiae Atrebatensis*, ed. Lottin, *Psychologie et morale*, 5: 431. On this point see Marcia L. Colish, "Another Look at the School of Laon," *AHDLMA* 53 (1986), 12–14.

31. Anselm of Laon, *Liber Pancrisis*, no. 59, ed. Lottin, *Psychologie et morale*, 5: 54.

32. Anselm of Laon, *Liber Pancrisis*, no. 96, ed. Lottin, *Psychologie et morale*, 5: 81.

33. William of Champeaux, *Sentences*, ed. Lottin, *Psychologie et morale*, 5: 216.

34. *Summa Sententie* 5.6, *PL* 176.133A.

35. *Sententiae magistri Gisleberti* I 7.20, p. 151.

36. Peter Abelard, *Sic et non: A Critical Edition*, ed. Blanche B. Boyer and Richard McKeon (Chicago: University of Chicago Press, 1976), q. 106, pp. 343–46.

37. *Sententiae magistri Gisleberti* I 7.28, p. 152; *Sententiae magistri Gisleberti* II 7.28, p. 73; *Ysagoge in theologiam*, pp. 187–88.

38. Peter Lombard, *Sententiae* 4. d. 3. c. 7, 2: 249–50.

39. *Summa Sententiae* 5.4, *PL* 176.130A–B.

40. *Sententiae magistri Gisleberti* I 7.13–14, p. 149.

41. Franz Bliemetzrieder, ed., *Anselms von Laon systematische Sentenzen* (Münster: Aschendorff, 1919), pp. 148–49; and *Sentences of the School of Laon*, no. 409, ed. Lottin, 5: 288.

42. *Sententiae magistri Gisleberti* I 11.39, pp. 161–62.

43. Peter Lombard, *Sententiae* 4. d. 35. c. 4. 2: 471–72.

Approaches and Attitudes to a New Theology Textbook: the *Sentences* of Peter Lombard

Nancy Spatz

*E*ach university faculty in the Middle Ages centered its teaching and classes around certain authoritative writings. The arts faculty had as its focus the writings of Aristotle and Priscian, medicine had works by Hippocrates and Galen, civil law had the *Digest* and *Code* of Justinian, canon law had Gratian's *Decretum* and the papal *Decretals*, and theology, of course, had the Bible and the *Four Books of the Sentences* of Peter Lombard. Peter was a famous theology master in Paris for many years; due to his prestige as a master he became a canon at Notre Dame in 1145 and bishop of Paris in 1159. The *Sentences* was composed in the 1150s, undergoing its final revision 1157–58. As Peter Lombard says in his prologue, he intended it to be "a small volume consisting of patristic views together with their testimony, so that the inquirer would not have to search through numerous tomes, for the synthesized brevity which he seeks is offered here without much labor."[1]

However, the *Sentences* was not adopted as a textbook in theology without some notice and controversy. The reactions of the more vocal and/or illustrious supporters and opponents of this move are well known to historians. Theology master Alexander of Hales and Pope Innocent IV were among those advocating its use as a textbook for ordinary lectures, while Bishop of Lincoln Robert Grosseteste and Master of Arts Roger Bacon were among its detractors; they bemoaned what they saw as the loss of prestige of the Bible in classes.[2] Nevertheless the *Sentences* would soon become the chief textbook in schools of theology until the mid-sixteenth century.

Although this work met some initial opposition it was eventually widely accepted by students and masters alike. Modern scholars, perhaps assuming that anything so broadly popular must be inferior or defective, have generally expressed a low opinion of the *Sentences*. Josef Pieper compiled some typically disparaging early twentieth-century scholarly opinions about the *Sentences* in his brief book on scholasticism.[3] It is charged with being mediocre: "The classical textbook for the following centuries was not the greatest and best *Summa* [of Hugh of St. Victor], but a mediocre book of sentences, the *libri quatuor sententiarum* of Peter Lombard."[4] Others assert that its popularity was due only to "a propaganda campaign" carried out by a student of Peter Lombard, Peter of Poitiers,[5] or that its "almost incomprehensible attractiveness" almost defies explanation.[6] Pieper's own explanation that the success of the *Sentences* was due to its "somewhat boring solidity which is after all one of the prime qualities of a good textbook" is faint praise, at best.[7]

Marcia Colish has challenged conventional wisdom in a recent article and two-volume study of the *Sentences*. In her work she points out the notable improvements and innovations of the *Sentences* of Peter Lombard as compared to other compilations of *sententiae*, i.e., patristic opinions. Having analyzed several contemporary collections of *sententiae*, she has found that Peter Lombard's comprehensive yet orderly and succinct treatment of theological material, consistent use of clear terminology, and balanced handling of authorities made his textbook superior to those of his competitors. His wide coverage of speculative doctrines such as the nature of Christ and the Trinity contributed to the book's popularity among the best minds of the following generations of theological students.[8] In this study I will also investigate the reasons for the exceptional popularity of the *Sentences* by examining students' and masters' reactions to it. I will attempt to answer four interlocking questions: When did the *Sentences* become a required textbook? How did students and masters use this textbook? What sorts of writings emerged from these studies? And, finally, what opinions did they express about the work, its author, and its place in theological studies?

The earliest surviving statutes of the theology school at Paris requiring the study of the *Sentences* date from ca. 1335–66. These regulations specify that students in theology must lecture on the Bible and on the *Sentences* before they could become masters.[9] Historians agree that these statutes reflect, at least in general outline, procedures that had been in place probably one hundred years before, if not earlier.[10] Before we can pinpoint when the *Sentences* became a customary theological textbook we must first look for its origins in the teaching methods of theology masters at Paris.

In the early twelfth century, courses in theology centered around the Bible. Traditionally, the master would lecture on the literal and spiritual meanings of the Bible, with a large component of spiritual readings focusing on moral typologies and *exempla*. Theological questions that arose, i.e., points to be addressed by means of questions and counter-arguments, were reserved for a separate course.[11] Evidently it was difficult to lecture and discuss the faith in any coherent manner during classes focusing solely on Scripture. So several different compendia known as *sententiae* were compiled by masters of the schools to help facilitate and organize theological study. Among these some of the better known are Abelard's *Sic et Non* (ca. 1121–22), the anonymous *Summa Sententiarum* (ca. 1138–41), and the *Sententiae* by Gilbert of Poitiers (ca. 1140s), Robert Pullen (ca. 1142–44), Roland of Bologna (ca. 1150), and Robert of Melun (ca. 1152–60).[12]

Thus, in the twelfth century the *Sentences* of Peter Lombard were just one of many compendia of opinions read and commented upon in the schools of Paris. Most of the earliest writings based upon Peter's work are marginal and/or interlinear glosses that concentrate on elucidating the literal meanings in the text.[13] Another sort of work deriving from Peter Lombard's *Sentences* were *summae*. These works, only loosely based on the *Sentences*, incorporate its main divisions of theology but do not comment on the text *per se*; examples of these are the *summae* and *sententiae* of Peter of Poitiers (ca. 1168–70) and Praepositinus (ca. 1206–10).[14]

In addition to writing marginal and/or interlinear glosses some masters also wrote academic prologues to the *Sentences*. An academic prologue was typically intended for the classroom and, as such, offered students a brief introduction to the work, its author, and its place in the scheme of human knowledge. One of the earliest of these prologues to the *Sentences* is by Peter Comestor, a Parisian theology master best known for his work the *Historia scholastica*.[15] As a student in Paris, he heard Peter Lombard lecture on theology. His interlinear gloss and prologue to the *Sentences*, composed ca. 1165–70, were instrumental in introducing it as a classroom textbook in the theology schools of Paris.[16] This prologue, probably the earliest written for the *Sentences*, inspired a whole series of prologues that borrow heavily from it.[17] Three will be discussed in this paper: a late twelfth-century work falsely attributed to Peter of Poitiers;[18] an *introitus* by Hugh of St. Cher, composed ca. 1231–32, which precedes his commentary on the *Sentences*;[19] and an anonymous prologue from the late twelfth or early thirteenth century found in Vatican manuscript Vat. Lat. 2186 that borrows from Peter's prologue but is more far-reaching and complex in its treatment of the *Sentences* and the subject of theology.[20]

By the late 1220s systematic commentaries on the *Sentences* were being written at the University of Paris.[21] These complete commentaries differ from the earlier glosses because, in addition to making a division and exposition of the text, the student raised and solved a series of questions connected to the distinctions given by Peter Lombard. A commentary usually included a preface to each of the books of the *Sentences* in which its subject matter and its connection to the other books were outlined. Of the four, generally the commentator's preface to the first book is the longest and most elaborate. Usually the preface to the first book is a meticulously detailed commentary on Peter Lombard's initial prologue to the *Sentences*. Often the commentator uses the preface as an opportunity to talk about his task at length, and in this aspect it is similar to an academic prologue. These prefaces to the *Sentences* are often in question-and-answer format and are rather lengthy and intricate. I include all the questions the author raises and solves about the prologue of Peter Lombard as part of the preface.

We have two complete commentaries on the *Sentences* with prefaces from the theology school at Paris in the 1220s. One commentary, mentioned above, is by Hugh of St. Cher, who was the second Dominican regent master in theology and was later made a cardinal.[22] Hugh is famous for organizing efforts at the Dominican *studium* that produced a *postilla*, a concordance, and a correction for the entire Bible. The first Dominican master at Paris, Roland of Cremona, lectured on the *Sentences* but wrote a *summa* based on them instead of a complete commentary.[23] The other *Sentences* commentary of the 1220s is by Alexander of Hales, a secular master, who composed his *Glossa in IV Libros Sententiarum* ca. 1222–29. Alexander later became the first Franciscan regent master in theology in 1236 or 1237 and taught until his death in 1245. By being the first to lecture ordinarily on the *Sentences* in the classroom, Alexander contributed to the growing popularity and renown of this textbook.[24] No other masters or bachelors at Paris wrote commentaries on the *Sentences* in this decade, although many of them continued the tradition of writing *summae* based loosely on Peter Lombard's work.

We have no surviving commentaries from the next three Dominican regent masters or the second Franciscan regent master, all of whom held their positions in the 1230s and early 1240s. Of these Dominicans, John of St. Giles wrote a commentary that did not survive, Guerric of St. Quentin wrote questions on the *Sentences* but no complete commentary, and Godfrey of Bleneau apparently wrote nothing on the *Sentences*. The Franciscan master John of La Rochelle is thought to have written a *summa* based on the *Sentences* but no commentary.[25] An anonymous gloss on the *Sentences* found in Vatican Lat. 691 has been tentatively attributed to John of La Rochelle, but this is far from certain.[26] In the margin of the first page of this gloss is a short *introitus* to the *Sentences*, "En lectulum Salomonis . . ." that will be discussed below. In general, from the paucity of surviving commentaries, it can be assumed that in this period writing a commentary on the *Sentences* was still an optional requirement for bachelors in theology.

However, by the mid-1240s the *Sentences* appears to have become a required textbook for all bachelors of theology at Paris. There is evidence of lectures being presented on it by at least nine bachelors: Franciscans Bertrand of Bayonne, Odo of Rosny, and Odo Rigaud; Dominicans Albertus Magnus and John of Moussy; and the seculars Peter l'Archevêque, Adam of Puteorum Villa, Stephen of Poligny, and John the Page.[27] This paper will consider the prefaces written by just two of the above, Albertus Magnus and Odo Rigaud.[28] Their commentaries appear to have been the most widely disseminated and copied, and both men had outstanding careers as teachers and churchmen. Albertus, one of the best known thirteenth-century philosophical figures, was the third Dominican regent master. He was the master of Thomas Aquinas and was later Bishop of Regensburg. Odo, who along with Alexander of Hales was the master of Bonaventure, served as the third Franciscan regent master and had a long active career as archbishop of Rouen.

The prologue from another commentary written in the 1240s, that of Richard Fishacre, will also be considered. Fishacre was a Dominican master in theology at Oxford. He is credited with having composed the first *Sentences* commentary at Oxford.[29]

How did these commentators treat the *Sentences* as a literary work? The earliest commentators used the mode of literary analysis prevalent in the twelfth century, which was based on rhetorical and philosophical divisions deriving from Boethius. Academic prologues were used as a pedagogical device in the schools to organize the introductory description and analysis of a work. The particular type of academic prologue we are concerned with here has been dubbed "type C" by Richard Hunt and Alastair J. Minnis.[30] In this type of prologue the commentator states the title of the work, the author, the *intentio* or intention of the author, the *materia* or subject matter, the *modus agendi* or method of proceeding in the work, the *ordo* or organization of the work, its utility, and the branch of learning to which it belongs.[31] This scheme was employed for authors in the liberal arts, canon and civil law, and also for books of the Bible.[32]

Peter Comestor uses three parts of this scheme in his prologue to the *Sentences*: the *materia*, *intentio*, and *modus agendi*. He says that the *materia* of the *Sentences* is the Creator and the works of the Creator, or *res et signa*. He writes:

> His [i.e., Peter Lombard's] intention is to confute blasphemers, encourage the learned and stir up the lazy. He does this, teaching three things about the faith: namely, what ought to be asserted, what ought to be said to the contrary, [i.e., denied], and what ought to be piously doubted rather than rashly asserted.[33]

The *modus agendi* is to place at the beginning of the work a prologue, in which the author excuses himself of arrogance and his work of super-fluity.[34] The prologue by Pseudo-Peter of Poitiers and the preface to the *Sentences* by Hugh of St. Cher, which both rely heavily on Comestor, keep the same *materia* and *intentio* but leave out the *modus agendi*. They make a slight change in the *intentio* of the author: they replace the intention of encouraging the learned with the intention of recalling the timid students back to study.[35]

The later commentators in this study do not often use as many of these rhetorical terms. For instance, the author of the prologue in Vat. Lat. 2186, Odo Rigaud, and Alexander of Hales use only the term *materia*. For them it comprises the subjects of the four books of the *Sentences*, each of which they describe with a relevant scriptural verse.[36] Thus, these writers do not use the type "C" prologue to any great degree, nor do they use the Aristotelian rhetorical division of the four causes popularized in the thirteenth century.

In his commentary, Albertus Magnus analyzes the *Sentences* by means of Aristotelian causation as well as by the more traditional divisions of *auctor*, *materia*, and *modus agendi*.[37] Aristotelian causation began to be the dominant method of rhetorical analysis around the 1230s.[38] Albertus's use of Aristotelian causation as well as the traditional rhetorical divisions shows that his work is part of a transitional phase between the type "C" and the purely Aristotelian prologue. Albertus says that Peter Lombard's reasons for writing the *Sentences*, namely, "the destruction of heretics, and the exaltation of the lamp of truth," are the two moving causes of the work.[39] He says that the author is another cause of the work; although Albertus does not use the term *efficiens*, this is obviously equivalent to the efficient cause.[40] The *materia*, or material cause, is testimonies of the truth founded in eternity.[41] The *forma* or formal cause (the equivalent, perhaps, of *ordo*) is that of four books using proofs based on exempla of the ancients.[42] The *finis* or final cause of the work is the sincere profession of the faith and the discovery of heresy.[43] He also mentions Peter Lombard's *modus agendi*, which entails approaching the truth by reasoning about the faith and removing errors, following a moderate course between extremes, and taking responsibility for one's own work.[44]

Richard Fishacre, in his commentary on and prologue to the *Sentences*, also relates the Aristotelian causes to the older schema of the twelfth-century prologue. He writes:

> [there are] four genera of causes, namely necessity or utility which pertains to the final cause, the author which pertains to the efficient cause, the subject which pertains to the material cause, the unity and division which pertain to the formal cause.[45]

In his prologue to the *Sentences* Fishacre is applying this division directly to the *scientia* of theology and thus only indirectly to the *Sentences*. He says that the utility or necessity of theology is to know the Book of Life, i.e., the Divine Mind. According to Fishacre, the author of the Bible is God; the subject of theology is Christ; and theology is divided into speculative and practical.[46]

The commentators' varying literary treatments of this textbook show that they believed that Peter Lombard, as composer of the *Sentences*, was a significant *auctor*. In the twelfth and thirteenth centuries, academic prologues were written only for *auctores*. Minnis, speaking in the literary context, defines an *auctor* as "someone who was at once a writer and an authority, someone not merely to be read but also to be respected and believed."[47] Typical *auctores* were ancient classical writers such as Boethius, Ptolemy, and Aristotle, as well as the authors of the books of the Bible. The only other modern writer besides Peter Lombard to be considered an *auctor* in the thirteenth century was Gratian, the composer of the *Decretum*.[48] The fact that within ten years of Peter Lombard's death his work was being commented upon as if he were an *auctor* shows how highly his contemporaries and students regarded him.[49] Peter Comestor, the first to lecture on the *Sentences*, applied to it the type of academic prologue current in the twelfth century. The next commentators on the *Sentences*, borrowing from him, followed this scheme somewhat mechanically. As the use of the type "C" prologue gradually dwindled in the early thirteenth century, scholars enthusiastically embraced the new Aristotelian scheme of literary analysis. This demonstrates the thirteenth-century students' flexibility and confidence in approaching the *Sentences*. They did not hesitate to investigate and to re-formulate the literary nature of the *Sentences* even though it was written by an *auctor*.

At the same time, their prologues show how seriously they took the *Sentences*. They felt that the textbook merited analysis using all the new advanced techniques taken from Aristotelian methodology. Their commentaries and prologues are proof that new answers could be obtained with the new methods.

Now let us turn to the commentators' views on the place of the *Sentences* in theological studies and its relationship with the Bible. Peter Comestor uses an elaborate metaphor from Scripture, Exodus chapters 19 and 24, to explain the position of the *Sentences* as compared to the Bible in the program of theological study.

> Moses set boundaries around the mountain of the Lord lest the people ascend to see the Lord and the greater part of them die. Nevertheless, Moses, it is read, crossed over the boundaries when the Lord called him. Now, the elders, who had once received of the spirit of Moses, approached the boundaries; but while Moses was delayed with the Lord they grew tired of waiting and returned to the settlement. But the people did not even leave the camp.
>
> By this mountain is signified the truth of sacred Scripture, that is, the canon of both Testaments. Now, the Old and New Testaments are called truth, because they subsist in such a solidity of faith and truth, that it is necessary to believe them without contradiction. The boundaries placed around the mountain are the hagiographers, that is, the writings of the holy fathers, disclosing to us an understanding of both Testaments. However, certain ones, like Moses who was called by the Lord, crossed these boundaries, such as the earliest fathers who received an understanding of Scriptures by the revelation of God alone; thus it is read of the apostles that the Lord "opened their senses so that they could understand the Scriptures" [Lk. 24: 45]. But this is not true of us. Now, certain ones who, not called by the Lord, transgress these boundaries are pronounced, with merit, blasphemers and heretics. However, the elders, those who approach the boundaries and then retreat, stand for the learned who begin studying the volumes of the fathers, but, terrified by the magnitude and great number of books, and almost despairing, transfer to briefer studies such as natural science, law, and things of this kind. The people who do not leave the camp stand for the lazy and indolent who do not even wish to attempt to study books.
>
> On account of these three types of people, the Master, seeing that the boundaries had now grown up into huge trees, in order to prepare an easier ingress for us, as if brushing aside some little branches in the way, collected this brief work from many sources.[50]

The verb Peter uses in the phrase "brushing aside some little branches" is *prosterno*, which means, variously, "to strew in front of, to throw down, to overthrow, to prostrate."[51] If you were entering a thick woods of overgrown trees you would not be helped by having someone strew twigs in your path; thus here Peter Comestor is describing how the twigs and branches of the trees must be pushed aside or trimmed in order to gain ingress for students. In other words, Peter seems to be saying that this textbook is a tool for cutting our way through the thick growth of patristic writings that impede our progress in theological studies. This a curious and very strong metaphor to use to describe the purpose of the *Sentences*. It conjures up a picture of students being oppressed and perhaps frightened by a thick impenetrable trackless forest —is this how they regarded the authorities, the writings of the Fathers, in their more discouraged or fatigued moments? Or perhaps Peter merely envisoned pruning back the overgrowth of the patristic forest to achieve a formal garden for the students' enjoyment and convenience.[52] This metaphor suggests an element of conflict in Peter's assessment of the purpose of the writings of the Fathers. We must study the Fathers because they received revelation from God about Scripture that has been denied to us. But at the same time they can be a hindrance and a barrier to our reaching the Scriptures. Peter Comestor apparently viewed the *Sentences* as a means to reach as close to an understanding of Scripture as is permitted.

Peter, a noted exegete and avid scholar, perhaps borrowed this metaphor of the patristic authorities as a forest from the fourth-century Donatist exegete Tyconius. In the prologue to his highly influential *Liber Regularum* Tyconius writes:

> I believed it necessary to write a book of rules [about the exegesis of scripture] . . . these rules will be like paths of light, thanks to which one can go into the immense forest of prophecy without the risk of getting lost.[53]

On the other hand, perhaps a forest is a common enough metaphor to apply to some area of knowledge that one is trying to come to terms with and penetrate. Alternatively, perhaps Peter Comestor was struck by the appearance of the pages of some Bibles of his time in which a brief scriptural text is surrounded and almost overwhelmed by a dense margin of patristic glosses and commentaries: this could suggest an overgrown forest obscuring a long-sought object.

Peter Comestor sees a further connection between the Bible and the *Sentences* in terms of content. He says that Peter Lombard chose the subject matter of the *Sentences* based on study of the Bible: "When, therefore, the master was about to put this work together from various volumes of the saints, he considered that the whole series of Sacred Scripture is concerned with only two things, namely, the Creator and the Creator's handiwork."[54] Thus, Peter Comestor believes that the content of the *Sentences* is based exclusively on the two main themes of the Bible, God and Creation. Obviously there is not yet any concept of a division of theology into practical and speculative, or moral and doctrinal. The *Sentences* is simply a tool for approaching closer to the truth of Scripture, which is its subject matter.

Pseudo-Peter of Poitiers sees the *Sentences* as a means of keeping us in the path of truth of the Fathers. He writes: "The boundaries put around the mountain [of Scripture] are understood mystically as the commentaries of the saints, whose footsteps we are compelled to follow lest we transgress the boundaries which our fathers set up."[55] Here he elaborates on the metaphor of a pathway first used by Peter Comestor. Once again some resentment to the weight and strictures of authority are showing—or is it just resignation?

Hugh of St. Cher, in his prologue, follows Peter Comestor and Pseudo-Peter of Poitiers rather closely in most respects. Although he does not mention that the *Sentences* create a path through the forest of patristic literature, he does make an important distinction between the classroom treatment of the Bible and the writings of the Fathers. Hugh says:

> Sacred Scripture is comparable to a mountain for two reasons: not only on account of the loftiness of its knowledge, but because it was instituted by God so that it is not lawful to oppose it. Hence it is that we often determine the authority of the saints, namely Ambrose, Jerome, Augustine, but it is in no wise permitted to determine the authorities of the scriptural canon, unless there be an obvious reason. For no one dares "to set his mouth against heaven" (Ps.

72: 9). We understand mystically the boundaries put around the mountain as hagiography, that is, the commentaries of the saints, whose footsteps we are compelled to honor and follow, lest we transgress the boundaries which our fathers set up.[56]

"To determine" is the right of a duly licensed and appointed master to put forth a determination or solution to some theological question. Thus a master is free to dispute patristic writings but not the Bible. Scripture, as a revealed work, is in a different category; one cannot dispute it, at least in most circumstances. The author does allow for the possibility of a compelling reason, but he cautions the reader with a warning drawn from the Psalms against presumption and arrogance. This distinction prepares the way for the widespread adoption of the *Sentences*, which facilitates discussion of doctrinal questions by opposing conflicting authorities and determining a solution. Nonetheless, Hugh points out that masters are still bound to honor the writings and decisions of the fathers as their guide.

The author of the first prologue to the *Sentences* found in Vat. Lat. 691 also uses a passage of the Old Testament as an allegory to explain the relationship between modern masters and the patristic *auctoritates*:

Their [i.e., the theologians'] master, Christ, established for them a house for weapons where this weapon, namely, the Books of the Sentences, is placed, in which are contained the authorities and reasons for the defense of the faith and the repulse of heresy. This is said in II Chron. 9: 15–16, that "King Solomon made two hundred spears and three hundred golden shields and put them in an arsenal," namely, "in the house of the forest" as III Kings 10: 17 says. The arsenal, which is called the house for weapons, can be said to be the Book of the Sentences; the spears of the Lord are the direct and sharp arguments of the faithful; the shields are the divine opinions (*sententiae*) destroying the cunning of the heretics through faith and truth. It is said "three hundred" on account of the perfection of knowledge and the indivisible Trinity. Again, it is said "two hundred spears" on account of authorities and reason, because the adversaries are defeated at one time by the javelins of authority, at another time by the javelins of reason.[57]

In this martial metaphor patristic authorities seem to pose no obstruction to the modern masters; rather, they are defensive weapons, shields that the successful master uses adroitly. The offensive weapons, the spears, are the sharp and direct arguments of the masters themselves based on reason and authorities. Perhaps here we see the growing confidence of masters who are becoming bolder and more self-confident in using patristic authorities. They no longer feel bound to follow in the Fathers' footsteps or paths, but instead manipulate them howsoever they wish in the verbal and intellectual scrimmage against the errors of heretics. In this allegory, the opinions and authorities of the Fathers are useful but essentially inert defensive weaponry, not a hurdle to intellectual progress.

The later commentators—the Anonymous in Vat. Lat. 2186, Albertus Magnus, and Richard Fishacre—present us with a picture of a bifurcation in the study of theology. They see theology as existing in two parts, differentiated both in content and in the method of its study.

The author of the commentary in Vat. Lat. 2186 defines theology, namely, knowledge of the Catholic religion, as the knowledge of piety, which has two parts: that which is the truth of piety and that which is the good of piety. The former teaches about the truth: what should be believed and its principles and causes, and what should be done. This knowledge seeks to move the intellect through rational syllogisms and proofs; this is the methodology of the *Sentences*. The other sort of knowledge, the good of piety, is that which is beatifying in this life and in the afterlife. It instructs both by illuminating our understanding of the conception of true belief and actions and by appealing to the affective part of a person, i.e., the will, in order to attain the beatifying good and the sorts of things required for this. The Bible is the means of this study; it teaches us through "examples, parables, warnings, threats, miracles, promises, and terrors." These sorts of rhetorical devices have a mobilizing effect on our emotions and promote in us the desire to do good.[58]

Albertus Magnus also says that theology is divided into two parts, based on the different rhetorical strategies of Scripture and the *Sentences*. The Scriptures proceed in the rhetorical mode of exhortation—persuasion —encouraging us in sound doctrine. The *Sentences* proceeds in the dialectical mode of argumentation, enabling us to refute contradictions to the faith by proving the truth and exposing errors.[59] Here Albert, like the previous writer, divides theology based not only according to content but also according to the rhetorical mode of the work studied.

Richard Fishacre also divides theology in two parts while providing insights about the methods of theological study in Oxford in the 1240s. He tells us that the modern masters teach morals when they lecture on the Scriptures. Only after this instruction in morals may the students study the part of theology that deals with the more difficult questions about the faith. The students' textbook for this class is the *Sentences*, which contains the most difficult part of the canon of the Scriptures. Richard points out that both parts of theological studies are ultimately based on the canon of Scripture.[60]

This brief survey of the first prologues to and commentaries on the *Sentences* of Peter Lombard adds to our understanding of medieval students' attitudes toward the *Sentences*. From the very beginning Peter Lombard as Master of the *Sentences* was treated as an *auctor*, for he was accorded the traditional academic prologue reserved for authoritative texts. Although students treated their textbook with reverence, they did not hesitate to subject it to new evaluation and scrutiny during the period when Aristotelian science was being rediscovered. For them it was obviously a living, vital text worthy of their time and energy. The *Sentences* did not lose its relevance for them as did so many other works from the twelfth century that were superseded by the new Aristotelian science. Rather, the opposite is true: by the 1240s Peter Lombard's book was a required or at least favored textbook for speculative theology at both Paris and Oxford, the premier theological schools of the day.

These prologues also reflect changing methods in theological study and offer a rationale for these changes. The students were quite aware that the division of theology into moral-scriptural studies and systematic textbook-based studies was a recent innovation. They seemed to find it necessary to explain the reason for this new program of study.

It was during this time of the growth in popularity of the *Sentences* that speculative theology flowered. There is no way to gauge to what extent the *Sentences* of Peter Lombard was actually responsible for this surge in speculative theology. But his work was an instrument used in furthering this split between the study of the Bible and the study of speculative theology. The study of the *Sentences* was taken up so enthusiastically that some feared, rightly or wrongly, that the Bible was being ignored in favor of this upstart text. This fear would reappear in later centuries. One of the motivating factors of Erasmus's and Luther's opposition to the study of speculative theology was the perceived neglect of the Bible in favor of scholastic speculation: their opposition to "arid" scholasticism helped to trigger the Reformation.

Appendix

Three brief *introitus* to the *Sentences* are in the margins of Vatican Lat. MS 691, a thirteenth-century manuscript containing an anonymous gloss on the *Sentences* composed ca. 1230–40 at the Franciscan *studium* in Paris. This gloss was very influential in the early Franciscan school at Paris: according to Bougerol, "La Glose sur les *Sentences*," p. 171, it was used by the redactors of Alexander Hales's *Summa*, and by Odo of Rigaud and Bonaventure in their commentaries on the *Sentences*.

The first *introitus*, Vat. Lat. MS 691, bottom left margin fol. 1ra, "En lectulum Salomonis," is transcribed below. Capitalization and punctuation are added where necessary to conform to modern practice. I have added the material in brackets. This work is listed in Stegmüller, *Repertorium* 1: 502, no. 1322, and A. Pelzer, *Codices Vaticani latini*, vol. 2, *679–1134* (Rome: Typis Polyglottis Vaticanis, 1931), pp. 11–12; for complete bibliography see Bougerol, "La Glose sur les *Sentences*," p. 117.

Cant. III [7–8]. *En lectulum Salomonis LX fortes ambiunt ex fortissimis Israel, omnes tenentes gladios et ad bella doctissimi. Salomon* qui dicitur pacificus, ipse est rex noster Christus. *Lectulus* eius est militans ecclesia quia in cordibus fidelium quiescit et dormit. Unde sponsa *Indica mihi ubi cubes*, etc. [Cant. 1: 6] hanc ecclesiam. *LX fortes* dicuntur custodire, scilicet, universi doctores fidem defendo et hereses impugnando qui possunt dici LX propter duplicem perfectionem, scilicet, custodiam mandatorum et opera misericordie. Composita enim LX ex denario et senario quia decies sex sunt LX. Hii sunt *ex fortissimis Israel* fortes per passionem, tolerantiam, sive patientiam, sed de Israel propter astuciam et cautelam. Hii sunt *tenentes gladios*, id est, auctoritates et sententias ad refellendum et impugnandum hereticos, sed *ad bella doctissimi* per defensionem. Magister eorum, Christus, constituit eis domum armorum ubi reposita hec arma, scilicet, Librum Sententiarum in quo continentur auctoritates et rationes ad fidei defensionem et heresis impugnationem. Hoc est quod dicitur II Paralip. IX [15–16] quod *rex Salomon fecit CC hastas et CCC scuta aurea et posuit in armamentario*, scilicet, in *domo saltus* ut dicit III Reg. X [17]. *Armamentarium* quod dicitur domus armorum potest dici Liber Sententiarum, *haste* Domini directa et acuta fidelium argumenta, *scuta* sunt divine sententie versucias hereticorum dirimentes per fidem et veritatem, *CCC* dicitur propter perfectionem scientie et indivisibile Trinitatis. Item *CC haste* propter auctoritates et rationes, quia nunc auctoritate nunc ratione iaculis adversarii consumantur. Hec inquam sunt arma contra pseudo de quibus dicit Apostolus II Cor. X [4] *Arma militie nostre non sunt carnalia sed potentia Deo ad destructionem munitionum*. Unde Cant. II [15] *Capite nobis vulpes parvulas que demoliuntur vineas*. De hac armorum domo dicitur Cant. IIII [4] *Sicut turris David collum tuum que edificata est cum propugnaculis*. Item per nemus quo terre datum est armamentarium significantur scientie seculares quibus imbuti debent carpentari quasi ligna silvestria. Et hoc fugit captivando intellectum per obsequium fidei [cf. II Cor. 10: 15].

Notes

This article is based on a paper presented at the Twenty-Fourth International Congress on Medieval Studies at Kalamazoo, Michigan, May 4–7, 1989. The author wishes to thank Robert E. Lerner, Joseph Goering, Marcia Colish, and Nancy Van Deusen for their comments on this paper. She owes special thanks to James J. John for his kind assistance in translating numerous Latin texts. All opinions and mistakes in this paper are solely the responsibility of the author.

1. Peter Lombard, *Sententiae in IV libris distinctae*, 2 vols., ed. Ignatius Brady (Grottaferrata: Editiones Collegii S. Bonaventurae ad Claras Aquas, 1971–1981), 1: 3: ". . . brevi volumine complicans Patrum sententias, appositis eorum testimoniis, ut non sit necesse quaerenti librorum numerositatem evolvere, cui brevitas collecta quod quaeritur offert sine

labore." I have used here the translation by James A. Weisheipl, *Friar Thomas d'Aquino: His Life, Thought, and Work* (Garden City, N.Y.: Doubleday, 1974), p. 68. For the fullest treatment of Peter's life and works see Marcia L. Colish, *Peter Lombard*, 2 vols. (Leiden: Brill, 1994).

2. R. James Long, "The Science of Theology According to Richard Fishacre: Edition of the Prologue to his *Commentary on the Sentences*," *Mediaeval Studies* 34 (1972), 71–98, here 72–73. See also Weisheipl, *Friar Thomas*, pp. 68–69.

3. Josef Pieper, *Scholasticism: Personalities and Problems of Medieval Philosophy* (New York: McGraw-Hill, 1964).

4. Pieper, *Scholasticism*, p. 95, quoting Alois Dempf, *Die Hauptform mittelalterlicher Weltanschauung. Eine geisteswissenschaftliche Studie über die Summa* (Munich: R. Oldenbourg, 1925), p. 108.

5. Pieper, *Scholasticism*, citing Martin Grabmann, *Die Geschichte der scholastischen Methode: nach den gedruckten und ungedruckten Quellen*, 2 vols. (Freiburg, 1909, 1911; repr. Berlin: Akademie-Verlag, 1956), 2: 406.

6. Pieper, *Scholasticism*, p. 97, citing Bernard Geyer, *Die patristische und scholastische Philosophie*, vol. 2 of *Friedrich Überwegs Grundriss der Philosophie*, 11th ed. (Berlin: E. S. Mittler and Sons, 1928), p. 275.

7. Pieper, *Scholasticism*, p. 98.

8. Marcia Colish, "Systematic Theology and Theological Renewal in the Twelfth Century," *Journal of Medieval and Renaissance Studies* 18/2 (Fall 1988), 135–56; see also Colish, *Peter Lombard*, 1: 34–77.

9. These earliest surviving statutes that include the *Sentences* as part of the theology curriculum are in Heinrich Denifle, Emile Louis Marie Chatelain, et al., *Chartularium universitatis Parisiensis*, 4 vols. (Paris: Ex typis fratrum Delalain, 1889–97), 2: 691–96, no. 1188; p. 692, art. 16: "Item, nota, quod illi qui legerunt cursus suos in theologia, debent expectare, postquam inceperunt legere Bibliam, per duos annos, antequam admittantur ad lecturam Sententiarum." The purpose of these statutes was to consolidate and regularize traditional theological school practices and curriculum, as is seen from the opening sentence (p. 691): "Hic sequuntur regule seu consuetudines aut statuta observata ab antiquo tempore in venerabili facultate theologie." Other documentary evidence suggests that the *Sentences* formed part of the curriculum by ca. 1240 (see below, note 27).

10. Palémon Glorieux, "L'Enseignment au Moyen Age. Techniques et méthodes en usage à la faculté de théologie de Paris au XIIIe siècle," *Archives d'histoire doctrinale et littéraire du moyen âge* (hereafter cited as *AHDLMA*) 43 (1968), 65–186, esp. 94–99; and Glorieux, "Sentences (Commentaires sur les)," *Dictionnaire de Théologie Catholique* (hereafter cited as *DTC*), 15 vols. (Paris: Letouzey, 1860–84), 14b, *Scholarios–Szczaniecki*. The most comprehensive guide to commentaries on the *Sentences* is Friedrich Stegmüller, *Repertorium Commentariorum in Sententias Petri Lombardi* (hereafter cited as *Repertorium*), 2 vols. (Würzburg: Schoning, 1947).

11. Beryl Smalley, "The Bible in the Medieval Schools," in *The West from the Fathers to the Reformation*, vol. 2 of *The Cambridge History of the Bible*, ed. G. W. H. Lampe (Cambridge: Cambridge University Press, 1969), pp. 197–220, here 198–99; and Smalley, *The Study of the Bible in the Middle Ages*, 2nd ed. (Notre Dame, Ind.: University of Notre Dame Press, 1964), pp. 196–213.

12. For editions of these works see Peter Abelard, *Sic et non: A Critical Edition*, ed. Blanche B. Boyer and Richard McKeon (Chicago: University of Chicago Press, 1976); Hugh of St. Victor, *Summa Sententiarum*, *PL* 176, cols. 41–174; Nikolaus M. Häring, ed., "Die *Sententiae magistri Gisleberti Pictavensis*," parts 1 and 2, *AHDLMA* 45 (1978), 83–180 and 46 (1979), 45–195; Robert Pullen, *Sententiarum libri octo*, *Patrologia cursus completus . . . series latina* (hereafter cited as *PL*), ed. Jacques-Paul Migne, 217 vols. (Paris, 1878–90), 186, cols. 639–1010; Ambrosius M. Gietl, ed., *Die Sentenzen Rolands Nachmals Papstes Alexander III* (Freiburg: Hemdersche Verlagshandlung, 1891); and Raymond M. Martin, ed., *Oeuvres de Robert de Melun* (Louvain: Spicilegium sacrum lovaniense, 1947–52). For a discussion of these works and their authors see Colish, "Systematic Theology," and her *Peter Lombard*, 1: 34–77.

13. See Glorieux, "Sentences," *DTC*, cols. 1873–74; and Odon Lottin, "Le Premier commentaire connu des *Sentences* de Pierre Lombard," *Recherches de théologie ancienne et médiévale* (hereafter cited as *RTAM*) 11 (1939), 64–71, here 71.

14. Lottin, "Le Premier commentaire," p. 71. Peter of Poitiers' *Libri quinque sententiae* is in *PL* 211, cols. 789–1280; books 1 and 2 ed. Philip S. Moore and Marthe Dulong, *Sententiae Petri Pictaviensis*, 2 vols. (Notre Dame, Ind.: University of Notre Dame Press, 1943, 1950). See also Philip S. Moore, *The Works of Peter of Poitiers, Master in Theology and Chancellor of Paris (1193–1205)* (Washington, D.C.: Catholic University of America Press, 1936). Praepositinus's commentary is unedited; see Stegmüller, *Repertorium* 1: 340–41.

15. For information on Peter Comestor see David Luscombe, "Peter Comestor," in *The Bible in the Medieval World: Essays in Memory of Beryl Smalley*, ed. Katherine Walsh

and Diana Wood (Oxford: Basil Blackwell, 1985), pp. 109–29. Peter Comestor's gloss on the *Sentences* survives only in fragments; see R.-M. Martin, "Notes sur l'oeuvre littéraire de Pierre le Mangeur," *RTAM* 3 (1931), 54–66; Peter's prologue is edited pp. 60–62.

16. Luscombe, "Peter Comestor," p. 110. Luscombe bases this conclusion on evidence in Walter of St. Victor, *Contra IV Labyrinthos Francie*, ed. Palémon Glorieux, "Le *Contra Quatuor Labyrinthos Francie* de Gauthier de Saint Victor," *AHDLMA* 19 (1952), 187–335, here p. 320, lines 12–35. On this subject see also Ignatius Brady's introduction to Peter Lombard, *Sententiae in IV libris distinctae* 2: 40*–42.*

17. Luscombe, "Peter Comestor," p. 116. See also Artur Landgraf, "Les écrits de Pierre le Mangeur," *RTAM* 3 (1931), 341–72.

18. The first sixty lines of the Pseudo-Peter of Poitiers prologue are edited by Martin, "Notes sur l'oeuvre," pp. 63–64, based on a manuscript from London, British Library, Royal MS 7 F XIII. The next sixty lines are edited by Odon Lottin, "A Propos des *Glossae super Sententias* attribuées à Pierre de Poitiers," in his *Psychologie et morale aux XIIe et XIIIe siècles*, vols. 5–6, *Problemes d'histoire litteraire* (Gembloux: J. Duculot, 1960), pp. 119–24, here 121–22, based on a manuscript from Paris, B.N. Lat. MS 14423.

19. This date is according to Thomas Kaeppeli, *Scriptores ordinis praedicatorum medii aevi*, vol. 2 (Rome: Ad S. Sabinae, 1975), pp. 269–81. Stegmüller, *Repertorium*, 1: 174–75 gives the date ca. 1230–32, and Palémon Glorieux, *Répertoire des maîtres en théologie de Paris au XIIIe siècle* (hereafter cited as *Rép.*), 2 vols. (Paris: Vrin, 1933–34), 1: 43 suggests 1229–30. Hugh's prologue, *introitus*, and first distinction to *Sentences* book 1, and his prologue and first distinction to book 4 are edited by Friedrich Stegmüller, "Hugo de Sancto Caro": Commentarius in I et IV *Sententiarum*," in Stegmüller, ed., *Analecta Upsaliensia theologiam medii aevi illustrantia*, vol. 1, *Opera systematica* (Uppsala: Lundequistska bokhandeln and Wiesbaden: O. Harassowitz, 1953), pp. 33–95. The prologue to Hugh's *Sentences* commentary, a discussion of the correct terminology to be used in analyzing the Trinity, is discussed by John Fisher, "Hugh of St. Cher and the Development of Medieval Theology," *Speculum* 31 (1956), 57–69. In this paper I am focusing on the *introitus* to the first book of the *Sentences*. For Hugh see also Robert E. Lerner, "Poverty, Preaching, and Eschatology in the Revelation Commentaries of 'Hugh of St. Cher'," in Walsh, *The Bible in the Medieval World*, pp. 157–89; and Beryl Smalley, "The Gospels in the Paris Schools in the Late Twelfth and Early Thirteenth Centuries: Peter the Chanter, Hugh of St. Cher, Alexander of Hales, John of La Rochelle," *Franciscan Studies* 39 (1979), 230–54, and 40 (1980), 298–369, repr. in Beryl Smalley, *The Gospels in the Schools, c. 1100–c. 1280* (London: Hambledon Press, 1985), pp. 99–196 (page references are to this version), here 118–43.

20. Jeanne Bignami-Odier, "Le Manuscrit Vatican Latin 2186," *AHDLMA* 12 (1937), 133–66; prologue on pp. 140–53.

21. For lists of the thirteenth-century theology masters at Paris see Glorieux, *Rép.* For the following information on commentaries see Glorieux, "Sentences," *DTC*, cols. 1862–63, 1871–73.

22. For information on Hugh of St. Cher see works cited above, note 19.

23. For Roland's life and works see Glorieux, *Rép.*, 1: 42, no. 1. For the text of the prologue to his *Summa* and bibliography see Giuseppe Cremascoli, "La 'Summa' di Rolando da Cremona: Il testo del prologo," *Studi Medievali* series 3, 16/2 (December 1975), 825–76.

24. For biography and bibliography see the Prolegomena to Alexander of Hales, *Glossa in Quatuor Libros Sententiarum Petri Lombardi*, 4 vols. (Quaracchi: Collegium S. Bonaventurae, 1951–57), 1: 110*–116*; for Alexander's *introitus* and exposition of the prologue of Peter Lombard see 1: 1–6. See also Smalley, "The Gospels in the Paris Schools," pp. 120–23, 144–71.

25. The above information is taken from Glorieux, *Rép.*, 1: 52–61, nos. 3, 4, 5, and 2: 25–30, no. 302.

26. Jacques-Guy Bougerol summarizes the scholarship on this manuscript and offers his own observations in "La Glose sur Les *Sentences* du Manuscrit Vat. Lat. 691," *Antonianum* 55 (1980), 109–73. Although Bougerol is primarily concerned with the authorship of the *Sentences* commentary in the body of the manuscript that he believes is by John of La Rochelle, he briefly discusses the three *introitus* on pp. 117–19.

27. This is based on students' classroom notes preserved in Paris, B.N. lat. 15652 and 15702, described respectively in the Prolegomena to Alexander of Hales, *Summa theologica*, 4 vols. (Quaracchi: Ex Typographia Collegii S. Bonaventurae, 1924–48), 4: CCCL; and in M.-D. Chenu, "Maîtres et bacheliers de l'Université de Paris v. 1240," in *Etudes d'histoire littéraire et doctrinale du XIII siècle* 1 (Paris and Ottawa: J. Vrin and Institut d'études médiévales, 1932), 11–39. The contents of both manuscripts are also discussed by Glorieux, "Les Années 1242–1247 à la Faculté de théologie de Paris," *RTAM* 29 (1962), 234–49. Bibliographic and biographical information for some of these masters is available in Glorieux, *Rép.*: for Bertrand see 2: 52, no. 306; for Odo of Rosny 2: 53, no. 307; for Odo Rigaud 2: 31–33, no. 303; for Albertus 1: 62–77, no. 6; for Peter 1: 333, no. 151; and for Adam 1: 335, no. 154. For Stephen, John of Moussy, and John the Page see *Rép.*, 1: 388, 229–30, and 230, respectively.

28. The most recent general work on Albert's life and thought is *Albert and Thomas: Selected Writings*, ed. and trans. Simon Tugwell (New York: Paulist Press, 1988). For Albert's prologue see Albertus Magnus, *Opera Omnia*, ed. Auguste Borgnet, vol. 25, *Commentarium in I Sententiarum (Dist. I–XXV)* (Paris: Apud Ludovicum Vives, 1893), pp. 1–20. For Odo see the articles by F. M. Henquinet, "Les manuscrits et l'influence des écrits théologiques d'Eudes Rigaux O.F.M.," *RTAM* 11 (1939), 324–50; and "Eudes de Rosny, Eudes Rigaud et la Somme d'Alexander de Hales," *Archivum Franciscanum Historicum* 33 (1940), 3–54. See also Franz Pelster, "Beiträge zur Erforschung des schriftliches Nachlasses Odo Rigaldis," *Scholastik* 11 (1936), 518–42. I have transcribed part of the prologue of Odo Rigaud, *Commentarium in IV Libris Sententiarum*, based on Paris, B.N. lat. MS 14910 f. 1r–v, compared with Troyes MS 824 f. 1r–2r, and Troyes MS 1245 f. 1r–2v.

29. For Richard Fishacre see Long, "The Science of Theology" (see above, note 2); this includes an edition and discussion of Fishacre's commentary, pp. 79–98. For another discussion of this prologue to the *Sentences* see Stephen F. Brown, "Richard Fishacre on the Need for Philosophy," in *A Straight Path: Studies in Medieval Philosophy and Culture: Essays in Honor of Arthur Hyman*, ed. Ruth Link-Salinger Hyman (Washington, D.C.: Catholic University of America Press, 1988), pp. 23–36.

30. Richard W. Hunt, "The Introductions to the 'Artes' in the Twelfth Century," in *Studia Mediaevalia in honorem admodum Reverendi Patris Raymundi Josephi Martin, O.P.* (Bruges: De Tempel, 1948), pp. 85–112; and Alastair J. Minnis, *Medieval Theory of Authorship: Scholastic Literary Attitudes in the Later Middle Ages* (London: Scolar Press, 1984). More about these prologues, especially regarding legal texts, can be found in Edwin A. Quain, "The Medieval *Accessus ad Auctores*," *Traditio* 3 (1945), 215–64.

31. Minnis, *Medieval Theory of Authorship*, pp. 19–25.

32. Minnis, *Medieval Theory of Authorship*, pp. 40–41.

33. Martin, "Notes sur l'oeuvre," p. 62: "Intencio sua est confutare blasfemos, confirmare doctos, excitare pigros. Quod facit, docens tria circa fidem, scilicet, quid de ea sit asserendum, quid est contra dicendum, quid pie dubitandum pocius quam temere sit asserendum."

34. Martin, "Notes sur l'oeuvre," p. 62: "Modus agendi talis est: prologum premittit et prescribit operi, in quo excusat et se de arrogancia, et suum opus de superfluitate."

35. See Stegmüller, "Hugo de Sancto Caro," p. 46; and O. Lottin, "A Propos des *Glossae*," p. 121.

36. Alexander of Hales, *Glossa in IV libros*, 1: 1; Bignami-Odier, "Le Manuscript Vatican," pp. 149–50; and Odo Rigaud, Paris B.N. lat. MS 14910 1rb, line 18.

37. Albertus Magnus, "In prologum magistri expositio," *Comm. in I Sent.*, pp. 6–12.

38. Minnis, *Medieval Theory of Authorship*, p. 80, writes that the moving causes are "a heading which could designate some or all of the four causes, or a causal system in which the four causes were said to play a major part."

39. Albertus Magnus, *Comm. in I Sent.*, p. 10: "In hac parte ex causis moventibus etiam alias hujus operis causas concludit. Et habet sex partes: in quarum prima repetit breviter causas moventes duas, scilicet eversionem haereticorum, et exaltationem lucernae veritatis. . . ."

40. Albertus Magnus, *Comm. in I Sent.*, p. 11: "In secunda tangit Auctorem. . . ."

41. Albertus Magnus, *Comm. in I Sent.*, p. 11: "In tertia tangit materiam, cum dicit: 'Ex testimoniis veritatis in aeternum fundatis, etc.', id est, in aeternitate. . . ."

42. Albertus Magnus, *Comm. in I Sent.*, p. 11: "In quarta tangit formam duplicem, scilicet distinctionis materiae secundum illum actum formae, quo distinguit formatum ab aliis, cum dicit: 'in quatuor libris, etc.' Et modum probationum suarum quibus utitur secundum actum formae quo agit, et est principium actionum, cum dicit 'In quo majorum exempla, etc.' Et exempla referuntur ad similitudines quibus utitur: doctrina autem ad auctoritates, et rationes alias."

43. Albertus Magnus, *Comm. in I Sent.*, p. 11: "In quinta tangit finem, cum dicit: 'In quo per Dominicae, etc.' Et sincera professio fidei est finis per se: proditio autem haeresis est finis per accidens. . . ."

44. Albertus Magnus, *Comm. in I Sent.*, p. 11: "In sexta et ultima tangit modum agendi triplicem, scilicet, pertingentiae ad veritatis aditum per rationes fidei, et excludendo errores, et hoc, ibi, 'Aditum demonstrandae.' Secundo, tangit modum inter subtile et grossum, cum dicit: 'Temperato inter utrumque.' Tertio, tangit modum inter proprium inventum, et alienum, ibi, 'Sicubi vero parum, etc.'"

45. Long, "The Science of Theology," p. 80: ". . . quattuor genera causarum, scilicet necessitatem vel utilitatem quod spectat ad causam finalem, auctorem quod spectat ad efficientem, subiectum quod spectat ad causam materialem, unitatem et divisionem quod spectat ad causam formalem."

46. Long, "The Science of Theology," pp. 80–81, 88, 92, 93.

47. Minnis, *Medieval Theory of Authorship*, p. 10. On *auctores* and *auctoritates* see also M.-D. Chenu, *Toward Understanding Saint Thomas* (Chicago: Henry Regnery, 1964), pp. 126–39.

48. Minnis, *Medieval Theory of Authorship*, p. 13.

49. Minnis, *Medieval Theory of Authorship*, pp. 160–61, writes that although prologues were reserved for *auctores* of antiquity (with the exception of Gratian and Peter Lombard) in the twelfth and thirteenth centuries, in the fourteenth century Aristotelian academic prologues began to be attached to modern texts developed for teaching grammar such as the *Parvum doctrinale* of Alan of Lille. Occasionally, the author of a new work would write for it his own Aristotelian prologue, e.g., Robert of Basevorn discusses the four causes in the beginning of his *Forma praedicandi,* which he completed in 1322 (ed. Th.-M. Charland, *Artes Praedicandi: Contribution à l'histoire de la rhetorique au moyen âge* [Paris and Ottawa: Vrin, 1936], pp. 233–35).

50. Martin, "Notes sur l'oeuvre," p. 61: "Statuit Moyses terminos iuxta montem domini ne ascenderet populus ad videndum dominum, et ex eis plurima multitudo periret. Legitur tamen Moyses domino vocante terminos transcendisse; seniores vero, qui de spiritu moysis acceperant, ad terminos pervenisse, sed, Moyse moram faciente cum domino, exspectacionis tedio affectos ad castra rediisse; populum vero nec castra eciam exivisse.

Per montem istum sacre scripture veritas, id est utriusque testamenti canon significatur. Vetus autem testamentum et novum ideo veritas dicuntur, quia tanta fidei et veritatis solididate subsistunt, ut absque contradictione eis credi sit necesse. Termini circa montem positi sunt agiographi, id est, sanctorum patrum scripta, utriusque testamenti intellectum nobis aperiencia. Hos autem terminos quidam sicut moyses domino vocante transierunt, uti primitivi patres qui solius dei revelatione intelligenciam scripture perceperunt: sicut legitur quod dominus apostolis *sensum aperuit ut intelligerent scripturas.* Sed de his nichil ad nos. Quidam autem hos terminos domino non vocante transgrediuntur. Unde merito blasphemi vel heretici dicuntur. Per seniores quidem ad terminos pervenientes, sed postea regredientes, designantur docti accedentes ad legenda patrum volumina, sed tam magnitudine quam numerositate librorum exterriti, quasi desperantes, ad breviores artes se transferunt, ut ad phisicam, leges et huiusmodi. Per populum castra non exeuntem intelliguntur pigri et desides, qui nec eciam ad legendos libros accedere volunt.

Propter hec tria genera hominum, Magister videns terminos illos iam in magnas arbores excrevisse, ut faciliorem ac . . . incessum nobis prepararet, quasi quosdam ramusculos in via prosternens, hoc breve opus de multis collegit. . . ."

51. Charlton T. Lewis and Charles Short, *A Latin Dictionary* (Oxford: Clarendon, 1975, s.v. "prosterno."

52. I wish to thank Joseph Goering for this second interpretation.

53. *PL* 18, cols. 15–66; col. 15: "Necessarium duxi ante omnia quae mihi videntur, libellum Regularum scribere . . . ut quis prophetiae universam silvam perambulans, his regulis quodammodo lucis tramitibus deductus, ab errore defendatur." For a modern edition and complete translation see *Tyconius, The Book of Rules,* trans. William S. Babcock (Atlanta: Scholars Press, 1989). I wish to thank Charles Kannengiesser for pointing out to me Tyconius's use of the metaphor of the forest.

54. Martin, "Notes sur l'oeuvre," p. 62: "Collecturus ergo Magister hoc opus ex diversis sanctorum voluminibus, consideravit universam scripture sacre seriem circa duo tantum, scilicet creatorem et creatoris opus versari."

55. Martin, "Notes sur l'oeuvre," p. 64: "Termini circa montem positi sanctorum expositiones mistice intelliguntur, quorum tenemur sequi vestigia, ne transgrediamur terminos quos posuerunt patres nostri."

56. Stegmüller, "Hugo de Sancto Caro," p. 44: "Sacra Scriptura monti comparatur propter duo, tum propter eminentiam scientiae, tum quia a Deo est instituta, ut eo non sit fas obviare.

Hinc est, quod sanctorum auctoritates, scilicet Ambrosii, Hieronymi, Augustini, saepe determinamus; auctoritates vero canonis nequaquam fas est determinare, nisi sit evidens ratio. Nemo enim audet *os suum* ponere *in coelum* (Ps. 72: 9).

Terminos positos circa montem mystice hagiographa intelligimus, id est sanctorum expositiones, quorum tenemur adorare vestigia et sequi, ne transgrediamur terminos, quos posuerunt patres nostri" (Prov. 22: 28).

57. The following is my edition of the text of Vatican Lat. 691, fol. 1ra. For the complete text see the appendix to this paper. "Magister eorum, Christus, constituit eis domum armorum ubi reposita hec arma, scilicet, Librum Sententiarum in quo continentur auctoritates et rationes ad fidei defensionem et heresis impugnationem. Hoc est quod dicitur II Paralip.IX [15–16] quod *rex Salomon fecit CC hastas et CCC scuta aurea et posuit in armamentario,* scilicet, in *domo saltus* ut dicit III Reg. X [17]. *Armamentarium* quod dicitur domus armorum potest dici Liber Sententiarum, *haste* Domini directa et acuta fidelium argumenta, *scuta* sunt divine sententie versucias hereticorum dirimentes per fidem et veritatem, *CCC* dicitur propter perfectionem scientie et indivisibile trinitatis. Item *CC haste* propter auctoritates et rationes, quia nunc auctoritate nunc ratione iaculis adversarii consumantur."

58. Bignami-Odier, "Le Manuscrit Vatican." The initial question, p. 140, is "Scientie religionis catholice intendentes . . . 5 de partibus eius, 6 qualiter se habeant partes eius ad inuicem et de modo tractandi in illis partibus. . . ." The reply is on pp. 147–48: "Ad 5 sic: huiusmodi res habet duas differentias tanquam formales, quia circa huiusmodi rem attenditur ueritas et bonitas . . . secundum hoc sunt due partes scientie pietatis, una est de uero pietatis, scilicet de uero credibili, et hec docet quid credibile et cuius et principia et causas et quid operabile, altera est de bono pietatis, scilicet quod est beatificans tam in uia quam in patria. Unde scientia pietatis docet et ea per que illuminatur intelligens ad cognitiones ueritatis credibilium et operabilium et ea per que mouetur affectus ad amorem et aquisitionem boni beatificantis et genera eius que exiguntur ad hec; . . .

6 patet ex iam dictis . . . sicut speculatiue ad actiuam uel theorice ad praticam. Nam prima docet quid et que et cuius sint credibilia et operabilia talia, secunda est mouens et instruens ad operandum iuxta precognita scilicet credere operari ut aquiratur finis. Hec secunda determinatur in libris *Ueteris* et *Noui Testamenti*, post in *Libro Sententiarum*. Et quia per exempla et parabolas et moniciones et comminaciones mirabilia et promissa et terrores et huiusmodi affectus et non per syllogisticas rationes, propter hoc illa pars doctrine non utitur sillogismo aut demonstratione sed narratione predictarum et entimematibus que sunt ex ycotibus [sic] et signis ad modum rethoricorum . . . intellectus uero mouetur per rationes sillogisticas et demonstrationes, ideo illi parti que traditur in *Libro Sententiarum* competit procedere per syllogismum et demonstrationem."

59. Albertus Magnus, *Comm. in I Sent.*, pp. 19–20, dist. 1, A, art. 5, "De modis exponendi sacram Scripturam": "Et quoad exhortationem habet quadruplicem exposicionem, scilicet historialem, allegoricam, moralem, et anagogicam: quorum modorum numerus dupliciter potest accipi, scilicet quoad exponentem, et quoad exposita. . . .

Penes exposita numerus iste accipitur sic: Scriptura potest attendi penes intentum a scribente, vel penes intentum a Spiritu inspirante et illuminante. . . .

In quantum autem finis est, scilicet contradicentes revincere, habet alium modum. Contradicens enim non revincitur nisi duobus, scilicet probatione veritatis, et manifestatione erroris. Hoc autem non fit nisi per argumentationem congruam a ratione auctoritatis, vel naturalis rationis, vel similitudinis congrue sumptam: et sic hoc modo argumentatio talis erit instrumentum ejus, et (ut patet in prooemio) iste modus est scientie istius libri, alii autem modi sunt observati in Biblia."

60. Long, "The Science of Theology," p. 97: "Utraque fateor harum partium in sacro Scripturae sacrae canone—sed indistincte—continetur. Verumtamen tantum altera pars, scilicet de moribus instruendis, a magistris modernis cum leguntur sancti libri docetur. Alia tamquam difficilior disputationi reservatur. Haec autem pars difficilior de canone sacrarum Scripturarum excerpta in isto libro qui Sententiarum dicitur ponitur. Unde non differt hic legere et disputare.

Et quia ut dicitur Sap. 1: 'In malivolam animam non introibit sapientia,' prius est ut affectus informetur sanctis moribus, quam aspectus desudet in quaestionibus circa fidem difficilibus. Alioquin parum aut nihil proficiet. . . . Quia ergo in praecedentibus de moribus instruendis audistis, ratio ordinis et consummationis exigeret ut et secunda pars, quae est de quaestionibus circa fidem difficilibus, nunc convenienter legeretur."

A Re-evaluation of the Contribution of Thomas Aquinas to the Thirteenth-Century Theology of the Eucharist

Gary Macy

*I*n David Burr's superb study of eucharistic presence and conversion in late thirteenth-century Franciscan thought, he argues that Thomas and Bonaventure made a major contribution to eucharistic theology by insisting that eucharistic conversion is "both an adequate and necessary explanation of eucharistic presence."[1] Dr. Burr points out that this teaching marks a significant advance over the teaching of both Thomas's and Bonaventure's predecessors despite their reliance on previous teaching. The main focus of his study goes on to show how the achievement of Thomas and Bonaventure was soon challenged by later writers and never received the widespread recognition that later historians sometimes attribute to it.

Given the self-imposed limits of Dr. Burr's study, the conclusions he draws are certainly justified by his careful textual analysis, but as he himself points out, Albert the Great, William of Melitona, Bonaventure, and Thomas all produced lengthy discussions of the Eucharist, only part of which dealt with conversion and presence. Based not only on Dr. Burr's research but also my own studies on the theology of reception of the Eucharist in thirteenth- and fourteenth-century theologians, I would like to put forward the tentative hypothesis that the theology of Albert the Great, rather than that of his student Thomas or that of the great Franciscan Bonaventure, marked a turning point in the theology of the Eucharist. In a distinct departure from his predecessors, and in a more thorough manner than even Thomas, Albert placed eucharistic conversion

53

at the heart of his theology, emphasizing the role of metaphysics over that of theology. Thomas would enthusiastically follow the lead of his teacher, while Bonaventure would accept Albert's theology only up to a point.

In order to highlight the novelty of Albert's teaching, it needs to be placed in the context of the theology of the Eucharist during the first half of the thirteenth century. At the beginning of the century, the three greatest influences on eucharistic thought were Hugh of St. Victor in his *De sacramentis*, Peter Lombard's discussion in the *Sentences*, and Innocent III's *De mysteriis*. These three sources emphasized, first, that the risen Lord was truly present in the sacrament and, second, that this presence, though real, was a sacramental presence, a presence in sign, accessible only through faith.

These concerns mirrored the theological concerns of the day. The first emphasis, traditional at least since the Berengarian heresy of the mid to late eleventh century, was particularly emphasized in opposition to the Cathars, who completely denied the validity of the Eucharist. In fact, it was in the creed directed against the Cathars and Waldensians, written at the Fourth Lateran council in 1215, that the term *transubstantiation* was first used in an official church document. Despite the tenacity of the assertion, this usage did not constitute a "definition" of transubstantiation, as several studies, starting with Hans Jorissen's magisterial *Die Entfaltung der Transsubstantiationslehre bis zum Beginn der Hochscholastik*, have shown.[2] Contemporaries certainly did not view it that way. William of Auvergne, in his discussion of transubstantiation, written between 1223 and 1240, concluded with the following advice:

> It suffices for the piety of faith, which we intend to establish here, to believe and hold that after the priestly blessing has been correctly performed, the bread of life is placed on the altar before us under the form of material and visible bread, and the drink of life is placed before us under the form of visible wine.[3]

A second and equally important emphasis stressed the non carnal nature of the presence of the Lord. Again, William of Auvergne would warn his readers that one of the two causes of heresy was the belief that the body and blood of the risen Lord were carnally eaten in this ritual.[4]

My own speculation would be that the theologians were trying to counter the popular notions of the sacrament that stressed the miraculous presence of Jesus in the numerous miracle host stories.

This emphasis on the spiritual nature of the Eucharist would be developed into a fully elaborated and very influential theology by the Parisian secular master and later convert to the Franciscans, Alexander of Hales. Basing himself on earlier writers, and especially Pope Innocent III, Alexander argued that reception depended upon the recognition of the sign value of the sacrament by the recipient.[5] In Alexander's commentary on Peter Lombard's *Sentences*, written ca. 1222–23,[6] he explained that since the body of Christ is spiritual food, only an intellectual nature is capable of receiving it. As Augustine had pointed out, the outward sign leads to the inner reality, and only the intellect can so reach beyond the sign to the reality behind it. Animals then receive simply the outer forms, the taste of bread and wine, whereas humans can understand symbols. Therefore, only humans can access the presence of the Lord underlying the *sacramentum* of bread and wine.[7]

Writing between 1220 and 1236 in a work now known as the *Quaestiones disputatae "Antequam esset frater,"* Alexander suggested that there are three kinds of union possible in the Eucharist. One can be united in thought, in love, and in nature to Christ. Those who existed before the coming of Christ could be united in thought and love, but not in nature. Angels, too, having a different nature than Christ, cannot receive him naturally. Then, too, Christ can be received with more or less love, and more or less understanding. This means that there are different degrees of reception of Christ. Perfect reception would take place only in heaven, Alexander intimated. Those who receive the sign alone, like Jews and pagans, are united only to the sign, as if it were mere bread. Again, there is a union of those who both believe and understand the reason for the sign. Finally, there is the greater union of those who believe and love, and this is spiritual reception.[8]

Alexander discussed the question of whether only rational creatures have the ability to receive this sacrament. It would seem that irrational creatures must be able to receive, since once transubstantiation takes place, the body of Christ remains as long as the species of bread and wine remains. If an animal receives the species of bread, it ought as well to receive the body of Christ. If, however, by sacramental reception is meant that the recipient touches the reality behind the sign as well as the sign alone, then neither animals, nor Jews, nor pagans can be said to receive sacramentally. True to the principles established earlier, Alexander asserted that to receive sacramentally, properly speaking, is to be united either in nature or faith or charity with Christ. Certainly animals cannot then receive. Even Jews and pagans, however they might share in the same human nature as Christ, do not receive sacramentally since they do not understand the reality underlying the signs.[9]

Alexander's discussion of reception is extremely important. I know of no earlier medieval author who had so explicitly argued that reception was dependent on the intentionality of the receiver, and Alexander's theology would be very influential. At least three important theologians of the next generation directly or indirectly followed Alexander's theology. The Franciscans William of Melitona and St. Bonaventure and the Dominican Albert the Great followed Alexander in asserting the importance of a true theology of sign in the reception of the Eucharist.

William of Melitona, writing ca. 1245–49, followed Alexander in including a lengthy and elaborate explanation of reception. Because it is a sign, understood only by reason or faith, only rational creatures are capable of reception of the *sacramentum et res* of the Eucharist. Irrational animals are capable of receiving only the accidents of the species, that is the *sacramentum*.

Humans can actually consume the body of Christ, although it is not digested. Since the species still exists, the body does enter the stomach. The species when vomited contains only the accidents, although it is possible that the substance of the bread is miraculously returned.[10] Only rational creatures can receive, though, because the content of the sign can only be reached by faith or knowledge. Animals receive only the accidents with no substance, so it cannot even be called eating. Further, William argued that reception by unbelievers is only accidental as well, but with the potential for sacramental reception.[11]

William summarized his thought in the following manner: "Therefore an animal is united with the accidents alone; for unbelievers, who inwardly believe nothing, is added an aptitude for sacramental or spiritual reception; for those having a deformed faith is added a knowledge of that to which they are united; to those having a true faith, in which charity is included, is added a union of love."[12]

These theologians were not the first to suggest that animals consuming the species receive only the accidents. This had already been the teaching of the authors associated with the school at Laon in the twelfth century.[13] Their contribution was to offer an explanation for this teaching based on intellectual intention. Only humans can understand symbols, and therefore only humans can make contact with the presence of the Lord underlying the symbols of bread and wine.

Bonaventure, perhaps the greatest of the Franciscan theologians, followed his predecessors in emphasizing the importance of the disposition of the recipient in the Eucharist. A long discussion of this issue occurs in his commentary on the *Sentences*. Probably written in the late 1240s or early 1250s, the commentary was possibly revised during his teaching career, which ended with his election as Minister General in 1257.[14] According to Bonaventure, three conditions are necessary for true reception: first, one must be capable of intending the *res* of the *sacramentum*; second, one must believe; and third, one must understand the significance of the sacrament in order to receive. It is because animals and angels cannot meet these requirements that they are incapable of reception.[15]

Bonaventure pointed out that true sacramental reception involves acceptance of the *sacramentum* as a real sign. First, this means that the species must be received as food with the intention of eating them as food. Second, the recipient must be capable of understanding a sign and, in fact, of understanding *this* sign. The recipient must intend to receive the body and blood of Christ as the Church believes. Therefore, only humans can receive sacramentally. Bonaventure disagreed slightly with William of Melitona over the question of heretics. Bonaventure conceded that a heretic might receive sacramentally if the heretic intended to accept what the Church believes to be present. With this one exception, Bonaventure's presentation is very similar to William's. Bonaventure, however, articulated more clearly the central role that intention plays in accessing the presence of the Lord by the recipient.[16]

Bonaventure also made clear the distinction between *situs* and *actum* in sacraments. If one objects that the species cannot be separated from the substance of the body and blood after the consecration, Bonaventure argued that while this might be true as far as *situs*, that is, that the body and blood are linked to the place of the species, the two may be separated *ad actum*, that is to say that whatever happens to the species does not also happen to the body and blood contained under the accidents. Just as the species is broken by the priest and nothing happens to the body and blood, so too the species can be received by an animal or infidel without touching the body and blood that are contained under this sign. Only through the intention of the recipient to receive what is believed to lie under the species can the body and blood by attained.[17]

In his commentary on Distinction 13 of Lombard's fourth book, Bonaventure discussed what would happen if a mouse ate the consecrated species. First, he argued that a mouse receives some food, but does not receive sacramentally or spiritually. Second, he argued that just as a mouse cannot be baptized, so a mouse cannot receive the Eucharist.[18] Bonaventure then went on to discuss two different opinions as to what a mouse eats in the sacrament. First he described the thought of those who argue that since the presence of the body and blood lasts as long as the species, therefore as long as the species subsists in the stomach of the mouse, the body and blood are also present. The mouse is not truly said to eat the body and blood in this case, however, for the mouse cannot reach the body and blood either in nature, nor through knowledge, nor in love. Bonaventure rejected this opinion, for it is an offense to piety to think that the body and blood of the Lord might be in the stomach of a mouse.[19]

Bonaventure next discussed the opinion of those who argue that the mouse could never eat the body and blood of the Lord, for Christ is only under the sign insofar as this sign is directed to human use, and since a mouse is incapable of this, the body and blood disappear and substance of the bread returns. Bonaventure called this opinion "more common, more honest and more reasonable."[20] Bonaventure then asked whether the body and blood of Christ might descend into the stomach of a human. He clearly stated that insofar as the effect of the sacrament is concerned, the body and blood never descend into the stomach but pass into the mind of the believer. Whether the *substance* of the body and blood descends into the stomach is a more doubtful issue, however. Bonaventure cited four different opinions here. The first argues that wherever the species subsists, the substance of the body and blood exists, even in the stomach of a mouse. The second opinion states that the body and blood descend into the stomach of humans alone, and that the substance remains there as long as the species is suitable for refection. A third opinion also holds that the substance descends into the stomach of a human insofar as that act is part of reception, but the substance does not remain in the stomach of the recipient. The final opinion recorded by Bonaventure describes the presence as lasting as long as any part of the species is sensed. After the species is no longer sensed, the further presence of the Lord is spiritual, not physical.[21]

Bonaventure pointed out that all four opinions have reasons to support them and that it is difficult to judge among them. He rejected the first opinion because it would be impious to think of the body of the Lord in the stomach of a mouse. He also rejected the fourth opinion because it lacks rigor. A human being, after all, can also sense food in his or her stomach. Bonaventure would, however, accept both of the other positions as probable. It is probable, therefore, that the body and blood are present only so long as the eating takes place but that they do not remain in the stomach of the recipient. It seemed to Bonaventure more probable, and more plausible, to say, however, that the body and blood remain in the stomach of the recipient so long as the species has its proper form and is suitable for human consumption. In opposition to William of Melitona, therefore, Bonaventure argued that when the species is vomited up by a sick person, the body is still present if the species is still recognizable as human food, and so great care must be taken in giving communion to a sick person.[22]

Bonaventure clearly carried on the teaching of both the Franciscan theologians who preceded him. The faith and reason of the recipient determined whether the body and blood of the Lord would be present, even in unworthy reception, for that individual recipient. This would seem to add another dimension to Bonaventure's linking of eucharistic conversion and presence as Dr. Burr describes it. Bonaventure appears to be asserting two different relationships in the Eucharist. The accidents of the bread and wine are united to the substance of the body and blood of the risen Lord by their sign value through transubstantiation. This relationship is secondary, however, to the more important relationship between the risen Lord and the recipient. Therefore, Bonaventure, following Alexander and William, argues that the transubstantiation is simply undone in the case of an animal eating the consecrated bread. One cannot assert that the real presence accompanies the accidents of bread and wine under all circumstances, as transubstantiation would seem to suggest. The final relationship between recipient and the risen Lord is determined by the intention of the believer, not the metaphysics of the change.

It is not that these theologians denied the usefulness of transubstantiation as a means of describing how the Lord could become really present in the sacrament. Since Dr. Burr has an extensive discussion of the role of transubstantiation in William of Melitona, and of the importance of that means of conversion in Bonaventure, I will merely repeat that this is the case. Alexander of Hales, writing earlier than these two theologians, also asserted the aptness of describing the change that takes place as transubstantiation. "To that which was asked next, what manner of change is this, whether according to quality, or according to quantity, I say that it is a change according to substance, of course, transubstantiation. Nor is this generation, nor corruption, because the same subject does not remain."[23]

Even more emphatically than Bonaventure, however, Alexander denied that transubstantiation could override the importance of the sign value of the Eucharist. When discussing the question of whether only rational creatures can eat the sacrament, Alexander included the argument *contra* that . . .

> given that transubstantiation might occur, once transubstantiation has taken place, as long as the species of the bread remains in the form of species, the *res sacramenti* remains under the species. Therefore, if it befalls the species to be consumed by an irrational creature, under which is the body of Christ, it follows that it eats sacramentally.[24]

Alexander completely rejected this argument in his *responsio*:

> I respond: to eat sacramentally, properly speaking, is to attain to the reality underlying the sign. Therefore, where this reality is in no way attained to, neither by means of belief, nor by means of cognition, there can by no means be sacramental eating. Eating by irrational creatures, therefore, is neither sacramental eating nor eating sacramentally; but it is some sort of carnal eating, yet, properly it is not even carnal eating, since there is here no division of substance, as there is nothing here but the division of accidents alone.[25]

The argument vetted and then rejected by Alexander will become important later, for it is precisely that argument which Albert and his student Thomas will insist upon.

Albert the Great discussed the question of reception several times during his long career. His earliest treatment, that contained in his *De sacramentis*, was written ca. 1240. In this short discussion he followed the teaching first expounded by Alexander of Hales. He explained that since the body of Christ is spiritual food, only an intellectual nature is capable of receiving it. As Augustine had pointed out, the outward sign leads to the inner reality, and only the intellect can so reach beyond the sign to the reality behind it. Animals then receive only outer forms, the taste of bread and wine. Only humans can understand symbols, and therefore only humans can make contact with the presence of the Lord underlying the *sacramentum* of bread and wine.[26]

A much longer and more important discussion of the reception of the Eucharist takes place in Albert's commentary on the *Sentences*, written in 1249.[27] Since this text is central to the argument of the paper, and since the Borgnet edition is unreliable, I have checked the text against the manuscript of Albert's commentary contained in Yale, Beinecke MS Z.109.04. Although there are important variations in the text, they do not affect the thrust of Albert's presentation.[28]

Albert distinguished two ways in which the Eucharist might be said to be received sacramentally, as opposed to spiritually. One could say that, in one sense, only the sign is received, with no understanding of what the sign meant. In another sense, one could receive the sign while understanding its meaning. Infidels can only receive in the first sense.[29]

In discussing the requirements for either sacramental or spiritual reception, Albert specified more clearly his concerns in this matter. It is necessary for sacramental reception that some sort of relationship exist between the recipient and the thing received. Therefore, at least some sort of faith is required, so infidels cannot be said to receive. Yet Albert did not wish to deny that the body of the Lord must be present wherever the species of the bread and wine exists.[30]

Albert attempted to resolve his dilemma in discussing the further question of whether the body of the Lord can be said to pass into the stomach in reception. He answered by arguing that there are two ways that the Lord's body can be said to enter into the stomach. The body could enter the stomach and be digested like any other food, and this is clearly impossible. Or, the body could be said to merely exist in the place where the bread happens to be, that is, in the stomach. In this case, one might say that the Lord's body does enter the stomach. Albert's problem here has to do with the metaphysics involved in the change. "I do not see, rationally, how the body of Christ cannot pass into all places into which the species of bread and wine passes, they being the sign under which the whole Christ is contained, according to the truth of the reality signified (res)."[31] In saying this, however, Albert was aware that his opinion ran counter to that of at least some of the other masters, including, although he does not mention him by name, Alexander of Hales, and he was careful to put his ideas forward cautiously. He ended his discussion with the caveat, "And I say this without prejudice, because some masters say the opposite."[32]

Albert made explicit in his commentary that a tension existed between a true sacramental theology and the metaphysics involved in the eucharistic change. If the Eucharist is truly a sign, then only those capable of understanding such a sign can be said to be capable even of unworthy reception of the body and blood of the risen Lord. Yet if a true substantial change takes place in the Eucharist, then the body and blood must be present wherever the species of bread and wine exists. Albert's solution seems to be similar to that of Bonaventure. The body and blood exist as long as the species can be sensed, but no connection exists between the recipient and the risen Lord except in faith. Albert did go further than any of his predecessors, however, in emphasizing the importance of metaphysics over the theology of sign by insisting that the body and blood must be present *everywhere* the species exists. This at last implies that the body and blood must be present in the stomach of an animal or infidel, a suggestion Alexander, William, and Bonaventure rejected. It is no wonder that Albert made this suggestion tentatively.

This would also add greater significance to Albert's insistence in the *Liber de sacramento eucharistiae*, written after 1260, that any other explanation of the change in the Eucharist, apart from transubstantiation, would be heresy, or tantamount to heresy.[33] Dr. Burr did note this insistence, but he argued that the assertion "is entirely innocent of any notion that conversion might be linked necessarily to eucharistic presence."[34] I agree with Dr. Burr, but would add that when this assertion is coupled with Albert's deliberate break with his colleagues in his teaching on the continued presence of the received species, an important shift seems to take place in Albert's work. Some time between the writing of his *De sacramentis* and his *Commentary on the Sentences*, Albert decided that the metaphysical change that takes place in transubstantiation cannot be undone, even if that leads to unacceptable theological conclusions. Since transubstantiation is the only acceptable explanation for eucharistic change, the consequences of that change take precedence over the relationship between the recipient and the risen Lord. Not surprisingly, Albert again insists in the *Liber de sacramento eucharistiae* that Christ would be present in the mouth, the throat, the stomach, or even the guts of a mouse, as long as the species retained its sensible form.[35]

These tentative suggestions would find a full-fledged defense in the work of the most famous of Albert's students, and indeed the most famous of the Dominicans, Thomas Aquinas. Thomas first tackled the subject of eucharistic reception in his commentary on the Lombard's *Sentences*, thought to reflect his teaching in Paris from 1252 to 1256.[36] Thomas accepted two forms of reception, sacramental and spiritual. Sacramental reception entails reception both of the species and of the body and blood. Thomas was aware that some theologians admitted forms of reception that included either reception of the species alone or participation in the Mystical Body alone. He accepted the latter, but the former he rejected as inappropriate to the Eucharist, for this would entail a purely accidental reception.[37]

In discussing whether a sinner can receive the body of Christ, Thomas abandoned the usual arguments in favor of such a reception based on the faith of the sinner. Thomas firmly insisted that sinners receive the body and blood of Christ because the change of the substance of the bread and wine into the body and blood of the Lord, once it takes place, cannot be reversed except by another substantial change. As long as the accidents of bread exist, the body and blood of the Lord continue in the sacrament. Only when digestion so changes the species that it is unrecognizable are the body and blood separate from the species. Thomas clearly followed Albert on this point: "As long as the species is not changed, there is no way for the body of Christ to cease to be here."[38] This principle made Thomas's further discussions of this question awkward, for it assumes that both animals and infidels can receive the sacrament, a difficult position to maintain.

Thomas answered this question by distinguishing, as Bonaventure did before him, between reception as understood in terms of the thing received and reception in terms of the receiver. In terms of what is received, anyone who receives the species receives the body and blood of Christ. In terms of the receiver, however, only those receive the species who understand this food to be a visible sign of the spiritual reality underlying it. In this sense, neither infidels nor animals can be said to receive the body and blood. Thomas explicitly rejected the opinion of Bonaventure, however, that animals cannot receive the body and blood as it exists under the signs of bread and wine. "This reason is not valid because of two things," Thomas insisted. First, the species is not changed immediately in the stomach of the animal, and therefore no change can take place in the substance supporting these accidents. The host could be removed and still be used. Second, the fact that a thing is not used for its intended purpose does not mean that it ceases to exist. Therefore, Thomas explained, the body and blood of the Lord are received into the mouths of animals and descend into their stomachs.[39]

Even Thomas seemed somewhat uneasy with this rather disgusting conclusion, and in one passage Thomas seemed momentarily to forget that he had rejected reception of the accidents alone based on his own metaphysical principles. "Irrational creatures in no way spiritually eat, nor sacramentally, because they neither use this eating as a sign, nor eat the sign for the reason that it is a sign. Therefore infidels are not said to eat sacramentally who intend to receive what the Church receives, but believe nothing to be here. Similarly someone who eats a consecrated host, not knowing that it is consecrated, does not eat sacramentally in that way, because he does not eat the sign except *per accidens*."[40]

Writing some twenty years later, Thomas, in one of his last works, merely repeats his insistence that the metaphysics of the sacrament outweigh the importance of the intentionality of the believer. In the *pars tertia* of the *Summa theologiae*, Thomas presented virtually a repetition of his arguments in the *Commentary on the Sentences*, and once again he explicitly rejected Bonaventure's argument against reception by animals.[41]

Conversion takes center stage for Thomas in his discussion of the Eucharist. As Dr. Burr has noted in his analysis of the *Summa theologiae*, "For Aquinas, only he who understands eucharistic conversion can understand eucharistic presence."[42] The same statement could also be made of Albert, at least in his *Commentary on the Sentences*, in a way that it could not for either Bonaventure or any other of their contemporaries. With Albert and Thomas, an important shift has taken place. Metaphysics has replaced theology as the explanatory force driving their discussions of the Eucharist.[43] Thomas may have worked out the implications of this shift more carefully and certainly less tentatively than Albert, but the shift in focus seems to me to occur already in Albert, especially when one compares the quite different discussions of the presence which occur in his earlier and later works.

In summary, the theology of Albert and Thomas differs significantly from that of not only Bonaventure but also other contemporary theologians in insisting that any reception of the accidents also includes reception of the body and blood. The necessary metaphysical connection between the accidents of the bread and wine and the substance of the body and blood overrides the theological understanding of the Eucharist as a true sign. Both theologians, however, were reluctant to speak of reception by animals or infidels as true sacramental reception. It was, more precisely, no reception at all. If metaphysically the connection between the accidents of bread and wine and the substance of the body and blood could not be broken by the intention of the recipient, neither could it be said that there was any connection, even a sacrilegious one, between an unintentional recipient and the body of the risen Lord contained in the sacrament.

If I am correct in my analysis, several interesting implications seem to follow. First, and most obviously, Thomas was not so original in his theology of the Eucharist as has sometimes been presumed. Second, the emphasis that Albert and Thomas placed on the centrality of the metaphysical change did not meet with widespread approval. Both Dr. Burr's work on the medieval teaching on eucharistic presence and my own research into the medieval theology of eucharistic reception[44] would demonstrate that opposition to this approach was widespread and continued up until the time of the Reformation and, of course, beyond.

Finally, I find it intriguing that it would be the Dominicans who were most emphatic about the metaphysical change, since this position would, knowingly or not, enhance the mediatory role of the priest in producing salvation. As long as presence depended on intention, at least to some extent, the Eucharist did not so much produce salvation as it celebrated a salvation already attained through a union of faith and love between the individual believer and the risen Lord. Sacraments, then, could be understood by the Waldensians or other even more explicitly anti-clerical heretics as dispensable signs of a personal salvation. Not surprisingly, in the studies of spiritual communion by Heinz Robert Schlette and Franz-Josef Nocke, it is Albert and Thomas who deny that spiritual communion can take place apart from sacramental communion, while their Franciscan counterparts, including Bonaventure, accept this possibility.[45]

Could, then, Albert and Thomas be concerned not only to introduce the more rigorous metaphysics of Aristotle into sacramental language but also to oppose the heretics of their day, as their order was formed to do? Such an assumption would help explain Albert's and Thomas's insistence that all other accounts of eucharistic change apart from transubstantiation would be heretical. Perhaps even in the esoteric discussion of eucharistic presence, Albert and Thomas were not quite the coolly dispassionate scholars often pictured in neo-scholasticism, but more members of a revolutionary new order formed to protect a church under attack.

Notes

An earlier version of this paper was read at the Annual Meeting of the Medieval Academy of America at Princeton University in April, 1991.

1. David Burr, *Eucharistic Presence and Conversion in Late Thirteenth-Century Franciscan Thought* (Philadelphia: American Philosophical Society, 1984), p. 15.

2. Münsterische Beiträge zur Theologie, vol. 28, 1 (Münster: Aschendorffsche Verlagsbuchhandlung, 1965). See now Gary Macy, "The Dogma of Transubstantiation in the Middle Ages," *Journal of Ecclesiastical History* 45 (1994), 11–41.

3. William of Auvergne, *Magisterium divinale, De sacramentis*, in *Opera omnia* (Paris: Pralard, 1674, repr. Frankfurt, 1963), p. 434.

4. "Primum autem declarabimus tibi duas causas istius videre, et credere prohibiti sunt. Harum prima est errantium circa veritatem comestionis; vocabuerunt enim puerili insipientia comestionem ipsam cibi praeparationem, dicentes ipsam masticationem cibi comestionem, dicentes cibum comedi, cum in ore teritur dentibus, aut molitur, aut cum in ventrem trajicitur, ignorantes quia corpus animalis est velut domus sufficientia officinarum et vasorum ornata atque munita, seu praeparata, aet quia os est sicut molendimum, aut sicut mortarium cum instrumentis, quae necessaria sunt ad terendum, sive pistandum," William of Auvergne, *Magisterium divinale*, pp. 430B–431A.

5. Ideas similar to those espoused by Alexander exist in late twelfth- and early thirteenth-century writers. See, for instance, Innocent III, *De sacro altaris mysterio*, liber 4, cap. 16: "Nam in quo similitudo deficeret, in eo sacramentum non esset, sed ibi se proderet, et fidei locum aufferret, neque jam crederetur quod ita fieri non oportet. Itaque quantum ad nos servat per omnia corruptibilis cibi similitudinem, sed quantum ad se non amittit inviolabilis corporis veritatem," *Patrologia cursus completus . . . series Latina* (hereafter cited as *PL*), ed. Jacques-Paul Migne, 217 vols. (Paris, 1878–90), 215.867D. See also Peter of Capua, *Summa "Uetustissima ueterum"* (1201–02): "Et potest dici quod etiam

in ipso sumente manet materiale corpus donec in eo est aliqua forma ipsius panis. Non tamen incorporatur ei quia cibus est anime non corporis ut dicit Augustinus," Vatican City, Biblioteca Vaticana, Vaticana latina MS 4296, fol. 70rl; and Jacques de Vitry, *Historia occidentalis* (ca. 1219–25): "Forma igitur gustatur, sentitur, dentibus atteritur. Corpus autem non in uentrem descendit, sed ob ore ad cor transit. Comeditur sed non consumitur," in *The Historia Occidentalis of Jacques de Vitry*, ed. John F. Hinnebusch (Fribourg: The University Press, 1972), p. 231.

6. On the dating of Alexander's works see Alexander of Hales, *Quaestiones disputatae "Antequam Esset Frater,"* ed. Collegium S. Bonaventurae (Quaracchi: Ex Typographia Collegii S. Bonaventurae, 1960), pp. 34*–36*.

7. E.g., "Quaestio est propter quid, si corpus Christ ibi est, non sumitur a brutis animalibus. —Responsio est ad hoc, quod differt sensus in brutis et in nobis. Est enim in nobis ordinatus ad rationem, in brutis vero non. Quia ergo corpus Christi sub sacramento non dicit tantum quod ad sensum pertinet, sed quod ad rationem, quod sensus est a brutis sumitur, scilicet species panis; quod in ordine ad rationem est non sumitur, scilicet corpus Christi," Alexander of Hales, *Glossa in quatuor libros sententiarum Petri Lombardi*, ed. Collegium S. Bonaventurae (Quaracchi: Collegium S. Bonaventurae, 1957), p. 204. See also pp. 161–62.

8. *Quaestiones disputatae*, pp. 966–67, no. 199, esp. p. 967: "Item, alia est unio speciei tantum, ut in iis qui manducant secundum quod est sacramentum solum, sicut panem aliquem, ut Iudaei vel pagani. —Item est unio secundem rationem signi, ut in eo qui credit et intelligit; et maior adhuc est eo qui credit et diligit, ut in iis qui spiritualiter accipiunt; et sic secundum quod maior unio, maior manducatio."

9. Alexander of Hales, *Quaestiones disputatae*, p. 699–700, no. 205–10. E.g.: "Respondeo: manducare sacramentaliter, ut proprie dicitur, est attingere rem sub sacramento; ergo ubi nullo modo attingitur, nec per modum crediti, nec per modum cogniti, nullo modo est manducatio sacramentalis vel sacramentaliter; sed est quodam modo manducatio carnalis, et adhuc, proprie non est ibi manducatio carnalis, quia non est ibi divisio substantiae, cum non sit ibi nisi divisio accidentium solum. . . . Ad hoc quod obicitur de Iudaeo vel pagano, dico quod plus est in hac manducatione quam in manducatione irrationalis creaturae, quia unio est ibi in natura. Tamen quia non est ibi cognitio rei sub specie, et cum manducatio sacramentalis importet accipere species et attingere rem quae est sub sacramento fide, non manducant sacramentaliter."

10. This is the opinion of Pope Innocent III, *De sacro altaris mysterio*, liber 4, cap 11, *PL* 215.863B.

11. William of Melitona, *Quaestiones de sacramentis*, ed. C. Piana and G. Gál (Quaracchi: Ex Typographia Collegii S. Bonaventurae, 1961), pp. 695–700. For the dating of this work see the introduction, pp. 5*–33*.

12. William of Melitona, *Quaestiones de sacramentis*, p. 701: "Unde brutum unitur solum accidentibus; infidelis nihil penitus credens superaddit quandam aptitudinem ad sacramentalem vel spiritualem manducationem; habens fidem informem superaddit quod unitur cognito, habens formatum credito, in quantum habet caritatem unitur ut dilecto."

13. A. Landgraf, "Die in der Frühscholastik klassiche Frage Frage quid sumit mus," *Dogmengeschichte in der Frühscholastik,* vol. 3, part 2 (Regensburg: Friedrich Pustet, 1956), p. 207. See also Gary Macy, "Of Mice and Manna: *Quid mus sumit* as a Pastoral Question," *Recherches Théologie Ancienne et Médiévale* 58 (1991), 157–66.

14. See Burr, *Eucharistic Presence and Conversion*, p. 8.

15. Bonaventure, *Commentaria in quatuor libros sententiarum Magistri Petri Lombardi,* in *Opera Omnia*, vol. 4 (Quaracchi: Ex Typographia Collegii S. Bonaventurae, 1889), p. 204.

16. Bonaventure, *Commentaria*, p. 204–05.

17. Bonaventure, *Commentaria*, p. 205.

18. Bonaventure, *Commentaria*, p. 307.

19. Bonaventure, *Commentaria*, p. 308.

20. Bonaventure, *Commentaria*: "Et haec opinio communior est et certe honestior et rationabilior."

21. Bonaventure, *Commentaria*, pp. 310–11.

22. Bonaventure, *Commentaria*, p. 311.

23. Alexander of Hales, *Quaestiones disputatae*, p. 928, no. 88: "Ad hoc quod postea quaeritur, cuiusmodi mutatio est hic, vel secundum qualitatem, vel secundum quantitatem, dico quod est mutatio secundum substantiam, scilicet transubstantiatio; nec tamen est generatio vel corruptio, quia non manet idem subiectum."

24. Alexander of Hales, *Quaestiones disputatae*, p. 969, no. 205: " . . . posito enim quod

transsubstantiatio fiat, facta transsubstantiatione, quamdiu manet species panis in forma
speciei, manet res sacramento sub specie; ergo, si contingit speciem ab irrationali creatura
sumi, sub qua est corpus Christi, sequitur quod manducat sacramentaliter."

25. Alexander of Hales, *Quaestiones disputatae*, p. 970, no. 208: "Respondeo: Manducare
sacramentaliter, ut proprie dicitur, est attingere rem sub sacramento; ergo ubi nullo modo
est manducatio sacramentalis. Irrationali ergo creaturae non est manducatio sacramentalis vel
sacramentaliter; sed est quodam modo manducatio carnalis, et adhuc, proprie non est ibi
manducatio carnalis, quia non est ibi divisio substantiae, cum non sit ibi nisi divisio
accidentium solum."

26. *De Sacramentis*, in *Opera omnia*, 26 (Münster: Aschendorff, 1985), pp. 65A–B.

27. On the dating of Albert's works see Burr, *Eucharistic Presence and Conversion*, p. 16.

28. I would like to thank Dr. Robert Babcock and Ms. Daria Ague of the Beinecke
Library for their kind assistance in providing me with a microfilm of this work.

29. *Commentarii in Sententiarum*, vol. 29 of *Opera omnia*, ed. August and Emil Borgnet
(Paris: Apud Ludovicum Vives, 1890–99), liber 4, dist. 9, art. 3, p. 218; Beinecke MS
Z109.04, fol. 39v1.

30. *Commentarii in Sententiarum*, art. 4, p. 219; Beinecke MS Z.109.04, fol. 39v2.

31. *Commentarii in Sententiarum*, art. 5, p. 221; Bienecke MS Z.109.04, fol. 40rl: ". . .
quia non video rationabiliter qualiter corpus Christi non transit ad omnem locum, ad quem
transeunt species panis et vini, sub quibus secundum veritatem rei continetur totus
Christus."

32. *Commentarii in Sententiarum*, art. 5, p. 221; Bienecke MS Z.109.04, fol. 40rl: "Et hoc
dico sine præjudicio: quia quidam Magistri dicunt oppositum."

33. Dist. II, tract. II, in *Opera omnia*, vol. 38, ed. Auguste and Emil Borgnet, 306B;
308A–309B.

34. Burr, *Eucharistic Presence and Conversion*, p. 26.

35. *Opera omnia*, vol. 38, ed. Auguste and Emil Borgnet, p. 309: "Dissolutio antem
(*recte*: autem) formarum fit vel in ore muris, vel collo, vel stomacho, vel in aliis
visceribus muris: et tunc nullo modo est ibi Christus. Quamdiu autem sunt ibi formae
sensibiles quae descerni possunt sensu, tandiu est ibi Christus, et non amplius."

36. On the dating of Thomas' works see James Weisheipl, *Friar Thomas D'Aquino: His Life, Thought, and Works* (Washington D.C.: Catholic University of America Press, 1983), pp. 358 ff.

37. Thomas Aquinas, *Scriptum super sententiis magistri Petri Lombardi*, ed. M. F. Moos (Paris: Lethielleux, 1947), pp. 365–66.

38. Aquinas, *Scriptum super sententiis*, pp. 368–69. See p. 369: ". . . ideo quamdiu species non mutatur, nullo modo desinit ibi esse corpus Christi. . . . "

39. Aquinas, *Scriptum super sententiis*, pp. 370–71.

40. Aquinas, *Scriptum super sententiis*, p. 371: "Ad tertium dicendum quod creatura irrationalis nullo modo spiritualiter manducat, neque sacramentaliter; quia neque utitur manducatio ut sacramento, neque manducat sacramentum dicitur manducare infidelis qui intendit recipere hoc quod recipit Ecclesia, quamvis hoc credat nihil esse. Et similiter etiam ille qui manducaret hostiam consecratam, nesciens eam consecratam esse, non manducaret sacramentaliter aliquo modo, quia non manducaret sacramentum nisi per accidens; nisi quod plus accederet ad sacramentalem manducationem, inquantum est aptus natus sacramentum ut sacramentum manducare: quod bruto non competit. Nec tamen oportet quod sit alius modus manducationis tertius a duobus praedictis; quia hoc quod est per acccidens, in divisionem non cadit."

41. *Summa theologiae tertia pars*, q. 80, ed. P. Caramello (Rome: Marietti, 1956), pp. 488–91.

42. Burr, *Eucharistic Presence and Conversion*, p. 13.

43. The significance of this difference has not gone unnoticed by historians. As early as 1939, Yves de Montcheuil pointed out the significantly different understandings of a sacrament that underlie this divergence between Thomas and Bonaventure in "La Raison de la Permanence du Christ sous les Espéces Eucharistiques d'apres Saint Bonaventure et Saint Thomas," in his *Mélanges théologiques*, 2nd ed. (Paris: Aubier, 1951), pp. 71–82. More recently the importance of this disagreement has been pointed out by the liturgist and historian Pierre-Marie Gy. See, for instance, his "La Relation au Christ dans l'Eucharistie selon S. Bonaventure et S. Thomas d'Aquin," *Sacrements de Jésus-Christ*, ed. J. Dore et al. (Paris: Desclee, 1983), pp. 70–106.

44. Gary Macy, "Reception of the Eucharist According to the Theologians: A Case of Theological Diversity in the Thirteenth and Fourteenth Centuries," in *Theology and the*

University, ed. John Apczynski (Lanham, Md.: University Press of America, 1990), pp. 15–36.

45. Heinz Robert Schlette, *Die Lehre von der geistlichen Kommunion bei Bonaventura, Albert dem Großen und Thomas von Aquin* (Munich: Hueber, 1959); and Franz-Josef Nocke, *Sakrament und Personaler Vollzug bei Albertus Magnus* (Münster: Aschendorff, 1967), pp. 194–203.

Intellectual Mathematical Activity in the Thirteenth Century

Barnabas Hughes, O.F.M.

A ny discussion of learning in the medieval university does well to begin with remarks about the goal of learning and what is necessary to achieve that goal. Educators have always recognized the impact of early instruction upon future learning. Hence, its goal can be well described in the words of Richard of St. Victor as quoted by the Dominican Vincent of Beauvais (*fl.* 1245) in *The Education of Royal Children*:

> To know anything is to know its form and nature. Form is found in exterior arrangement; nature lies in interior qualities. Every arrangement uses number which arithmetic controls or proportion the focus of music or place which is the province of geometry or motion the concern of astronomy. . . . The lower sciences are rightly ordered to the higher.[1]

In this one reference Vincent identified both the means and the end. The end or the highest science is, of course, theology, the divine science toward which all studies must tend. St. Bonaventure has much the same idea and influence in his own *Reduction of the Arts to Theology*. The means rest in the seven liberal arts.

"At Oxford," so Father Weisheipl wrote some twenty-two years ago, "the faculty was called *facultas septem artium liberalium* and *fundamentum, origo et principium aliarum scientiarum*."[2] The "other sciences" in the four to five years undergraduate sequence were the three philosophies: natural, moral, and metaphysical. Among the seven liberal arts, however, some arts were more fundamental than others. Both Robert Grosseteste and Roger Bacon saw in the mathematical arts "the gateway and key to all the other sciences."[3] And among the mathematical sciences, arithmetic held the first place.

This arithmetic is the theory of numbers, a philosophic study. Its scope is the nature of unity, equality and inequality, and ratio and proportion. (Medieval supermarket computations belonged to the *compotus*.) Pearl Kibre, in her noteworthy essay, "The *Quadrivium* in the Thirteenth-Century Universities (with special reference to Paris)," wrote, "The importance of arithmetic in the university curriculum, regardless of where it was placed in the listing of the quadrivial arts, appears to have been generally accepted."[4] The high ranking that was accorded to arithmetic may well have been due to Boethius. He wrote in *Theory of Arithmetic*:

> Which of these disciplines, then, is the first to be learned but that which holds the principal place and position of mother to the rest? It is arithmetic. It is prior to all not only because God the creator of the massive structure of the world considered this first discipline as the exemplar of His own thought and established all things in accord with it; or that through numbers of an assigned order all things exhibiting the logic of their maker found concord; but arithmetic is said to be first for this reason also, because whatever things are prior in nature, it is to these underlying elements that the posterior elements can be referred.[5]

As for texts, that of Boethius was certainly used from the earliest days of the universities. But a newcomer appeared. Sometime during the thirteenth century the *De arithmetica* of Jordanus de Nemore began to replace Boethius's text. The recorded existence of twenty-three more or less complete manuscripts[6] of Jordanus's tract leads one to suspect that its value was fairly widely recognized. In the early fourteenth century, works on the theory of numbers were read at Oxford in just three weeks or fifteen days.[7] One century later, the reading time was extended to thirty days.[8] Hopefully, the extension was due to demands by the students for more time; they were also expected to get well into Euclid's theory of numbers, namely, Books VII to X of *The Elements*.

Of equal interest, I believe, is the thinking of Godfrey of St. Victor on arithmetic. In *The Fountain of Philosophy* he wrote:

Might have guessed this river is   twice two branches sending,
Which the crowd quadrivium   as a name is lending—
——— those disciplines   in one group is blending
For they're fused right from start,   just as in their ending.
At their source a basin forms   in which pebbles nestle:
. . . .
Sitting on that bank there's a   varied delegation:
Computists play pebble-games. . . . [9]

This viewpoint is directly related to the topic at hand.

The number game played by the computists was to form a number with pebbles in a geometric shape. For instance, ten could be shown as a triangle (see Figure 1). Or, twelve can take the form of a pentagon (see Figure 2). For young students in medieval schools figurate or polygonal numbers were *new numbers*. Yet the figures had been in the mainstream of arithmetic since their invention or discovery by the Pythagoreans.[10] Boethius's translation[11] of Nicomachus's *Arithmetic* was the depository for what medieval students might have begun to learn about polygonal numbers.

Figure 1.   Figure 2.

An unknown but quite knowledgeable writer, possibly a university teacher seeking to create an innovative approach to number theory for his young bachelors, wrote the tract *New Numbers* (*In novis numeris*). The new numbers are figurate numbers easily formed by arranging pebbles in various patterns. The tract is an advance upon the work of Boethius because it offers additional concepts and skills not found in his treatise. Furthermore, the format itself is interesting. It is written in verse and surrounded by a commentary. I offer an analysis of both treatise and commentary together and, in the Appendix, critical editions of each.

Content Analysis

Descriptors of figurate numbers and rules for finding certain ones are offered, rather than a theory of polygonal numbers wherein the reader would expect such things as definitions, axioms, and properties, together with consequent generalizations. After reading the tract, one knows what the author proposed to do; but at the beginning one is not so sure. Whereas the idea of "new numbers" in the title of the commentary is attractive, the introduction in the treatise is abrupt: "Bino equales trigonales tetragonali." Having been exposed to the versified *Carmen de algorismo* of Alexander de Villa Dei (in the Gonville and Caius MS), the reader is somewhat prepared to supplement the treatise with necessary words and phrases. Thus it is comparatively easy to interpret the initial line to mean that a four-sided number is composed of two equal triangular numbers. Nonetheless, whether the commentary accompanies the treatise (as in the Gonville and Caius MS) or stands alone, it is welcomed. Somewhat more than twice as long as the versified treatise, it leads the reader gently through introductory ideas about figurate numbers and rules for finding them; all of this is in the treatise, compactly. The commentator was careful to reference it by quoting a few words of the passage about to be remarked upon as a signal to the reader. (I have marked these phrases in **boldface**, both in the treatise and in the commentary.) Accompanying the commentary in the margins of the manuscripts are geometric figures exemplifying the various polygonal numbers, such as the following.

pentagonal

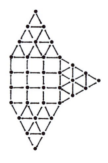

heptagonal

Note that the dots are connected by lines to enable the reader to distinguish the figures composing the named figurate numbers; for example, the pentagon is constructed from a square and one triangle. Finally, both texts assume that the reader knows the squares of at least the first ten whole numbers together with the seven[12] arithmetic operations. With this background I offer a mathematical analysis of the versified treatise, seldom differentiating between its contents and that of the commentary. Indeed, the commentary adds nothing substantive to the treatise. Remarks about the Latin mathematical vocabulary conclude the analysis.

The treatise may be divided into three sections: names of simple polygonal numbers; two ways of viewing their distinguishing characteristics; and rules for finding specific figurate numbers given any arbitrary number. The first section limits the discussion to just five of the polygonal numbers: triangular; pentagonal; hexagonal; heptagonal; and octogonal. Two others, the rectangle and the square, will be assigned auxiliary roles.

In the second part, distinguishing characteristics of the figures are identified. Each polygonal number is shown first to be composed of so many triangular numbers. From a second viewpoint one sees them (except for the triangular numbers) as being constructed from a square and one to four triangles. Each case is illustrated in the margin. In this section several remarks are made. The first notes that the square contains two unequal triangles. While the statement is true, the word used in the treatise for square is *tetragonus* rather than *quadratum*, which the commentary also recognizes. The author chose this terminology poorly, for in the introductory sentence he has the *tetragonus* composed of two equal triangles, which is impossible for a square. Nonetheless, the second remark flows from the inequality of the triangles composing the square: one side of the larger triangle is the diameter of the square. Furthermore, upon it another square may be constructed whose area is twice that of the first, even though the sides of both squares are incommensurable.

The third section, somewhat more than 80 percent of the treatise, offers answers to three questions asked about each polygonal number, namely:

1. Given an arbitrary number, how does one find whichever polygonal number is immediately less than it?;
2. Given any polygonal number, how does one find the immediately smaller polygonal number of the same kind?; and
3. Given any polygonal number, how does one find the immediately larger polygonal number of the same kind?

The ability to ask these questions coupled with the contents of the first two sections suggests that the author had a good understanding of the fundamental theory of polygonal numbers. At least the following concepts and skills were at his command.

1.a. *Any polygonal number greater than three can be decomposed into a finite number of equal triangular numbers, T, and one linear number, L.*
     While neither author nor commentator wrote here of linear numbers, it is clear from the context that both had the concept if not the terminology.[13] A linear number is simply a number represented by a sequence of dots in a row, having the same number as the side of the polygonal number. The decomposition is formulated as: $(k - 2)T + L = k$-gon, for $k = 4, 5, 6, \ldots$ For instance: $k = 6$; $k = 8$.

1.b. *Any polygonal number greater than four can be decomposed into one square, S, and a finite number of equal triangles, T.*
     This is a corollary from 1.a. As a formula it reads: $S + (k - 4)T = k$-gon, for $k = 5, 6, 7, \ldots$ The squares in the centers of the diagrams above are easily seen.

2.a. *A numerical procedure for finding any triangular number.*
     The method of finding any polygonal number requires the searcher initially to find a triangular number quite near some given number. First, double the given number. Second, find the square number immediately less than twice the number. Third, add the square root to the square. Finally, halve the sum to produce the triangular number near the given number. The clever part of the procedure is doubling the arbitrary number to find the square number, say n^2. Thereafter, the procedure is a straightforward application of the usual formula

for finding any triangular number: $(n^2 + n)/2$, n a positive integer. For instance, to find the triangular number near 52: 1) $2(52) = 104$; 2) The square 100 is just less than 104 and its root or side is 10; 3) $100 + 10 + 110$; and 4) $110/2 = 55$, the triangular number near 52.

2.b. *A numerical procedure for finding any polygonal number near a given number.*

It is assumed that the given number is larger than the required polygonal number. Now, since any polygonal number can be decomposed into a finite number of triangles, the first step is to find the triangular number whose multiple leads to the desired polygonal number. This is done by dividing the given number by the difference between two and the characteristic number of the desired polygon. Then one finds the triangular number that is immediately less than the integral part of the quotient. Next, multiply the triangular number by the aforementioned divisor and add to the product the linear number equal to the side of the triangular number (from 2.a.) increased by one. And thus you have the required polygonal number. All of this is equivalent to the construction formula noted in 1.a. For example, given 52, to find the nearby pentagonal number: 1) $52/(5-2) = 17\ 1/3$; 2) Near 17 is triangular number 15 whose side or root is 5; 3) $3(15) = 45$; and 4) $45 + (5+1) = 51$, the required pentagonal number.

3.a. *The names of polygonal numbers are generic words, admitting for each an infinite sequence of specific terms with the same characteristic construction.*

The sequence is generated by the formula: $n([k - 2]n - [k - 4])/2$, where k is the characteristic number of the polygon and n ranges through the set 2, 3, 4, ... For instance, the sequence of pentagonal numbers is 5, 12, 22, . . . , $n(3n - 1)/2$, all of which show pentagonal shapes.

3.b. *Given any term but the first in a sequence of a specific polygonal number, its predecessor can be found.*

Theoretically, the method is easily described: remove the numerical difference that makes one number larger than its predecessor. Before finding the difference, the author assumes that the inquirer has just found a specific polygon and, therefore, knows the length of its side. Hence, in order to find its predecessor: first, subtract 1 from the side; then, multiply the remainder by 2 less than the characteristic number of the polygon; third, add 1 to the product; finally, subtract the sum from the given polygon. The remainder is its predecessor. For example, the pentagonal number 22 has a side of length 4. Consequently, by the preceding algorithm: $22 - [(5 - 2)(4 - 1) + 1] = 12$, and 12 is the predecessor of 22. The generalization of the procedure is to subtract from the specific number the quantity $(k - 2)(n - 1) + 1$, where k is the characteristic number of the polygon and n is the length of its side, a positive integer.

3.c. *Given any term in a sequence of a specific polygonal number, its successor can be found.*

The method is analogous to the preceding, with its assumptions. Simply add $(k - 2)n + 1$ to the given polygon. For example, to find the successor to pentagonal 22 whose side is 4, add $(5 - 2)4 + 1 = 13$ to 22 to obtain its successor, 35.

The mathematical vocabulary of commentary and treatise merits attention as a witness to medieval terminology. Two sets of nouns may be distinguished: those referring to general arithmetic concepts and skills; and those pertinent to polygonal numbers. In the first group are: *monos*; *unitas*; *numerus*; *radix*; *quadratum*; *medietas*; *multiplicatio*; *productum*; and *quotiens*. The second includes: *costa*; *latus*; *diametrus*; *trigonus*; *tetragonus*; *pentagonus*; *exagonus*; *eptagonus*; and *octogonus*. Of the latter, the first three are linear terms; the others are polygonal. Most of the adjectives refer to polygonal numbers, namely: *trigonalis*; *tetragonalis*; *pentagonalis*; *exagonalis*; *eptagonalis*; and *octogonalis*. Some, however, are generically arithmetic: *equalis*; *cubicus*; *quadratus*; and *incommensurabilis*. The verbs look to various operations and their results: addition: *addere* (with dative or *ad* with accusative), *coniungere*, *iungere*; subtraction: *delere ab*, *demere de*, *minuere de*, *subtrahere*, *tollere ab* or *de*; multiplication: *ducere in, multiplicare per, triplare, triplicare, quadruplicare*; duplication: *duplere, duplicare*; division: *dividere per*; mediation: *dimidiare, mediare*; to operate in general: *facere, producere*; and result of operation: *componere, occurere, remanere, resultare, superesse*.

Author, Time of Composition, and Resources

Neither treatise nor commentary identifies its author. Nonetheless, there is some evidence in the Gonville and Caius MS for suggesting that Alexander de Villa Dei is the author of *De numeris trigonis*. First, he wrote *Carmen de algorismo*, which immediately precedes our treatise in the codex, and both tracts were written in verse with generally fourteen syllables to the line. Second, the commentary begins "Quia autem superius dictum est de numeris quadratis et cubicis et progressis." Clearly this refers to the immediately preceding tract by Alexander de Villa Dei. Third, identical terminology is used in *Carmen* and *De numeris trigonis* where the context is the same or similar. Fourth, the two edited versions[14] of *Carmen* do not have the same conclusion. Halliwell's resources lack pages 27–28 in the Gonville and Caius rendition, and Steele's sources want page 28. Hence, it may be argued that Gonville and Caius contains the complete conclusion of *Carmen*, which includes *De numeris trigonis*. It seems to me, therefore, that despite the thinness of the evidence, the conjecture about authorship deserves attention until such time as a critical edition of all known manuscripts (there are more than two hundred copies) of *Carmen de algorismo* is published.

Fixing a time of composition depends, of course, upon settling the question of authorship. If my conjecture is borne out, then *De numeris trigonis* was composed early in the thirteenth century when Alexander was teaching. Otherwise, a later date must be advanced, such as late thirteenth or early fourteenth century. This lowest upper boundary is fixed by the Gonville and Caius codex, which was penned in the first quarter of the fourteenth century. It is clearly a copy of a manuscript that, if it still exists, has not been found. For all appearances the commentary was written after the treatise.

Regardless of the time of composition there were only two substantive arithmetic tracts available that discussed polygonal numbers in any practical detail: Boethius's *De institutione arithmetica*; and Jordanus de Nemore's *De arithmetica*. Our author certainly did not draw his innovations from Boethius, for the following reasons. First, Boethius used the words *triangulus numerus* and *triangularis figura*[15] where our author employed *trigonus* and *trigonalis*. Second, Boethius divided every *k*-gon into *k* triangles,[16] but our author divided them into (*k* - 2) triangles. Third, Boethius recognized the number 1 as the first number in the sequence of whatever polygonal number while our author did not. Finally, Boethius did not have our author's rules 2.a, 2.b, 3.a, 3.b, and 3.c.

Does that leave Jordanus's tract as the springboard for *De novis numeris*? Not necessarily. Jordanus expounded on polygonal numbers in Book VIII. There, in Proposition 23, he used the word *trigonus*. But he also used *triangulum* and *triangularis*. And there is no evidence of *triangularis* in *De novis numeris*. Furthermore, Jordanus did not offer the rules our author does. However, Jordanus did state a proposition that may have prompted our author to think along similar lines, namely, proposition VIII, 18: "Latere proposito, exagonum equiangulum constituere." If one can find a hexagon given its side, how might one find the antecedent or consequent hexagon? The answer lies in our author's rules. I am inclined to think that he had read Jordanus's *De arithmetica*, and it was this to which he made reference in line 34 below.

Sources for the Critical Edition

Only two codices that contain treatise and/or commentary have been found. The first is Cambridge, University Library, G.g. VI.3, ff. 309va–315vb, English hand, s. xiv *med.*:

commentary
running head: *Algorismus in numeris*
    title: *Incipit algorismus in nouis numeris.*
     incipit: *Quia autem superius dictum est de numeris quadratis et cubicis et progressis. . . .*

The codex is a compilation of mathematical tracts: arithmetic; algebraic; geometric; astronomic; and astrologic.[17] They seem to be merely a collection rather than an organized entity. The text of the commentary is in double columns. Noteworthy for its absence is our versified treatise, *De numeris trigonis*. Each of the figurate numbers under discussion is illustrated in a margin of the manuscript. The second codex is Cambridge, Gonville and Caius College Library, 141 (191), pp. 29a–34b, English hand, s. xiv *in.*:

> **commentary**
> running head: *Algorismus Figurarum*
> title: *Incipit algorismus in novis numeris*
> incipit: *Quia autem superius dictum est de numeris quadratis et cubicis et* progressionibus
> **treatise**
> title: *De numeris trigonis et exagonis et eptagonis et ceteris*
> incipit: *Binos equales trigonales tetragonalis.*

Whoever assembled this codex organized a collection of mathematical tracts whose clear purpose was to cover in orderly sequence the practical topics leading to proficiency in astronomy, including the construction and use of the quadrant.[18] *De numeris trigonis* sits in the lower part of each page surrounded on the sides and above by the double columns of the commentary. The margins hold the necessary diagrams of the figurate numbers (which follow the commentary, below). As noted in the apparatus, one correction was made between the lines of the commentary at a later date.

The Gonville and Caius manuscript clearly offers the better version of the commentary. As the apparatus shows, the other MS suffers from many omissions, most of which are cross-references to the treatise. Since Gonville and Caius lacks one clause (lines 184–85) found in the University Library MS, neither copy is the exemplar for the other.

Appendix

(p. 29)
De numeris trigonis et exagonis et ceteris

Binos equales trigonales tetragonalis
Alterius que latus monademque similiter tenet in se
Si tres pentagonus. Bis binos exagonabis(!).
Eptagonus 5 trigonus habet. Octagonus 6.
Et latus unius monadem petit sibi quisque.
Ex trigono cum tetragono fit pentagonalis.
Exagonus de tetragono trigonisque duobus.
Eptagonus tribus ex trigonis et tetragonali.
Quatuor ex trigonis cum tetragono sibi incursis
Octogonus. Monade radix sed in omnibus istis
Tetragoni latere trigoni* tibi maior habetur
in propositum duplum numeri. Si ducis et illum
Addas producto trigonum facis exagonalem.
Est impossibile tibi; sic operatio creatur.
Sed de producto numeri si triplixeris illum
Proximus est trigonus, remanens erit exagonusque.
Exagonalis erit trigonus quia tercius omnis
Et quia radices quadri plures trigonales
Non capiuntur. Modo de reliquis non est mihi cura.

---

*rep. trigoni

(p. 30)

Si tu scire velis **trigonus** quis maximus infra
Propositum numerum fuerit: duplicabis eundem
Et sua quadrato qui maximus esse probatur
In duplo radix addatur. Postea totum
In binas partes equales dimidiabis
Altera pars cuius numerus trigonalis habetur.
Et prius extracta radix latus fiet eius
Quo numerus est monade trigoni latus superioris.
Sed primum supra latus hoc excedit in uno.
Constat enim quam numerum trigoni latus esse.
Ergo prefatus trigonus quem composuisti
Equalis si proposito fuerit, trigoni sunt
Ambo. Si maior fuerit sibi proximus extat.
Sed si proposito minor, tunc maius eius.
Si trigono tibi proposito petis immediatum
Vicinum que supra: si coniungas latus eius
Et monadem. **Sed si queris inferiorem,**
Tollatur latus eius ei quem queris habere.

(p. 31)

Si tibi pentagonum queris qui maximus infra
Propositum numerum fuerit, tollatur ab illo
Tertia pars. Sed non curare de remanenti.
Et dicte partis trigonum qui maximus extat
Invenias. Eius que triplo trigoni latus adde
Dicti cum monade sit pentagonus tibi fiet,
Et latus eius erit dicta pars addita triplo.
Equalis si proposito fuerit, pentagoni sunt.
Sed si proposito minor est, est maximus eius.
Et si maior eo fuerit, sibi proximus extat.
Pentagono si maiorem petis immediatum,
Ad triplum lateris monadem adde. Deinde
Addas totale prefato pentagoni.
Occuret tibi pentagonus vicinus eidem.
Sed si vicinum tibi queres inferiorem,
Subtrahe de latere monadem. Reliquo que triplicatur
Illam iunge triplo, totum de pentagonali
Delens. Et remanet vicinus ei minor illo.

(p. 32)

Exagonum si tu queris quis maximus infra
Propositum numerum fuerit, tollatur eidem
Eius pars quarta, nec cures de remanenti.
Et dicte partis trigonum qui maximum extat.
Exqueras quam multiplicetur bis bina. Sed illi
Quem tu producis latus et monadem similiter addas
Exagonum faciens. Latus est pars addita cuius.
Qui si fortassis numero quem proposuisti
Equalis fuerit erit exagonalis uterque.
Sed si maior eo, tunc illi proximus extat.
Sed si proposito minor est, tunc maius eius
Exagonum. **Si tu proponis** et exagonalem
Vicinum supra, quartas tibi quadruplicabis.
Exagonale latus quo facto iungere debes
Producto monadem. Totum iungatur eidem
Exagono. Sic vicinum facis exagonalem
Et primum supra. **Sed si petis inferiorem,**
Tollas de latere monadem. Sed quadruplices
Quod superest. Quo producto coniunge. Deinde
Totalem numerum delebis ab exagonali
Exagonus remanet minor illo proximus illi.

(p. 33)

Eptagonum queres. Numerum quem proposuisti
Divide per 5; nil cures de remanenti.
Et quinte partis trigonum qui maximus extat.
Ducas in 5 latus et monadem sibi iunge.
Eptagonum facies. Latus est pars addita cuius.
Qui si prefato numero quem proposuisti
Equalis fuerit, erit eptagonalis uterque.
Sed si proposito minor est, est maximus eius.
Si sit maior eo, tunc illi proximus extat.
Eptagono si proposito petis immediatum,
Ducas in 5. Latus et monadem sibi iunge.
Quem tu producis totale sed eptagonali
Adde tuo. Sit maior eo vicinus ei que.
Sed si de latere monadem subtraxeris atque
Duxeris in 5 remanentem. Postea iunges
Producto monadem. Totum sed ab eptagonale
Traxeris, occurat minor illo proximus illi.

(p. 34)

Octogonum queres. Numerus quem proposuisti
divide tu per 6, nec cures de remanenti.
Illius et sexte partis qui maximus extat.
Invenies trigonum quem per 6 multiplicabis.
Producto latus et monadem coniungere debes
Octogonum facies. Latus est pars addita cuius.
Qui numero forsan equalis si sit eidem
Quem tu proponis, ambo sunt octogonales.
Sed si proposito minor est, est maximus eius.
Si sit maior eo, sibi tunc vicinior extat.
Octogono si proposito petis immediatum,
Multiplica per 6 latus eius et addere cures
Producto monadem. Totum iungatur et illi
Octogono. Sic vicinum facis octogonalem
Et primum supra. **Quod si petis inferiorem**
Tollas de latere monadem. Sed multiplicetur
Per 6 quod superest numero quem iungere debes
Producto. Totum delebis ab octogonali.
Octogonus remanet minor illo proximus illi.

(p. 29a./fol. 309ra)
Incipit Algorismus In novis numeris

Quia autem superius dictum est de numeris quadratis et
cubicis et progressionibus, unde quia adhunc sunt quidem
numeri qui sunt trigoni, quidem tetragoni, quidem pentagoni,
5   quidem exagoni, quidem eptagoni, quidem octogoni. Ideo de
his singillatim est dicendum. Et primo de differentie
eorum.

Binos equales: hic ponit auctor differentiam uniuscuiusque
eorum, dicens quod numerus tetragonus habet 2 trigonos
10   equales in se, et dicitur numerus tetragonus. Numerus
quadratus et dicitur a tetris quod est 4, quia habet 4
latera et angulos equales. Trigonus quia habet tres costas
equales et sic de ceteris est exponendum. Pentagonus habet
tres trigonos in se ut patet in exemplo. Exagonus 4 habet
15   trigonos. Eptagonis 5. Octogonus 6. Et unusquisque istorum
habet latus unum, hoc est quod si unum fuerit tres, oportet
quod omnia latera habeant tres, et sic deinceps.

Ex trigono: hic ponit aliam cognitionem eorum dicens quod
ex trigono et tetragono constat pentagonus, ut patet.
20   Exagonus constat ex tetragono et duobus trigonis, ut patet.
Eptagonus constat ex tetragono et **(p. 29b)** ex tribus
trigonis. Octogonus autem ex tetragono et 4 trigonis
constat, ut patet. Sed nota quod in omnibus istis debemus
uti uno radice scilicet in omnibus trigonis constituentibus
25   aliquod istorum, ut dictum est superius. Nunc nota quod
latus unum trigoni tetragoni est maior omnibus aliis
lateribus trigoni, et est hoc latus diametrus tetragoni.
Quia si hoc latus ducatur in se, erit resultans duplum ad
quadratum primum, ut probatur in geometria et hoc per
30   46am conclusionem primi libri Euclidis. Ideo si ei
addas trigonum habes exagonum. Sed quia hoc est

impossibile ducere diametrum in se, et hoc in numeris quia
diametrus est incommensurabilis coste, ut probatur in
arsmetrica.[19] Sed si subtraxeris istum trigonum, proximus

35   erit trigonus primi quadrati. Et remanens quod est
quadratum diametrus erit equales exagono **(fol. 309rb)** ex
lateribus primi quadrati componentis. Nam est duplum ad
primum quadratum. Et per consequens habet 4 trigonos primi
quadrati et sic exagonus per eius descriptiones. Sic dicto

40   de differentiis eorum, modo dicendum est de inventione
talium numerorum. **(p. 30a)**

Si trigono: hic ponit auctor regulam de inventione numeri
trigoni, dicens quod si proponatur alius numerus et velis
scire quis sit numerus trigonus maximus continens sub isto

45   numero proposito si ipsum non fuerit trigonus, tu duplicabis
numerum propositum et invenies radicem proximi numeri
quadrati contenti sub illo duplicato. Tunc adde radicem ad
suum quadratum et quod collectum fuerit media. Una autem
medietas est maximus numerus trigonus continens sub numero

50   proposito. Radix autem inventa est latus eius numeri
trigoni. Verbi gratia. Sit propositus 12. Dupla et est
24. Cuius extrahes quadratum maximum infra illum et est
16 cuius radix 4. Adde ergo istam radicem ad suum quadratum
scilicet 4 ad 16, et resultat 20 cuius medietatas 10 qui est

55   numerus trigonus quesitus, cuius latus est radix inventa
scilicet 4, ut patet in exemplo *a*. Latus autem proximi
numeri trigoni superioris est minus isto latere per
unitatem. Numerus vero proximus trigonus post istum numerum
habet latus excedens latus huius unitate, ut patebit postea.

60   **(p. 30b)** Propterea sciendum est quod si contingat quod
trigonus compositus sit equalis numero proposito, numerus
propositus erat trigonus. Si autem fuerit maior numero
proposito, est proximus trigonus post numerum propositum.
Si vero fuerit minor tunc est proximus trigonos infra

65   numerum propositum.

Si trigono: hic docet auctor invenire numerum trigonum
immediatum supra propositum numerum, dicens quod si addas
numero trigono invento latus eius et unitatem habes proximum
numerum trigonum supra. Verbi gratia. 10 fuit numerus
70   trigonus inventus cuius radix vel latus 4. Addas ergo huic
10, 4 et unitatem et resultat 15 qui est proximus trigonus
(fol. 309v) super trigonum inventum, ut patet in exemplo *b*.

Sed si queris inferiorem: hic docet auctor invenire numerum
trigonum inferiorem proximum numero trigono invento, dicens
75   quod debet tolli latus trigoni inventi ab isto trigono
invento et resultans erit numerus trigonus inferior ei
proximus. Verbi gratia. 10 erat trigonus inventus. Demas
ab eo 4 qui est latus eius et remanet 6 qui est numerus
trigonus inferior proximus numero invento scilicet 10, ut
80   patet in exemplo ultimo scilicet *c*. **(p. 31a)**

Si tibi pentagonum: hic ponitur auctor regulam de
inventione numeri pentagoni, dicens quod si proponatur alius
numerus et velis scire quis sit numerus pentagonus proximus
ei. Si non fuerit pentagonus, tollatur a numero proposito
85   tertia pars et non cures de remanente. Cuius tertie partis
accipies proximum trigonum quam triplicabis et addes ei
latus trigoni cum unitate. Et quod resultat erit numerus
pentagonos proximus numero proposito. Verbi gratia. Sit
propositus numerus 24 cuius accipies tertiam partem quae est
90   8. Cuius accipies proximum trigonum quod est 6 quem
triplicabis et erit 18. Cui addes latus trigoni quod est 3
cum unitate quod est 4. Et resultat 22 qui est numerus
proximus pentagonus, ut patet in exemplo *e*. Latus autem
eius est illa pars que additur triplo, scilicet quattuor.
95   Si autem fuerit equalis proposito numero, tunc sunt
pentagoni ambo, scilicet inventus et propositus, uti patet
in tractatu.[20] Si autem fuerit minor proposito ut in hoc
exemplo, tunc est maximus continens sub eo. Si autem fuerit

maior proposito, tunc est proximus post numerum propositum,
100   ut patet. Si queratur numerus pentagonus proximus huic
numero quod est 30 ut patet. **(p. 31b)**

Pentagono si maiorem: hic docet auctor invenire pentagonum
maiorem immediatum pentagono **(fol. 309vb)** invento. Et hoc sic
accipe latus pentagoni inventi et tripla eum et adde ei
105   unitatem. Et hoc totum adde pentagono invento et resultabit
proximus pentagonus maior. Verbi gratia. Pentagonus
inventus est 22 cuius latus 4. Quam triples et est 12.
Unitatem ei adde et resultat 13. Quem addes 22 scilicet
pentagono prius invento, et resultat 35 qui est proximus
110   pentagonus maior, ut patet in exemplo *f.*

Sed si vicinum: hic docet auctor invenire pentagonum
minorem proximum pentagono prius invento. Et hoc sic accipe
latus pentagoni inventi et ab eo tollas unitatem. Et quod
remanet triplica, et huic triplicato adde unitatem. Et quod
115   resultat tolle a pentagono primo invento. Et quod remanet
erit proximus pentagonus inferior. Verbi gratia: 22 est
pentagonus primo inventus cuius latus 4. Deme ab eo
unitatem et remanet 3 quem triplicabis. Addendo unitatem et
resultat 10. Quod tolles a 22. Remanet 12; quod est
120   propositum ut patet in exemplo *g.* **(p. 32a)**

Exagonum si tu scire velis: hic ponit auctor regulam de
inventione numeri exagoni, dicens quod si proponatur alius
numerus et velis scire quis sit proximus ei exagonus, tollas
a numero proposito quartam partem eius nec cures de
125   remanenti huius quarte partis. Invenies numerum trigonum
ei proximum. Quem trigonum multiplicabis per quattuor et
huic producto addas latus trigoni et unitatem. Et quod
resultat est exagonus quesitus. Verbi gratia. Sit numerus
propositus 30 quem divides per 4. Et quarta pars erit 7.
130   Cuius trigonus 6 quem multiplicabis per 4. Et resultat 24

cui addes latus trigoni scilicet 3, et unitatem. Et
resultat 28; quod est propositum **(fol. 310ra)** scilicet
exagonus quesitus. Latus autem eius est pars addita
scilicet 4, ut patet in exemplo *h*. Si autem equalis fuerit
135   numero proposito, tunc uterque est exagonus. Sed si maior
fuerit, tunc est proximus post numerum propositum. Si vero
fuerit minor, tunc est proximus numerus exagonus infra
predictum numerum propositum. **(p. 32b)**

Si tu proponis: hic ponit auctor regulam ad inveniendum
140   numerum exagonum proximum post exagonum primo inventum,
dicens quod debes quadruplicare latus exagoni et addere ei
unitatem et hoc totum addere exagono primo. Verbi gratia.
Latus exagoni est 4 quod multiplicabis per 4 et est 16. Cui
addes unitatem et resultat 17. Hoc totum adde exagono primo
145   invento scilicet 28. Et est 45; quod est propositum ut
patet in exemplo *i*.

Sed si petis inferiorem: hic docet auctor invenire minimum
exagonum inferiorem et proximum exagono invento, primo
dicens quod debes delere unitatem a latere exagoni, et
150   multiplicare quod remanet per quattuor, et quod resultat
accipe et addere ei unitatem, et hoc totum delere ab
exagono primo. Et habes propositum. Verbi gratia.
Exagonus primus est 28 cuius latus 4. Dele ab eo unitatem
et remanet 3. Quod multiplicabis per 4 et erit 12. Cui
155   addes unitatem et erit 13. Quod delebis ab exagono primo
quod est 28, et remanet 15. Qui est exagonus inferior et
proximus exagono primo scilicet 28; quod est propositum ut
patet in exemplo *k*. **(p. 33a)**

Eptagonum queres: hic ponit auctor regulam de inventione
160   numeri eptagoni, dicens quod si proponatur alius numerus et
velis scire quis sit ei proximus eptagonus, divide illum
numerus per 5 nec cures **(fol. 310rb)** de remanenti. Et huius

quinte partis accipies trigonum proximum. Quem trigonum
multiplicabis per 5, et resultanti ex multiplicatione adde
165 latus trigoni et unitatem. Et quod resultat erit eptagonus
quesitus. Verbi gratia. Sit numerus propositus 36. Hunc
numerum divides per 5, et erit pars quinta septem. Cuius
proximus trigonus est 6, latus vero eius 3. Hunc ergo
trigonum quod est 6 multiplicabis per 5 et resultat 30. Cui
170 addes latus eius trigoni quod est 3 et unitatem. Et
resultat 34 qui est numerus quesitus. Latus autem eius erit
pars addita scilicet 4, ut patet in exemplo *l*. Si autem
fuerit equalis numero proposito, tunc erit eorum uterque
numerus eptagonus. Si vero fuerit maior proposito, tunc est
175 proximus eptagonus post illum numerum. Si vero fuerit
minor, tunc est proximus numerus eptagonus infra numerum
propositum, ut patet cuilibet invenienti. **(p. 33b)**

Eptagono si proposito: hic ponitur auctor regulam docentem
invenire numerum eptagonum maiorem proximum eptagono dato,
180 dicens quod debes multiplicare latus eptagoni dati per 5 et
addere ei unitatem et hoc totum addere eptagono dato. Verbi
gratia. Sit eptagonus datus 34. Latus autem eius 4 quod
multiplicabis per 5. Et resultat 20 cui addas unitatem et
erit 21. Quod addes eptagoni dato scilicet 34 et resultat
185 55. Qui est proximus eptagonus maior eptagono dato, ut
patet in exemplo *m*.

Sed si de latere: hic docet auctor invenire numerum
eptagonum proximum minorem eptagono dato, dicens quod debes
demere unitatem de latere eptagoni dati et quod remanet
190 multiplicare per 5. Et huic producto addes unitatem et
quod resultat minue de eptagonali dato. Et quod remanet
erit eptagonus quesitus. Verbi gratia. Eptagonus datus sit
34. Latus eius 4 de quo deleas **(fol. 310va)** unitatem et
remanet 3. Quod multiplicabis per 5 et resultat 15. Cui
195 addita unitate resultat 16. Quo dempto ab eptagonali dato

scilicet 36, remanet 18; quod est propositum ut patet in
exemplo *n*. **(p. 34a)**

Octogonum querens: hic ponit auctor regulam docentem
invenire numerum octogonum, dicens quod si proponatur alius
200   numerus et velis scire numerum octogonum ei proximum, divide
numerum propositum per 6 nec cures de remanenti. Huius autem
sexte partis invenies trigonum proximum quod multiplicabis
per 6. Addes ergo resultanti ex multiplicatione latus
trigoni et preterea unitatem. Et quod resultat erit
205   octogonus proximus numero proposito. Verbi gratia. Sit
propositus numerus 50 quod divides per 6 et erit quotiens 8.
Cuius accipies proximum trigonum quod est 6, latus autem
eius 3. Hunc ergo numerus trigonum multiplicabis per 6 et
resultat 36. Cui producto addes latus trigoni scilicet 3 et
210   unitatem, et resultabit 40. Quod est numerus octogonus
quesitus. Cuius latus erit pars addita multiplicato ex
trigono in 6 quod est 4, ut patet in exemplo *o*. Quod si
fuit octogonus inventus equalis numero proposito, tunc ambo
sunt octogoni. Si vero fuerit minor proposito, tunc est
215   maximus infra numerum propositum. Si vero fuerit maior
proposito, tunc est proximus octogonus post numerum
propositum.

Octogono si proposito: hic docet auctor invenire numerum
octogonum proximum maiorem octogono dato, dicens quod debes
220   multiplicare per 6 latus octogoni dati et addere ei unitatem
et addere hoc totum octogonali dato. Et habes propositum.
Verbi gratia. Sit octogonus datus 40 cuius latus 4. Quod
multiplicabis per 6 et resultat 24. Cui addes unitatem et
erit 25. Quod addes octogonali dato scilicet 40, et
225   resultat 65. Qui est numerus octogonus proximus maior
octogono dato; quod est propositum ut patet in exemplo *p*.

Quod si petis inferiorem: hic docet auctor invenire numerum

octogonum **(fol. 310v)** proximum minorem octogono dato, dicens
quod debes delere unitatem a latere octogoni dati, et
230   remanentem multiplicare per 6, et resultanti ex
multiplicatione addere unitatem, et hoc totum minuere de
octogono dato. Et habes octogonus inferior proximus. Verbi
gratia. Octogonus datus est 40 cuius latus 4. Dele ab eo
unitatem et remanet 3. Quod multiplicabis per 6 et erit 18.
235   Cui addes unitatem et erit 19. Quod minues ab octogono dato
scilicet 40, et remanet 21. Qui est minor octogonus
proximus octogono dato, ut patet in exemplo *q*.

Explicit alogrismus in novis numeris.

APPARATUS VARIORUM

Note: all variants are in the University Library MS unless noted by G.

8–10. Binos equales . . . tetragonus] Prius tetragonus habet 2
        trigonos equales in se et dicitur numerus tetragonus.
    16. *om.* quod
    18. *om.* Ex trigono
    19. *om.* ut patet
    20. *om.* ut patet
    23. *om.* constat
    25. Nunc] Postea
    29. *om.* et hoc per
    30 *om.* libri
    42–43. *om.* Si trigono . . . trigoni,
    54. scilicet] hoc est
    66. *om.* Si trigonus
    72. *rep. G* inventus
    73. *om.* Sed si queris inferiorem
    81. *om.* Si tunc pentagonum
    96. *deleta in G* patet in tractatu
    102. *om.* Pentagono si maiorem

108. resultat] est
111. *om.* Sed si vicinum
119. *om.* a *sed add. G² supra.*
136. est] erit
137. *om.* exagonus
178. *om.* Eptagono si proposito
184–5. ut . . . exemplo m *om.* G *sed add. G² supra.*
187. *om.* Sed si de latere
198. *om.* Octogonum querens
204. *om.* preterea
218. *om.* Octogono si proposito
227. *om.* Quod si petis inferiorem
238. *om.* G algorismus in novis numeris

Notes

A synopsis of this report was delivered at the Fall, 1989, conference honoring the 30th anniversary of California State University, Northridge.

1. "Cognitio rerum consistit in forma et natura; forma est in exteriorum disposicione, natura in interiorum qualitate. Omnis autem disposicio siue in numero est, ad quam pertinet arismetica, uel in proporcione, ad quam musica, uel in situ, ad quem geometria, uel in motu, ad quem astronomia. Ad interiorem uero qualitatem spectat phisica. . . . Omnes igitur artes subseruiunt diuine sapiencie et inferior sciencia recte ordinata ad superiorem conducit"; Vincent of Beauvais, *De eruditione filiorum nobilium*, ed. Arpad Steiner (Cambridge, Mass.: The Mediaeval Academy of America, 1938), p. 57.

2. James A. Weisheipl, "The Place of the Liberal Arts in the University Curriculum during the XIVth and XVth Centuries," in *Actes du Quatrième Congrès International de Philosophie Médiévale [Arts Libéraux et Philosophie au Moyen Âge]* (hereafter cited as *Actes*) (Montreal: Institut D'Études Médiévales, 1969), p. 209.

3. Pearl Kibre, "The *Quadrivium* in the Thirteenth Century Universities (with special reference to Paris)," in *Actes*, p. 177.

4. Kibre, "The *Quadrivium*," p. 181.

5. Michael Masi, "Arithmetic," in *The Seven Liberal Arts in the Middle Ages*, ed. David L. Wagner (Bloomington: Indiana University Press, 1983), p. 151.

6. Ron B. Thomson, "Jordanus de Nemore: Opera," *Mediaeval Studies* 38 (1976), 113–14.

7. James A. Weisheipl, "Curriculum of the Faculty of Arts at Oxford in the Early Fourteenth Century," *Mediaeval Studies* 26 (1964), 143–85.

8. Weisheipl, "Place of the Liberal Arts in the University Curriculum," p. 211.

9. Edward A. Synan, ed., *The Fountain of Philosophy: A Translation of the Twelfth-Century* Fons Philosophiae *of Godfrey of Saint Victor* (Toronto: Pontifical Institute of Mediaeval Studies, 1972), p. 52, lines 341–50.

10. *Nicomachus of Gerasa. Introduction to Arithmetic*, ed. Martin L. D'Ooge (New York: Macmillan, 1926), p. 19, lines 239–49; see also *Nicomachi Gerasensis. Introductionis Arithmeticae Libri II*, ed. Richard Hoche (Leipzig: Teubner, 1866), pp. 87–99.

11. *Boethii. De Institutione Arithmetica, Libri Duo*, ed. Gottfried Friedlein (Leipzig: Teubner, 1867), pp. 86–104.

12. Alexander de Villa Dei identified the seven operations in *Carmen*, namely, addition, subtraction, mediation, duplication, multiplication, division, and extraction of roots. John of Holywood (ca. 1190–ca. 1250) added two operations, numeration and progression, to the list in *De arte numerandi*, ed. James O. Halliwell, *Rara Mathematica*, 2nd ed. (London: J. W. Parker, 1841), p. 2.

13. See John of Holywood, in Halliwell, *Rara Mathematica*, p. 20.

14. Halliwell, *Rara Mathematica*, pp. 73–83, and Robert Steele, ed., *The Earliest Arithmetics in English* (London: Oxford University Press, 1922), pp. 72–80.

15. *Boethii. De Institutione Arithmetica*, ed. Friedlein, p. 91.

16. *Boethii. De Institutione Arithmetica*, ed. Friedlein, pp. 91–92.

17. *A Catalogue of the Manuscripts Preserved in the Library of the University of Cambridge*, vol. 3, ed. Charles Hardwick (Cambridge: Cambridge University Press, 1858), p. 215; Neil R. Ker, *Medieval Libraries of Great Britain: A List of Surviving Books*, 2nd ed. (London: Royal Historical Society, 1964), p. 136; and Barnabas Hughes, *Jordanus de Nemore. De numeris datis: A Critical Edition and Translation* (Berkeley: University of

California Press, 1981), pp. 24–25.

18. Montague R. James, *A Descriptive Catalogue of the Manuscripts in the Library of Gonville and Caius College* (Cambridge: Cambridge University Press, 1907), pp. 155–58.

19. The exact source was not found. In another context, Robert Grosseteste remarked as though the concept were common knowledge, "Diametrum esse cost asymmetram"; see his *De libero arbitrio*, c. 8, in Ludwig Baur, *Die philosophischen Werke des Robert Grosseteste, Bischofs von Lincoln* (Munster i.W.: Aschendorff, 1912), p. 194.

20. See treatise above (p. 31, line 8).

Thirteenth-Century Motion Theories and Their Musical Applications: Robert Grosseteste and Anonymous IV

Nancy Van Deusen

$\mathcal{T}$he concept of motion infiltrates discussion in every discipline, lurks behind diverse problemata, and emerges suddenly as a seminal issue in thirteenth-century intellectual discourse. Motion, in the thirteenth century, is divisible according to maximum and minimum partitions. It is, as well, frequently compared to tremor and, as a concept, is given importance of place and seriousness of treatment over nearly every other subject matter. Recent secondary literature has, accordingly, extensively treated this question of motion,[1] but those with an interest in the problem have tended to investigate selective issues, with the result that some problems have been overworked to the exclusion of both the context of motion discussion in medieval writings and other, more crucial, considerations.[2] Often the real concerns, shared by thirteenth-century writers, have been ignored.[3]

Aristotle's *Physica*, a fundamental source of thirteenth-century attitudes toward motion, as well as commentaries on this work, discuss motion's nature and measurable constructive properties. Medieval writers, in their interpretation of the *Physica*, differentiate between locutionary, divisible, measurable motion on the one hand, and tremor on the other, topics which, for example, greatly interested Robert Grosseteste. His writings—although he himself used the *translatio vetus* for his commentary—were produced during the wave of response to Michael Scot's translation of the *Physica* (ca. 1220–35), of which there are sixty-five copies even today. A portion of Averroes's great commentary on the *Physica*, also available in the Latin translation of Michael Scot, would have been accessible to him.[4] Grosseteste's interest in motion, however, is obvious in works other than his commentary on the *Physica* of Aristotle, demonstrating that his concern for the subject was lively, continuous, and that he had noticed that motion as a theme was common to many disciplines. We find the subject of motion treated extensively, for example, in his treatises *De artibus liberalibus* and *De generatione sonorum*, in which Grosseteste achieved clarity concerning the most significant properties of motion.[5] Sensitive as well to music and its exemplary capacity, Grosseteste perceived that the ideal analogy to both the natural and philosophical aspects of the phenomenon of motion was indeed music. Because music existed invisibly within the course of time, its measurements demonstrated the longitudinal movement of time. Motion, therefore, for Robert Grosseteste could best be exemplified in music.[6]

Motion intrigued thirteenth-century intellectuals such as Robert Grosseteste for two reasons. First, it is the most significant aspect of Aristotle's *Physica*, which had recently been retranslated and newly incorporated into the curriculum of the medieval *artes* faculty by the middle of the thirteenth century. The *Physica* was an important component of the "new learning" and immediately generated written discussion as well as commentaries.[7] The second reason for this medieval preoccupation with motion was that all the liberal arts had it in common, as Grosseteste pointed out in his work on that subject.

Motion then was a pivotal concept; its significance could be directed by and understood as a comprehensible feature of each discipline. This idea of manifold facets of a phenomenon, differentiated according to the disciplinary window from which they were viewed, was prepared by Aristotle himself. Motion as an abstraction was explained in the *Metaphysica*,[8] as a locutionary artistic process in the *Poetica*;[9] and motion was compared to the continuum of a regime, or of life's conduct in the *Ethica*.[10] All of these countenances of motion were useful for an understanding of its total nature. All faces of motion influenced the discipline of music and, in turn, could be exemplified by music, as Robert Grosseteste demonstrated.[11] These multiple conceptualizations of motion as they occur in the *Metaphysica, Physica, Poetica,* and *Ethica* must all be taken into consideration in order to obtain a complete medieval impression of motion.

The harmonization of these features was one of the purposes of the many commentaries on the *Physica*; the multivalence of the Aristotelian concept of motion made these commentaries necessary. But if the concept itself had not interested Robert Grosseteste and others so much, they would not have written about it with the degree of interaction with the subject matter one notes. There appears to be a personal commitment to the subject matter, for example, in Robert Grosseteste's comments, because he returns to the subject even when his theme at hand does not directly require that he do so (as, for example, in his work on the *artes liberales*),[12] and because this particular concept, in all of its facets, could be observed in and substantiated by personal experience.[13]

Since it was, no doubt, the most important problem contained in the *Physica*, motion became the central issue of natural philosophy. Aristotle presents the problem of motion with careful exemplification in opportune, memorable moments of this treatise—at the beginning of the work and again at the beginning of book 3. It is generally true that the concepts that found the most resonance in the thirteenth century were those which had clear profile and were presented either shortly after the beginning or at the beginnings of significant divisions within Aristotle's works. In the *Physica*, Aristotle divides his discussion of motion into sections in order to make the subject more comprehensible. These sections include: the nature of motion; and examples and types of motion. He actually presents his categories of motion first, since they can be observed and thus are easier to understand than the nature of motion itself. Accordingly, the Philosopher discusses distinct types in the first two books of the *Physica*. These include: 1) *change*;[14] 2) *process*, as when a simple thing is said to become something else, a category which includes *survival* or persistence, as in survival through a process or within a process;[15] 3) *impulse*, which is particularly significant, since the term brings up the two essential dimensions of nature, that is, the capacity for being moved and for coming to or being at rest;[16] and finally 4) *growth* and *continuous change* toward some end.[17] Indefinite, spontaneous chance or arbitrary movement, for example, of fortune, is

especially difficult to classify, and Aristotle comments on the problem-
atic nature of fortune in several contexts.[18] The apparently irreconcilable
yet observable phenomenon of chance leads Aristotle to a subject to
which he frequently returns in his exposition, namely, that seemingly
contradictory statements or lines of reasoning can, at the same time, be
correct.[19]

Aristotle's discussion of the nature of motion, simply because it is
so basic—therefore self-evident—has frequently been overlooked. As a
matter of fact, Aristotle himself writes far more concerning the motion
of natures and does not introduce his discussion of the nature of motion
until the beginning of book 3, despite the fact that his discourse up to
that point has been exclusively centered around that subject. He writes:
"Nature is a principle of motion and change, and it is the subject of our
inquiry. We must therefore see that we understand what motion is, for
if it were unknown, nature too would be unknown"; and "Now motion
is supposed to belong to the class of things which are continuous; and
the infinite presents itself first in the continuous, that is, how it comes
about that the account of the infinite is often used in definitions of the
continuous; for that is infinity." Continuous motion is divisible.[20]

Aristotle's examples of motion include music, dogs, men, horses, and
mathematics.[21] Mathematicians abstract shape from motion: "Now the
mathematician, though he too treats of these things, nevertheless does
not treat of them as the limits of a natural body; nor does he consider the
attributes indicated as the attributes of such bodies. That is why he
separates them; for in thought they are separable from motion, and it
makes no difference, nor does any falsity result, if they are separated."[22]
The music historian would quickly notice that during the period of the
assimilation of the *Physica*, musical notation underwent a revolutionary
change, that is, from the abstraction of motion from shape to the representation of (rhythmic) motion by shape. This, of course, is discussed at
length by music theorists.

In summary, Aristotle states that a proportional relationship exists
between motion and nature, that motion, in fact, is nature. Motion is
continuous and infinite as well as measurable and divisible. Place, empty
space, and time are all necessary conditions of motion. Further, motion

is the fulfillment of what is potential. To quote Aristotle again, "The fulfillment of what is carried along is locomotion, which indeed has led some people to suppose that every mover is moved."[23] All of this—and one must admit it is rather a dense thicket of considerations—is exemplified, and therefore becomes obvious, in contraries.[24]

Musical analogies exist as examples of all of these aspects. Music, for example, exposes its nature by its motion in time. Conversely, the nature of motion itself can be demonstrated by music situated in time, but, since musical time flow is manipulated artistically, music also includes empty space, or constructed pauses. Music is the fulfillment of what motion is potentially. It therefore demonstrates continuity and interruption; the passage of time and time's measurable divisibility. Finally, in the thirteenth century, music would demonstrate continuous but contrary lines of motion brought together or reconciled in convincing, artistically-constructed consonance.[25]

Despite the fact that Aristotle defines motion, as he states, both generally and particularly, his concept of motion is difficult to understand because one must also understand potentiality, privation, process, activity, and passivity. The final properties of motion, activity and passivity, which were the same yet not identical, posed a particular problem, namely, how contraries could be simultaneously true, or how different things could be harmonized, reconciled, and made consonant with one another. This question is answered by stating that the resolution of contraries is accomplished *through* and *by* motion.

Music contained all of the properties of motion. It was continuous and capable of—at least theoretically—infinite divisibility into tones. This quality of infinite yet measurable division in fact distinguishes music from undifferentiated sound and noise. Music was the actualization of the potential; an actualization that took place at the moment of sound in a release of energy. At the same time, music was a process comparable to that of building. Finally, and most significantly, music exemplified the most important point of Aristotle's argumentation, namely, that two lines of music—each independent of the other, each capable of exerting energy in its own right—when combined could sound as a unity. This was accomplished as single tones sounded together in counterpoint, as point of sound against point of sound, within the longitudinal flow of separate melodic lines. Aristotle's thesis of the resolution of contraries was sensorily perceptible and intellectually comprehensible in the musical example of contrary motion.

Florence, Biblioteca Mediceo-Laurenziana, Pluteo 29, I, fol. 210r: Contrary Motion.

Although the reception of new Aristotelian ideas was rapid, many of the concepts presented were indeed unaccustomed and difficult to understand. Music had an important function during this early period of Aristotelian reception—to exemplify concepts that would have otherwise been nearly impossible to sufficiently comprehend. Encouragement for this musical exemplification came, after all, from Aristotle himself, who from the first sets up music's competency to function as an analogy to the principles he is explaining. This could not have been lost on his thirteenth-century audience.

Robert Grosseteste, for example, in his treatise *De generatione sonorum*, seized upon the concept of contrary motion and expressly related it to time and sound. He wrote:

> Et cum sit alterum tempus, quo formatur sonus vocalis et sonus consonantis. Et etiam sunt duo tempora discontinua, quia inter quoslibet motus contrarios est quies media: eo modo dicitur consonans, quasi cum alio sonans; et quasi per se non possit audiri, cum eius generatio praecedat, vel subsequatur tempore generationem vocalis.
>
> Ad hoc respondeo: quod virtus motiva, qua formatur vocalis continue a principio syllabae usque ad finem eius, inclinat spiritus et instrumenta ad formandum sonum vocalis sibi similem et etiam movet spiritus et instrumenta. Cum autem dictam inclinationem concomitatur inclinatio aliqua ad formandum sonum consonantis, egreditur in spiritibus et instrumentis motus unus compositus proveniens a duabus inclinationibus, sicut cum ponderosum inclinatur ad motum deorsum. . . .[26]

Two sound movements, generated by two separated inclinations, each moving in time and each distinct, could move in opposite directions. Simultaneously, from two inclinations could be formed one unified motion, brought about by separate points of rest (*motus contrarios est quies media*). The vocabulary Grosseteste used is a terminology that could be, and in fact was, loaded with musical significance. Many of his expressions, such as *tempus, proportio, sonus vocalis, motus contrarius*, and *sonus consonantis*, could also be understood as a musical conceptual language, a fund of words and concepts that immediately brought music to mind—also for Grosseteste himself. This fact demonstrates the intrinsic interdisciplinary nature of knowledge transfer, but it also shows that the richness of meaning of these terms can be assessed only when their entire multidisciplinary context is taken into consideration. For musicologists, I believe the specifically non-musical significance is crucial for the understanding of these terms.

Grosseteste's thought process follows. He had assimilated the categories of the nature of motion as they were presented in the *Physica*. Motion stands in a proportional relationship to and with nature.[27] It is continuous, that is, infinitely divisible.[28] Motion exists within place and time; empty space is also a necessary feature of its existence.[29] Finally, motion is a fulfillment of what is potential motion; locomotion is that fulfillment of motion as it moves along steadily to a goal.[30] Digested, reorganized, extended, with emphasis placed according to the strong selective will of the writer, these characteristics of motion find their place in Grosseteste's concept of locution.[31]

Locutionary continuous motion is distinguished by its divisibility into minute particles. It is therefore subject to close control and is measurable. Grosseteste presents a concept of measurable continuous movement, not unlike natural movement, leading to a goal. He presents a concept of longitudinal teleological continuity motivated by generative purpose. In *De artibus liberalibus*, Grosseteste writes: "Quinque ergo sunt proportiones, quarum tres sunt minime multiplicium et duae maxime superparticularium quia haec sunt inter maximas et minimas divisiones in motu secundum tarditatem, vel velocitatem, vel secundum utramque."[32]

Grosseteste's discussion of locutionary motion and its divisions occurs in the context of his writing on the liberal arts. In fact, motion is what all of the arts have in common.[33] Each of the liberal arts expresses motion in a way that is proper to its disciplinary territory. Grosseteste's care in laying out the characteristics and significance of locutionary is necessary for the further step, the concept of locutionary motion itself. It is directionally focused, controlled, and can be both constructed and analyzed because it can be measured. This motion reaches an end or goal through process.[34] It is a concept of locutionary motion which is multivalent in its applications. Aristotle, for example, applied it to the plot of a play in the *Poetica*.

Grosseteste was more interested in some examples of motion than in others. Theatre plots do not seem to have interested him, but direction and continuity of sound—especially the sound of the human voice, displaying the proportional divisions of long and short syllables and pursuing a purpose which arrived at an end—certainly did. He chose this example for discussion. In a rapid succession of important issues and terms, he presented an entire complex of aspects for his concepts of *virtus motiva* and contrary motion. These aspects are: 1) progression (*in progressione ad auditum*);[35] 2) the instrumental character of *virtutes motivae* (*et quia virtutes motivae corporis instrumenta*);[36] 3) an aspect of continuity or governance (*necessarium est regimen et adjutorium, quibus purgetur error et suppleatur defectus*),[37] which was 4) divisible (*Proportiones vero motuum secundum duplicem motus divisibilitatem considerantur. Est enim motus divisibilis divisibilitate temporis et secundum hanc divisibilitatem dicitur motus duplus ad alium, qui duplo mensuratur tempore . . .*);[38] leading to 5) perfection, completeness, or a goal (*et ad perfectionem deductiones sunt artes septenae, quae solae inter partes philosophiae ideo censentur artis nomine, quia earum est tantum effectus, operationes humanas corrigendo ad perfectionem ducere*).[39] Grosseteste's locutionary motion transcends natural motion because of its directional, longitudinal aspect, in its transverse diameter, and in its termination. *Tremor* is the opposite of longitudinal motion in nearly every respect, since it remains in one place, in one situation, and has no recognizable, orderly progression. Tremor therefore is useless as a type of motion in artistic construction. In contrast, longitudinal, divided motion is ordered and has distinctive measurable parts, whereas tremor is erratic, stationary, uncontrolled and indefinite.[40] Grosseteste carefully defined his principle of locutionary continuous motion first, then considered contrary motion. The format of his discussion, as R. W. Southern has pointed out, is a presentation of succinct areas, in a logical progression rather than developed in a *Summa*. Grosseteste's discussions contain very few examples, and his essay on the liberal arts primarily addresses music. One comes to the conclusion that, for Grosseteste, music, in its nature and gestures, was the outer perceptible example for both divisible and contrary motions.

I would take issue with both Smalley, who regarded Grosseteste as a conservative, habitually looking backward,[41] and Southern, who presents him as insular, fiercely independent, and original.[42] Grosseteste selected aspects of Aristotle's treatises that especially interested him, such as motion. His particular characteristic, however, lay in his ability to see the function, value, and special competency of music to explicate physical properties such as motion in sound. While Southern noticed what he considered to be Grosseteste's aptitude for music,[43] Grosseteste's substantial contribution to speculative music theory has not been noticed. Both Smalley and Southern, furthermore, have stated that Grosseteste's influence was minimal during his own lifetime. Both, however, over-looked an important emphasis in his writing, that is, his concern for the understanding and articulation of musical relationships.

One first notices Grosseteste's pronounced emphasis on music in his discussion of the liberal arts, in which he developed an entire system of contrapuntal rules. I shall summarize Grosseteste's term or rule first; then I shall give its direct musical application, as set forth by a con-temporaneous anonymous writer who, as far as we know, also lived and worked in England.[44] First, Grosseteste presented the term *contrary motion*, an important concept, also selected by music theory, where it can be visually observed—in the music itself—and where it was verbally explained.[45] Second, Grosseteste explained the concept of a "quiet median" or, as I understand it, a mid-point of rest within contrary motion, or between melodic lines that demonstrate contrary motion. In contrapuntal theory, consonances, or certain intervals which give a sense of musical repose, must be used when two tones occur together for a significant period of time. Consonances occurring on strong and longer-held beats have been important for the tradition of counterpoint throughout its history.[46] Third, sound is not continuous but is frequently interrupted according to artistic considerations. This tenet of Grosseteste's system is analogous to the appearance of the consideration of rests in thirteenth-century music theory.[47] Grosseteste's system also includes a concept of simultaneity or *concordantia temporum*, a concord of times. Counterpoint, from the onset, is a study, both analytical and prescriptive, of simultaneously occurring relationships.[48] Further, Grosseteste wrote of duple and triple proportions of movement as a concept of measurement (*proportiones temporum*). He considered proportions as progressive measurements of time, as well as quantitative relationships within time. The measurement of time, or the increasing refinement of rhythmic value indication, continues from the mid-thirteenth century onward. Proportions, when applied to musical time, illustrate the dynamic quality of proportions themselves.[49] Grosseteste's consideration of motion contains a concept of composition, as a composite containing elements. The concept of a "piece," or a self-contained composition, with a beginning, a middle progressive section, and a termination is not an earlier medieval idea; rather, it is increasingly important from the mid-thirteenth century onward.[50] Grosseteste's system elucidates both process and occurrence, connection and separation. His system sets forth both a concept of order and a notion of figures within that order. Figures, abstracted from an ongoing organization, and the ability to be figural have an important place in Grosseteste's argumentation. Figures are also abstracted from music's time flow. Musical notation exemplifies both continuity and configuration, and the concept of figure is given a great deal of place in mid-thirteenth-century discussions of music.[51] Finally, the principle of "rule" itself is discussed by Grosseteste (*quod sit regula nostrae operationes*).[52] Art is dependent upon and disposed by rules of operations. One does counterpoint. It is practical, operational, and procedural, but also it is characterized by its adherence to a body of rules. This makes it unique, as no other style in the history of Western music is based upon such an interlocking system of regulations.

In placing each rule before its musical counterpart, I have shown that each of Grosseteste's tenets within his system extends to thought on music, as he himself stated.[53] For Grosseteste, music was an example not only of the quadrivial but also of the trivial arts, in that it had an organizing, order-giving "ministry."[54] Accustomed as we are to distinct disciplines and special technical vocabularies as well as manners of expression, we are unaccustomed to the mutual dependency and interrelationship of all fields of learning. Repeatedly Grosseteste emphasized the collusion and conceptual dependency among all of the arts. Having established this, he then went on to the illustrative and organizational qualities of music, using a vocabulary that related his treatises to contemporaneous music-theoretical discussion: (in the order of their appearance) *proportiones*, *concordantia*, *motus dicitur duplus ad motum*, *motus contrarius*, *ordo*, *figura*, *mensurata*, *regula* and *imperfectum a perfecto*.

Robert Grosseteste did not thoroughly explain technical musical considerations in either *De artibus liberalibus* or *De generatione sonorum* because, I believe, he did this elsewhere. I would suggest the possibility that Grosseteste was the author of the music treatise *De mensurata et discantu* for which Edmond de Coussemaker, in the last century, assigned the designation Anonymous IV. This hypothesis is based on the fact that the treatise originated in England and conceivably could have been written during Grosseteste's lifetime. Among the sparse facts of both Grosseteste's and Anonymous IV's lives, what is known is that both were associated with the monastery of Bury St. Edmunds. In a factual region where very little can be indisputably proven, however, the most convincing reason for my conclusion is internal evidence. Stylistic similarities, methods of explication, the use of a common vocabulary, and the concise, forthright character of both works, as well as Grosseteste's own preoccupation with music, all make this explanation of ownership plausible. That the music treatise was conserved and cherished also points to a writer of reputation.[55]

In comparing Robert Grosseteste's style with that of Anonymous IV, one notices the following similarities. The subject, of course, demands a more detailed study. First, and most important, figures, for Anonymous IV, not only have music notational significance but also are analogous to geometric diagrams in the sense that they abstract and delineate material.[56] This emphasis, gauged by the frequency with which facets of the subject are discussed, is unique to this writer among contemporaneous writers on music. Anonymous's emphasis on the figural aspect relates to his perception of the associations between the other quadrivial arts.[57] A common dimension of both geometric figures and musical notation is the importance of joints, of lines converging so that they become significant. This emphasis on joints is shared by both Anonymous and Robert Grosseteste.[58]

Second, there are telling similarities in uncommon expressions used by both Anonymous IV and Grosseteste, such as *circularem processum donec circulatio perficiatus*, which is unique to Anonymous IV among writers on music but is shared by Robert Grosseteste.[59] Third, both writers emphasize the separation between vocal and instrumental means of tone production. This subject again reinforces Anonymous IV's interdisciplinary command of his material, and his particular insight into the quadrivial arts and their relationships to one another. The format of rhythm, for example, could best be exposed by instrumental delineation, just as geometric figures expose—by their delineatory power—the essence of the material contained. Anonymous IV's focus on instruments and their potential for exposing the outline of rhythmic shape shows his sensitivity to an important internal connection among the quadrivial arts, namely, that they all define, diagram, and delineate material. Finally, both writers share a pronounced concern for sign/property versus intellectual understanding. Signs, for both Anonymous IV and Grosseteste, indicate intellectual material.

In conclusion, I would like to place my hypothesis that Grosseteste wrote a treatise on music in what I believe to be a proper perspective. After all, the possible identity of an anonymous writer on the subject of music is admittedly of more interest to a small group of music historians working in the limited field of thirteenth-century music theoretical sources than to anyone else, and the fact that a treatise on music could conceivably be added to Robert Grosseteste's already lengthy list of writings is of more interest, again, to a relatively small group of scholars who study the life and works of this thirteenth-century personality. The circumference of interest in both cases is limited. I would, however, suggest that the impact of what I have set forth goes beyond the immediate considerations of music theory, Anonymous IV, and Grosseteste.

Music uniquely exemplified an absolutely pivotal concept. This concept was exposed by all of the major Aristotelian works, the *Metaphysica*, the *Poetica*, the *Ethica*, and the *Physica*. Motions—of discourse, of physical bodies, of thoughts, and, especially, of musical melodic lines—which appeared to oppose one another by their contrary impulses, their sources of directions, and their movements toward goals—could and should be reconciled to one another. This had an analogy as well, as the Apostle Paul pointed out, in the Christian life. The point of reconciliation, of simultaneous consonance, was the point of rest, the *quies medians*.[60]

The system of musical counterpoint—as point of sound against point of sound—made this plain to the ear and, in musical notation, to the eye as well. And so this difficult idea of contrary motion could be articulated, understood, and, conversely, influenced musical composition for the next 600 years. No other concept in the history of Western music has had such power.

Notes

1. James A. Weisheipl's article "Natural and Compulsory Movement," reissued in a collection of his essays, *Nature and Motion in the Middle Ages* (Washington D.C: Catholic University of America Press, 1985), pp. 25–48, includes in its footnotes a bibliography of this literature.

2. Writers, for the most part, have concentrated on the principle and problem, *Omne quod movetur ab alio movetur*. See especially Roy R. Effler, *John Duns Scotus and the Principle "Omne quod movetur ab alio movetur"* (St. Bonaventure, N.Y.: Franciscan Institute, 1962); and James A. Weisheipl, "The Principle *omne quod movetur ab alio movetur* in Medieval Physics," in *Nature and Motion*, pp. 75–97.

3. One of these concerns, the relationships among the *artes liberales*, which attracted intense and prolonged discussion in the thirteenth century, is a case in point. It is a subject that is no longer interesting. One reason for this is that those who do study the culture of the Middle Ages are more interested in—and, in fact, find their academic niches within—modern disciplines that have developed since the early nineteenth century, in order to give academic legitimacy to the subjective interpretation of the Middle Ages. These include history, art history, musicology as it exists today, and literature. Medieval disciplines, their overlapping areas of information and competence, and particularly the quadrivial arts and their interactions with one another attract less concern.

4. See Bernard G. Dod, "Aristoteles latinus," in *The Cambridge History of Later Medieval Philosophy: From the Rediscovery of Aristotle to the Disintegration of Scholasticism, 1100–1600* (Cambridge: Cambridge University Press, 1982), which includes a useful table of translators of Aristotelian works and extant copies of these translations, pp. 74ff.

5. *De generatione sonorum*, ed. Ludwig Baur, in his *Die philosophischen Werke des Robert Grosseteste, Bischofs von Lincoln* (Münster: Aschendorff, 1912), pp. 7–10; and *De artibus liberalibus*, ed. Baur, ibid., pp. 1–7. All subsequent references to Grosseteste's works are to this edition. Grosseteste treated motion in several other treatises, for example, *De motu corporali et luce*, ed. Baur, pp. 90ff., *De motu supercaelestium*, ed. Baur, pp. 92–100, and *De finitate motus et temporis*, ed. Baur, pp. 101–06.

6. Richard Southern comments on this sensitivity to music in *Robert Grosseteste: The Growth of an English Mind in Medieval Europe* (Oxford: Clarendon, 1986), pp. 209, 232, 318, but there are many internal evidences for an interest in and knowledge of music on the part of this author, as, for example his quotation of Augustine's *De musica VI, 5 n. 9, Patrologia cursus completus . . . series latina* (hereafter *PL*), ed. Jacques-Paul Migne, 217 vols. (Paris, 1878–90), 32.1168: "De hoc Augustinus in libro sexto musicae ita ait: Ego ab anima hoc corpus animari non puto, nisi intentione facientis; nec ab isto quicquam illam pati arbitror, sed facere de illo et in illo tanquam subiecto divinitus dominationi suae, aliquando tamen cum facilitate, aliquando cum difficultate operari, quanto pro eius meritis magis minusve ei subiecta est natura corporea. Corporalia ergo quaecunque huic corpori ingeruntur aut obiiciuntur extrinsecus, non in anima, sed in ipso corpore aliquid faciunt, quod eius operi aut adversetur aut congruat" (in *De intelligentiis*, ed. Baur, p. 119). But Grosseteste's understanding of music's special competence can be seen best by his frequent allusions to music as an example of the subject he is currently examining, even when neither text nor topic at hand directly invoke these references.

7. The extent of these Aristotelian commentaries can at least partially be seen in Albert Zimmermann's *Verzeichnis ungedruckter Kommentare zur Metaphysik und Physik des Aristoteles aus der Zeit von etwa 1250–1350*, Bd. 1 (Leiden: Brill, 1971).

8. Grosseteste points to the *Metaphysica*'s expository treatment of motion as an abstraction in *De motu supercaelestium* (ed. Baur, p. 94): "Item cum iste motor sit abstractus, neque movetur ab aliquo moto, remanet dubitatio de modo motoris ipsius, scilicet: quomodo facit motus? Et sermo Aristotelis [*Metaph*. XII, 7. 1072a 26–27] est hic et XII Metaphysicae, quod primum sic movet sicut desideratum et intellectum movet nos. Sed cum desideratum moveat nos per modum finis, tunc et iste motor in illis erit per modum finis: et quaestio nostra est de eo, quod movet per modum efficientis." See also *De motu*, ed. Baur, p. 100, in which Grosseteste refers to *Metaphysica* XII, 8.1073a 32–33; 1074a 18ff. for the same reason and directly relates the concept of motion to time.

9. The forward, continuous, successive motion of the plot is presented throughout the *Poetica*.

10. *Ductus/conductus* as successive motions with incremental particulars is a recurring concept in Aristotle's ethical treatises.

11. The concept of motion has seminal importance and occurs at the beginning of *De artibus liberalibus*: "In humanis vero operibus erroris purgationes et ad perfectionem deductiones sunt artes septenae, quae solae inter partes philosophiae ideo censentur artis nomine, quia earum est tantum effectus, operationes humanas corrigendo ad perfectionem ducere. Opera enim nostrae potestatis aut in mentis aspectu, aut in eiusdem affectu, aut in corporum motibus aut eorumdem motuum affectibus omnia consistunt. . . . Cum autem attendimus non ad illud, quod efficitur per motus corporeos, sed in ipsis motibus moderationem, modificatrix est musica," ed. Baur, pp. 1–2.

12. The concept of motion is used in discussing proportions: "Haec enim, ut asseruit Macrobius motuum proportionibus reperitur concordantia. Proportiones vero motuum secundum duplicem motus divisibilitatem considerantur. Est enim motus divisibilis divisibilitate temporis et secundum hanc divisibilitatem dicitur motus duplus ad alium, qui duplo mensuratur tempore, sicut etiam syllaba longa respectu brevis dupla est; et motus divisibilis et proportionalis proportionalitate et divisibilitate spatii: sicque motus dicitur duplus ad motum, qui in eodem tempore duplum pertransit spatium," *De artibus liberalibus*, ed. Baur, p. 2. In this context, Grosseteste returns to the subject of music: "Et cum a motibus coelestibus sit concordantia temporum et compositio et harmonia mundi inferioris et rerum omnium compositarum ex quatuor elementis, necesseque sit harmoniam efficientium in effectis reperire, ex extendit se speculatio musicae, ut proportiones temporum, et elementorum mundi inferioris constitutionem cognoscat, et etiam omnium elementorum compositionem," *De artibus liberalibus*, ed. Baur, p. 3; punctuation emended.

13. Personal experience substantiates both the concepts of procession, or the successive, and occurrence or simultaneity: "Cum inquam ita sit in numeris sonantibus protendit se musica speculatio ut harmoniam cognoscat, non solum in numeris sonantibus seu corporalibus, sed etiam in progressoribus et occursoribus, recordabilibus, sensibilibus et iudicialibus," *De artibus liberalibus*, ed. Baur, p. 4.

14. Change: "We say that one thing comes to be from another thing, and something from something different, in the case both of simple and complex things. I mean the following. We can say that the man becomes musical, as what is not-musical becomes musical, or the not-musical man becomes a musical man. Now what becomes in the first two cases—man and not-musical—I call simple, and what each becomes—musical—simple also. But when we say the non-musical man becomes a musical man, both what becomes and what it becomes are complex," *Physica*, 189b34 (trans. R. P. Hardie and R. K. Gaye, *The Complete Works of Aristotle: The Revised Oxford Translation*, 2 vols., ed. Jonathan

Barnes [Princeton: Princeton University Press, 1984], 1: 324). All quotations from the *Physica* are taken from this work.

15. Survival or persistence through process: "When a simple thing is said to become something, in one case it survives through the process, in the other it does not. For the man remains a man and is such even when he becomes musical, whereas what is not musical or is unmusical does not survive, either simply or combined with the subject," *Physica* 190a9.

16. Impulse: see *Physica* 192b16f for the presence or absence of an "innate impulse to change . . . which seems to indicate that nature is a principle or cause of being moved and of being at rest in that to which it belongs primarily in virtue of itself and not accidentally."

17. Continuous change towards some end: "By gradual advance in this direction we come to see clearly that in plants too that is produced which is conducive to the end. . . . Moreover, among the seeds anything must come to be at random. But the person who asserts this entirely does away with nature and what exists by nature. For those things are natural which, by a continuous movement originated from an internal principle, arrive at some end: the same end is not reached from every principle; nor any chance end, but always the tendency in each is towards the same end, if there is no impediment," *Physica* 199a24; 199b14.

18. Chance, spontaneous and arbitrary change: "Chance and what results from chance are appropriate to agents that are capable of good fortune and of action generally. Therefore necessarily chance is in the sphere of actions. This is indicated by the fact that good fortune is thought to be the same, or nearly the same as happiness, and happiness to be a kind of action, since it is well-doing. . . . The spontaneous on the other hand is found both in the beasts and in many inanimate objects," *Physica* 197b1f.

19. Correctness of apparently contradictory statements: "It is necessary, no doubt, that the causes of what comes to pass by chance be indefinite, and that is why chance is supposed to belong to the class of the indefinite and to be inscrutable to man, and why it might be thought that, in a way, nothing occurs by chance. For all these statements are correct, as might be expected," *Physica* 197b9f.

20. *Physica* 200b13; 17.

21. *Physica* 191b15–25.

22. *Physica* 193b32.

23. *Physica* 201a25.

24. *Physica* 201a33.

25. The specific Aristotelian sources of fundamental concepts in thirteenth-century writing concerning music is a subject for further, more exhaustive treatment. One source of the highly influential concept of six "modes of rhythm" is Aristotle's six "modes of causation" (*Physica* 195b13). The rhythmic modes, like modes of causation, exhibit motoric causality, originate from six separate tendencies or inclinations, and—again like Aristotle's modes of causation—have the common characteristic that each pair's two rhythms are contraries one of the other: ♪: ♪ . All of the modes together contain a complete compendium of the rhythmic figures able to be produced by the human voice.

26. *De generatione sonorum*, ed. Baur, p. 9.

27. Grosseteste discusses sound, motion, and nature in much the same manner in his commentary to the *Posterior Analytics* (II.4), *De artibus liberalibus* (ed. Baur, pp. 2–3), and *De generatione sonorum* (ed. Baur, pp. 7–8), as Baur's parallel edition makes clear. See his *Die philosophischen Werke des Robert Grosseteste*, pp. 58*–59.

28. "Proportiones vero motuum secundum duplicem motus divisibilitatem considerantur. Est enim motus divisibilis divisibilitate temporis et secundum hanc divisibilitatem dicitur motus duplus ad alium, . . ." *De artibus liberalibus*, ed. Baur, p. 2.

29. Space: ". . . et motus divisibilis et proportionalis proportionalitate et divisibilitate spatii: sicque motus dicitur duplus ad motum, qui in eodem tempore duplum pertransit spatium," *De artibus liberalibus*, ed. Baur, p. 2.

30. Locutionary motion: "Hinc motus locutionum intelligo, quae licet a motu efficiatur, a natura motus non censetur seiungenda," *De artibus liberalibus*, ed. Baur, p. 2.

31. Grosseteste's discussion of locutionary motion differentiates between divided, divisible, or measured motion and tremor, that is, between continuous percussive motion and sound that is "non esse continuum, sed interruptum et numerosum," *De artibus liberalibus*, ed. Baur, p. 3.

32. The entire context of this important passage is as follows: "Quinque ergo sunt proportiones, quarum tres sunt minime multiplicium et duae maxime superparticularium: quia haec sunt inter maximas et minimas divisiones in motu secundum tarditatem, vel velocitatem, vel secundum utramque. Haec numquam praestant in motibus perfectum moderamen. Hinc motus locutionum intelligo, quae licet a motu efficiatur, a natura motus

non censetur sejungenda. Cum enim corpus violenter percutitur, partes percussae et constrictae a situ naturali secedunt. Quas virtus naturalis ad situm naturalem inclinans fortiter metas debitas facit transscendere ipso impulsu naturali; iterum a situ naturali egrediuntur et de una inclinatione naturali situm transgredientes revertuntur generaturque hoc modo tremor in minutissimis partibus percussi corporis, donec tandem inclinatio naturalis non ultra situm debitum eas impellat. In hoc autem tremore et motu locali partium motarum necesse est, cum quaelibet pars per situm sibi naturalem transeat, eius diametrum longitudinalem esse in termino suae diminutionis et diametri transversales erunt in termino suae majorationis. Cum autem transierunt situm naturalem, diameter longitudinalis extenditur et transversales contrahuntur, donec perveniant ad terminum motus sui localis; eruntque tunc diametri transversales in termino suae diminutionis et longitudinales in termino suae majorationis. Deinde, cum redierit, erit extensio et contractio diametrorum via conversa. Hanc autem extensionem et contractionem ingredientem profunditatem materiae et praecipue id, quod est aereum subtile in corpore, sonativum esse intelligo. Cumque inter quoslibet motus contrarios sit quies media, necesse est, sonum quantumcumque parvum audibilem non esse continuum, sed interruptum et numerosum, licet hoc non percipiatur.

Cum itaque eisdem proportionibus humanae vocis, et gesticulationibus humani corporis modulatio temperetur, quibus soni et motus corporum reliquorum, speculationi musicae subjacet non solum harmonia humanae vocis et gesticulationis, sed etiam instrumentorum et eorum, quorum delectatio in motu sive in sono consistit et cum his harmonia coelestium sive noncoelestium. Et cum a motibus coelestibus sit concordantia temporum et compositio et harmonia mundi inferioris et rerum omnium compositarum ex quatuor elementis, necesseque sit harmoniam efficientium in effectis reperire et extendit se speculatio musicae, ut proportiones temporum, et elementorum mundi inferioris constitutionem cognoscat et etiam omnium elementorum compositionem," *De artibus liberalibus*, ed. Baur, p. 2–3.

33. See above, n. 11.

34. This concept of motion cannot be found in, for example, Martianus Capella's description of motion in *The Marriage of Philology and Mercury,* trans. William Harris Stahl and Richard Johnson with E. L. Burge (New York: Columbia University Press, 1977), p. 9: "Amidst these extraordinary scenes and these vicissitudes of Fortune, a sweet music arose from the trees, a melody arising from their contact as the breeze whispered through them; for the crests of the great trees were very tall and, because of this tension, reverberated with a sharp sound; but whatever was close to and near the ground, with drooping boughs, shook with a deep heaviness of sound; while the trees of middle size in their contacts with each other sang together in fixed harmonies of the duple, the sesquialtera, the sesquitertia also, and even the sesquioctava without discrimination, although

the semitones came between. So it happened that the grove poured forth, with melodious harmony, the whole music and song of the gods." Cf. Remigius of Auxerre's commentary on this passage (2 vols., ed. Cora E. Lutz [Leiden: Brill, 1962–65]), 1: 86–87). This concept of motion was highly influential in the Middle Ages, but, rather than locutionary motion, it corresponds to a concept of tremor. The concept of divided, interrupted, measurable time-lapse is exactly what occurs in a musical work of art, whereas tremor is nearly useless as an artistic time-lapse concept.

35. *De artibus liberalibus*, ed. Baur, p. 1.

36. "Virtutes motivae" is an expression used by Grosseteste at the onset of *De artibus liberalibus* (ed. Baur, p. 1). Furthermore, Grosseteste distinguished in several contexts between voices and instruments.

37. *De artibus liberalibus*, ed. Baur, p. 1.

38. *De artibus liberalibus*, ed. Baur, p. 2.

39. "Mentes ergo aspectum et affectum hac tres virtutes rectificant et ad perfectionem perducant," *De artibus liberalibus*, ed. Baur, p. 2 (cf. p. 1).

40. Grosseteste discussed tremor at length in *De generatione sonorum*, ed. Baur, pp. 7–10. After presenting the possibility of tremor, he proceeded to his discussion of characteristic motions, or figures, a subject that is the chief topic of Aristotle's *Poetica*.

41. See *Robert Grosseteste, Scholar and Bishop: Essays in Commemoration of the Seventh Centenary of his Death*, ed. Daniel A. Callus (Oxford: Clarendon, 1955), pp. 71–74.

42. Southern, *Robert Grosseteste*, pp. 1, 296–98.

43. Southern, *Robert Grosseteste*, pp. 1, 296–98, esp. 318.

44. A summary of the little that is known concerning this writer is given by Fritz Reckow in the introduction to his edition of Anonymous IV's treatise, *Der Musiktraktat des Anonymus 4*, 2 vols. (Wiesbaden: Franz Steiner, 1967), 2: 1–22. An indication of just how little is known about this individual is the fact that he has no name.

45. "Contrary motion" is expressed by Anonymous IV in several contexts and manners, as, for example: "Et isti modi sunt perfecti sicut alii; sed penes reductionem reducuntur ad modos contrarios, videlicet ad primum vel secundum, ita quod isti ultimi sexti ad

secundum et primi sexti ad primum, et sic in cognitione prima satis patet," *Der Musik-traktat*, ed. Reckow, 1: 34. "Mode," used frequently by both Robert Grosseteste and Anonymous IV, carries the connotation of "a way of moving": "Sed proprietas et perfectio istius erit in ordine ligatarum modo contrario et e contrario etc.," *Der Musik-traktat*, ed. Reckow, 1: 53. "Discantus est secundo procreatus vel factus supra tenorem concordatus. . . . De brevi autem sequenti non est cura, quia indifferenter ponitur secundum quod melius competit, et est unius temporis contra unum tempus in tenore. . . . Aliter: si fuerint tria puncta, et unus ascendit et operari, si naturaliter habet. . . . quoniam aliquando ipsis nescientibus descendunt vel ascendunt aliter in aliam concordantiam quam in consimilem," *Der Musiktraktat*, ed. Reckow, 1: 74–75.

46. Consonances on strong beats, or a concept of a "quiet median": "Est et altera medietas, quae dicitur armonica, quae partim convenit cum arsmetica, partim cum geo-metica, prout in *Musica* Boecii *Omnium quidem perceptio* etc. plenius habetur. Iterato proportiones relativae alio modo considerantur. Quaedam dicitur aequalis ut unum ad unum, duo ad duo, tria ad tria etc. quae apud musicos dicitur aequalitas et quoad sonum unisonus nuncupatur, sive fuerit in cordis sive in fistulis organorum sive in cimbalis benesonantibus etc.," *Der Musiktraktat*, ed. Reckow, 1: 65. "Et nota, quod primus punctus tenoris mediat continuando et quiescit in locis, in quibus magis competit secundum concordantias suprapositas, et quiescit secundum discordantias disconvenientes etc. prout melius competitit," *Der Musiktraktat*, ed. Reckow, 1: 83.

47. Pauses: "Sequitur de tertio <capitulo>, quod tractat de pausationibus temporum sonorum, et hoc per hunc modum: pausatio est quies vel dimissio soni in debita quantitate temporis vel temporum longae vel brevis alicuius modi modorum sex supradictorum. . . . Tempus vero eius consideratur iuxta ordinem longarum et brevium modi ante ipsam coniuncti immediate, sive fuerit primi vel secundi etc. Si fuerit primus modus perfectus ante ipsam coniunctim immediate, sic erit simplex pausatio brevis unius temporis. Et per continuationem discretionis modi antedicti post ipsam pausationem. . . . Et talis pausatio dicitur perfecta in se," *Der Musiktraktat*, ed. Reckow, 1: 57. "De duplici pausatione supradicta non intelligimus duplare brevem vel longam, sed prout in ordine alicuius modi intelliguntur, . . ." *Der Musiktraktat*, ed. Reckow, 1: 62.

48. Simultaneity or simultaneously occurring points of sound: "Sed puncta materialia sic distinguuntur: pone primo unam longam materialem; postmodum iunge duos currentes, . . ." *Der Musiktraktat*, ed. Reckow, 1: 37. ". . . prout universales antiqui nominaverunt, et hoc est, prout concordaverunt sonos cum sonis," *Der Musiktraktat*, ed. Reckow, 1: 71. "Seqitur modo, sicut diximus superius de concordantiis super duo puncta, et hoc secundum sex concordantias armonicas, . . ." *Der Musiktraktat*, ed. Reckow, 1: 73. The use of *cum, ad, ad invicem, contra* imply simultaneous occurence: "Et oportet, quod ad minus sint ibi duae voces concordantes ad invicem secundum quod dicam, et hoc est

secundum considerationem habitudinis illorum ad invicem, quod fit multiplici modo tam ex parte <dis>cantus quam ex parte tenoris," *Der Musiktraktat*, ed. Reckow, 1: 74. Time is the principal consideration in a concept of simultaneity: ". . . et est unius temporis contra unum tempus in tenore," *Der Musiktraktat*, ed. Reckow, 1: 74.

49. *Proportiones* and their dynamism (as expressed in the term *operari*): "Et nota, quod quando contingit operari per istam regulam, si termini unius proportionis multiplicentur per eundem numerum, semper resultabit eadem proportio," *Der Musiktraktat*, ed. Reckow, 1: 70.

50. The increasingly concrete concept of a "composition," culminating in the dating and titling of compositions, is a subject that requires thorough treatment. "Composition" contains and is influenced by the concept of a "composite," which I have treated in "The Latin Phaedo and its Concept of Simultaneous Harmony," in *Tradition and its Future in Music*, Report of SIMS 1990 Osaka (Proceedings of the Symposium of the International Musicological Society, Osaka Japan, 1991), pp. 309–20. Robert Grosseteste related "composite," the "letter" and "doctrine" in his commentary on the *Posterior Analytics*: "Est autem precognitionis et cognitionis duplex via, scilicet a simplicioribus ad compositiora vel econverso, quod innuitur in hac littera: *utraque enim per prius nota faciunt doctrinam, . . .*" *Commentarius in posteriorum analyticorum Libros*, ed. Pietro Rossi (Florence: Olschki, 1981), p. 95.

51. The thorough, perceptive discussion of *figures* is an especially important common subject matter for both Robert Grosseteste and Anonymous IV. Both concentrate on the configurational demonstrative competence of figures to express and delineate material, the relationship between figures and material, and the cognitive effect of figures. Both writers carefully describe figures, and both discuss the significance of shape and the joinings that connect lines and form figures. See, for example, Anonymous IV: "Puncta materialia, prout depinguntur in libris et prout significant melos et tempora supradictorum, duplici acceptione accipiuntur: uno modo per se et absolute sine sermone adiuncto . . . apud aliquos figurae vocantur, quare nota figura potest dici; apud aliquos simplices soni dicuntur, et sic materiali signo pro formali intelligitur," *Der Musiktraktat*, ed. Reckow, 1: 40–41. "Tres ligatae totaliter ascendendo sic notantur: fac quadrangulum et alium quadrangulum iungendo conum cum cono sive angulum cum angulo lateraliter protrahendo, iterato alium quadrangulum sibi iungendo et recte supraponendo, ut in duabus ligatis superius dictum est," *Der Musiktraktat*, ed. Reckow, 1: 42. See also the expanded discussion of the relationship and significance of mode and figure and their logical reductions in Robert Grosseteste's commentary on the *Posterior Analytics*: ". . . et causa una est quia in doctrinis est semper modus et figura sillogistica, et sic excluduntur a doctrinis fallacie que peccant contra modum et figuram. In aliis facultatibus arguitur

frequenter inductive et a simili et multis aliis argumentationibus que non habent modum et figuram sillogisticam licet possint reduci in figuram et modum.

Secunda causa est quod ea que sunt in mathematicis sponte se offerunt intellectui et perspicaciter videntur in intellectu; ea vero que sunt in logica et metaphysica propter remotionem eorum a sensu et subtilitatem nature sue subterfugiunt intellectum et speculantur velut a longe et non discernuntur eorum subtiles differentie. . . . Ponit autem exemplum manifeste visionis rerum mathematicarum et parve deceptionis in his. Si enim queratur an omnis circulus sit figura cum descriptione circuli, omni intellectui manifestum est quod sit. Si autem queratur an carmen sit circulus, ut ex his concludatur quod carmen sit figura, omni intellectui patet quod circulus non dicitur ex eodem sensu de carmine ex quo dicitur de figura, sed manifestissima est equivocatio," *Commentarius in posteriorum analyticorum*, ed. Rossi, pp. 178ff. It should also be noted in this context that Grosseteste wrote a treatise on the component parts of figures, *De lineis, angulis et figuris*, ed. Baur, pp. 59–65.

52. Rules are also important to Anonymous IV, who frequently uses this term as well as others, such as *reductio, frange*, which carry the connotation of analysis: "Frange ergo secundum possibilitatem vocis humanae et secundum quod melius competit iuxta similitudinem modi secundi vel primi praedictorum et iuxta puncta materialia," *Der Musiktraktat*, ed. Reckow, 1: 40. ". . . quatuor regulas regulare eiusdem coloris. . . . Sed habebant regulas regulatas ex aliquo metalo duro ut in libris Cartuniensium et alibi multis locis," *Der Musiktraktat*, ed. Reckow, 1: 60. "Et sic si una regula non sufficit, altera sufficit. Et nota, quod quando contingit operari per istam regulam, . . ." *Der Musiktraktat*, ed. Reckow, 1: 70. Cf. Grosseteste: ". . . et artis sit diffinitio seu dispositio, quod sit regula nostrae operationis, merito hae solae artis vocabulo nuncupantur," *De artibus liberalibus*, ed. Baur, p. 4.

53. "Cum inquam ita sit in numeris sonantibus, protendit se musica speculatio ut harmoniam cognoscat, non solum in numeris sonantibus seu corporalibus, sed etiam in progressionibus et occursoribus, recordabilibus, sensibilibus et iudicialibus," *De artibus liberalibus*, ed. Baur, p. 4.

54. "Musicae ministerium in philosophia naturali non minus utile, quam ad medendum, cum omnis aegritudo et inordinatione spirituum et intemperantia curatur, . . ." *De artibus liberalibus*, ed. Baur, p. 4.

55. See Reckow, 1: 1–18.

56. "Boni notatores in figurando sic depingunt supradicta: quidam faciunt quadrata puncta cum uno tractu vel sine, ut praedictum est, quidam non quadrata, sed per modum

quadranguli vel quadrangulorum ita, quod longitudo stando sit longior longitudine iacendo vel protrahendo, sive fuerit cum tractu vel sine. Elmuahim vero oblique saepe protrahitur; et quidam protrahunt ipsum simile elmuahim," *Der Musiktraktat*, ed. Reckow, 1: 41. Both *joints*, which are essential to the character and signifying properties of geometrical shapes, and each line contained within geometrical shapes are carefully discussed by Anonymous IV, a preoccupation which can be compared to Grosseteste's discussion of the triangle in his commentary on Aristotle's *Posterior Analytics*, ed. Rossi, p. 95.

57. Although this is a subject that deserves special treatment, the use of common vocabulary has blinded scholars to significant substantial differences in style and emphasis among writers on music in the thirteenth century. A fund of expressions used in common by thirteenth-century writers on music is not surprising, since they all shared Aristotelian sources. Differences in style, which make writers such as Johannes de Garlandia, whose interest is openly that of relating music to the *artes* of the trivium, and Anonymous IV, whose emphasis is music's place within the quadrivial arts, have not been sufficiently discussed.

58. On the relationship of lines and points to material, Anonymous IV had much to say. He discussed the relationship of sign to material property and the result of intellectual understanding: "Longarum materialium multiplex est <modus> . . . et dicitur recta brevis materialis, quia significat rectam brevem unius temporis," *Der Musiktraktat*, ed. Reckow, 1: 43–44. "Gallici vero Parisius habebant omnes istos modos supradictorum, prout in libris diversis a diversis notatoribus plenius patet, ad cognitionem quorum sic procedimus," *Der Musiktraktat*, ed. Reckow, 1: 51. "Per quas regulas potestis verificare exempla materialis significationis, quae notantur in principio . . . sicut de modis perfectis intelleximus," *Der Musiktraktat*, ed. Reckow, 1: 52.

59. "Et sic procedit iuxta numerum, quousque habueris circularem processum, . . . et sic procede de istis novem, sicut fecisti de sex supradictis suo modo, donec habueris circularem sufficientiam, et tunc reitera," *Der Musiktraktat*, ed. Reckow, 1: 35, see also p. 36.

60. Col. 1: 15–17.

The *De Musica* of Engelbert of Admont: The Transmission of Scholastic Musical Thought

Richard J. Wingell

O ver the course of history, treatises about music have reflected current trends in the history of thought as well as new developments in musical style. Important intellectual movements change the way people think and write about music. In the Carolingian age, for instance, when the rise of cathedral schools created a need for new ways of teaching music, writers such as Hucbald of St. Amand, Aurelianus Reomensis, and Guido of Arezzo filled that need by writing music treatises designed specifically for the schools. In the case of the early university, as new Latin translations of Aristotle's works were imported into Europe, the intellectual movement known as scholasticism led to a radical revision of medieval thought in all disciplines. Music, always central to medieval thought, was an important subject to study in the light of the new scholastic epistemology and methodology.

Several treatises come readily to mind as illustrations of the medieval university's approach to musical thought. The classic example of scholastic writing about music is the mighty achievement of Jacques de Liège, the *Speculum musicae*, which in seven long books reviews the traditional wisdom about music, reconciles the differences and contradictions within the speculative tradition, and discusses current musical developments.[1] Another interesting example is the *Pomerium* of Marchetto da Padua, a straightforward discussion of Italian Trecento notation and compositional practice cloaked in a thick layer of scholastic jargon added by Syphans of Ferrara, a Dominican monk commissioned by Marchetto for that purpose.[2] Syphans did his work so thoroughly that

Marchetto later felt compelled to publish the musical ideas, stripped of the elaborate overlay of scholasticism, in a *Brevis compilatio*.[3]

Another treatise, the *De Musica* of Engelbert of Admont, is often described as a typical music treatise from the age of the universities.[4] Nan Cooke Carpenter, in her study of music in the medieval and Renaissance universities, describes this work as "typical of the medieval university treatise—related to the teaching of music both as a mathematical science and as a practical art for use in the Church."[5] Klaus Niemöller, in the only article that discusses the treatise in any detail, describes it as a combination of abstract theory and the practice of sacred song.[6]

A careful reading of Engelbert's text, however, suggests that this treatise is not a typical example of musical thought from the universities, since it does not successfully combine the scholastic speculative tradition with practical teaching about current musical styles. Neither Engelbert's avowed purpose, as set forth in his prologue, nor the subsequent material on chant exhibits thorough familiarity with the practical problems of performing the chant repertoire. Rather, his purpose is to summarize fundamental scholastic teachings about music for his rural Benedictine community. In this light, the puzzling inconsistencies in the text, the occasional misunderstanding of the authorities he cites, and the problems concerning practical questions do not detract from the importance of this treatise. Its significance rests not on its questionable success in joining the speculative and practical traditions but on its transmission of scholastic teaching about the art and science of music.

Before turning to the text, we should briefly review Engelbert's career.[7] He was born in Volkersdorf in Styria around 1250 and entered the Benedictine abbey at Admont around 1267. After studies at the cathedral school of St. Vitus in Prague, he enrolled in the University of Padua in 1278. He spent nine years there, five years in the arts curriculum and four years studying theology in the Dominican college attached to the university. In 1288 he was elected abbot of the Abbey of Saint Peter in Salzburg, and in 1298 he was elected abbot of his home monastery in Admont; he was apparently a compromise candidate, acceptable to both Archduke Albert of Austria and the archbishop of Salzburg. After thirty years as abbot at Admont, he retired because of illness and died in 1331.

The University of Padua was established in 1222 as a branch of the University of Bologna and was a center for the study of mathematics and medicine, as well as the liberal arts.[8] Among the notable musical alumni of Padua were Marchetto of Padua, Johannes Gallicus, and Prosdocimus de Beldemandis, a prolific writer on both the science and current practice of music.

During his thirty years as abbot at Admont, Engelbert wrote twenty-seven theological treatises on typical scholastic topics.[9] Among the titles are *De libero arbitrio, De providentia Dei, De gratiis et virtutibus Beatae Mariae Virginis,* and *De causis longaevitatis hominum ante diluvium.* In addition, he wrote several commentaries on Aristotle and miscellaneous works on politics, ethics, history, and natural science. He also turned his attention to music, for reasons he explains in the first section of his prologue to the *De musica.*

> Propter amicorum et familiarium dilectionem et complacentiam, quibus totum volo et debeo quod possum, cogor ad iuventutis studia, quae dudum postposui, nunc redire, et eis affectantibus Introductionem, aliquam brevem et levem quasi summam quandam in artem musicam tradere, quae a Boetio primo translatore correctore et ampliatore ipsius musicae de graeco in latinum, et a multis aliis post Boetium multipliciter est declarata, et iteratis ac variatis modis tradendi et docendi renovata. Hunc ipsum laborem meum reputans neque superfluum neque vanum, cum multi nostro tempore docentes musicam et discentes, solo illa quae ad usum cantandi per notas et litteras vel claves musicas pertinent, amplectantur, quo usu adepto reputant se perfectos in arte, nihil ultra de his, quae ad musicae artificialem inquisitionem et discretionem et iudicium pertinent, curantes: cum tamen vera scientia in unaquaque facultate sit scire ipsius artis principia et radices, a quibus ipsa ars surgit, et ex quibus in ipsa, et secundum ipsam artem est infallibilis processus secundum viam et ordinem rationis ad cavendum errorum, et sciendum in singulis veritatem.[10]

Clearly, Engelbert wrote his treatise not to explain practical matters about music but to provide for his friends and his monastic family a brief *summa* of the art of music as taught by Boethius and his successors in the speculative tradition. Too many contemporary writers about music, according to Engelbert, concentrate only on those matters that pertain to *usum cantandi*, the practice of singing, rather than taking the next step and devoting themselves to scientific inquiry into the principles and roots of the art, which would lead to true knowledge. In other words, his motivation for writing was not to produce another practical manual about singing chant but to summarize scholastic teaching on music.

The same motive can be deduced from the definition of music, taken from Boethius, with which Engelbert begins his treatise: "Musica generaliter sumendo est scientia inquirendi et discernendi secundum proportiones harmonicas, concordantiam et consonantiam in contrariis et dissimilibus rebus sibi coniunctis et collatis."[11] This definition, like his opening declaration of purpose, comes down squarely on the side of speculation, as opposed to the practical definitions of music—"the art by which God is praised"—found in Carolingian treatises. Next he cites the triple division of music according to Boethius into *musica mundana, musica humana,* and *musica instrumentalis,* citing as further authorities Plato, Macrobius, Aristotle, and the commentary on Martianus Capella by Remi of Auxerre. At the end of this section, he states his purpose again in somewhat modified form and introduces the other authorities he will cite.

> Omissa igitur Musica mundana et humana, de sola organica musica intendimus aliqua dicere breviter, et in summa; non perfectionem artis, quae longa utique est et profunda et lata, quantum ad eliciendas conclusiones musicae ex suis principiis, et quantum ad conclusiones singulas in principia prima et propria reducendas, sicut in musica Boetius laboravit: sed introductionem ad artis notitiam, ex praesenti nostro labore et opere promittentes. Secundum quem modum et ordinem, post Boetium auctorem Guido Cantuariensis, et Odo Cluniacensis monachi, et Aribo scholasticus Aurelianensis libellos et tractatus de Musica conscripserunt.[12]

This statement of his goal is somewhat more limited that the previous one. He will confine his remarks to *musica organica,* a synonym for *musica instrumentalis,* and he promises not the perfection of the art but only an introduction to knowledge of the art of music.

The list of modern authorities at the end of this passage raises interesting questions. He garbles two of the three names; "Guido Cantuariensis" should clearly be "Guido Aretinus," and "Aribo scholasticus Aurelianensis" appears to be a composite of two different theorists, Aribo Scholasticus and Aurelian Reomensis. More important, all three were Carolingian theorists who produced practical texts for cathedral schools, and all flourished around the year 1000. The library at Admont contained manuscript copies of these treatises; the twelfth-century manuscript copy of Guido's *Micrologus* formerly in the possession of the monastic library of Admont, cataloged as Admont 494, is now housed in this country, in the Sibley Library of the Eastman School of Music.[13] The question is not how Engelbert knew these authors but why he cites only those treatises and not works from the nearly three centuries between the Carolingian writers and his own day. The long gap between his "modern" authorities and Engelbert's own period might even suggest that the *De musica* is an earlier work wrongly attributed to Engelbert, except that the language, thought patterns, and methodology of the treatise are so thoroughly scholastic. The answer to the question of authorities lies in Engelbert's limited purpose. The only music of interest to him is chant; he ignores polyphony altogether, except for two offhand references to the practice of discant in discussions of the upper reaches of the scale. One wonders why polyphony is not of interest to him; although he need not treat every topic that the modern reader might find interesting, the frequently discussed question of consonant and dissonant harmonic intervals might have appealed to his mathematical and systematic mind. Nor has he any interest in contemporary writings on instrumental music; whenever he mentions instruments, his list is an old one borrowed from Boethius—"lyre, pipe, psaltery, and cithara."[14]

Even granting his narrow focus on chant, Engelbert's choice of authorities raises interesting questions. It is understandable that he would cite Remi of Auxerre when discussing Latin translations of the traditional Greek string names for the various notes of the scale; Remi's commentary on Book Nine of the *De nuptiis Mercurii et Philologiae* of Martianus Capella is the sort of traditional line-by-line commentary that one imagines would have appealed to Engelbert.[15] Hucbald of St. Amans is another writer whose ideas Engelbert would have found compatible because of Hucbald's reliance on Boethius and Martianus Capella, his use of the Greek string names for the notes of the scale, and his explanation of the same pre-Guidonian scale that Engelbert favors as the basis for singing chant.[16] Any number of treatises from the twelfth and thirteenth centuries would have provided him with discussions of recent developments in the theory of chant.

Guido is a likely authority in one respect, because of the incredibly wide circulation his treatise enjoyed; copies of this text found their way to all corners of Europe.[17] However, Guido had little use for the speculative tradition so dear to Engelbert. In his famous preface, Guido promised to omit everything from previous writings that does not pertain directly to singing chant.[18] His purpose was to train young men in the cathedral schools so that they could learn the chant repertory as quickly and accurately as possible. Guido is also the source of the twenty-one-note scale organized in hexachords that eventually supplanted Engelbert's favorite scale, the two-octave scale organized in tetrachords.

The use Engelbert makes of Boethius and Guido is our central question. Engelbert is most comfortable dealing with mathematical patterns in questions regarding proportions, intervals, *mutatio* in the hexachord system, species of fourths, fifths, and octaves, and the theory of authentic and plagal modes. When discussing these matters, he delights in working systematically through all the permutations of a single idea, like the different octave species connected with the eight church modes. He has a scientist's love of elegant, symmetrical patterns, and his prose is clearest in these sections.

His treatise is not so successful, however, when matters are not so tidy and symmetrical, and he has difficulty reconciling the conflicts and contradictions within traditional musical thought. Significantly, whenever symmetrical theory conflicts with practice, he sides with theory, ignoring the resulting practical problems. His consistent preference for traditional theory over practical matters is clear in his discussion of two important topics, viz., scales and modes.

Engelbert's treatment of the scale illustrates the problem he has with practical matters. He is aware of the two traditional scales—the greater perfect system of Guido, with twenty-one notes organized into three classes of overlapping hexachords, and the earlier system, consisting of fifteen or sixteen notes organized into four tetrachords. He belabors this question endlessly, both in Book I, which is concerned with the basic information one should know about music, and in Book III, where he discusses the scale as one of the practical questions crucial to singing chant.[19] He prefers the earlier system; it is, after all, sufficient as a scale for chant, since it covers two octaves and provides all the notes one needs, at least for chants that stay within the theoretical limits of the eight modes. Figure 1 is Engelbert's version of the two-octave scale, found at the end of Chapter 14 of Book III.[20]

A B C D E F G a   c d e f g

Figure 1. Engelbert's two-octave scale.

This scale certainly exhibits the elegant symmetry dear to the scientific mind. Note that Engelbert leaves out the initial gamma, the added low note called *proslambanamenos* by the Greeks and included by many theorists. He acknowledges in his text that Odo of Cluny included the gamma; elsewhere, in his version of Remi's explanation of the Greek string names, Engelbert does include the gamma or *proslambanamenos*.[21] In his diagram of the tetrachord scale, however, following Aribo, he leaves out the gamma, presumably in the interest of symmetry. His version of the scale is certainly simple, elegant, and symmetrical. All the tetrachords are identical, proceeding by tone, semitone, and tone. Two pairs of conjunct tetrachords suffice, the second pair an exact duplicate of the first; this scale contains all the notes we need for singing chant. Engelbert goes on at some length about the sufficiency of this scale and its *convenientia* for the repertory of chant; he insists that the two-octave scale provides all the room and freedom that a composer could want.[22]

There is, however, a problem with this scale as the theoretical foundation for the repertory of chant. In the second octave, there is only one *B, B quadratum*; we also need a *B rotundum*, B flat, since this note is common in the chant repertory, particularly in the first, fifth, and sixth modes. Engelbert certainly knew of the importance of this note and its place in Guido's hexachord scale. In his discussion of the eight modes he acknowledges its importance in certain modes, but here he omits it from his basic scale. The Carolingian theorists who used a similar scale managed to include B flat by setting up a fifth overlapping tetrachord, as shown in Figure 2, based on Hucbald's treatise.[23]

A B C D E F G a b c d e f g aa

Figure 2. Hucbald's two-octave scale.

Note the differences between this scale and Engelbert's. Low A is the added note or *proslambanamenos*, and the tetrachords start on B. These are all similar tetrachords, proceeding by semitone, tone, and tone. Engelbert knows of the importance of B flat to chant but does not account for it in his basic scale. Later, in Chapter 17 of Book III, he designs another scale that includes B flat, but that chapter is a discussion of the various species of fifths within the scale, not the scale itself.[24] Engelbert chooses the simplest and most symmetrical scale, not because he is unaware of the practical problems inherent in it but because practical issues are of less concern to him than fundamental mathematical and theoretical questions.

When he discusses Guido's scale of twenty-one notes grouped into hexachords, Engelbert is accurate and thorough.[25] He is particularly fascinated with the possibilities of *mutatio* on those notes which have two or three hexachord syllables. Even here, however, he makes a small change from Guido's system, leaving out the top note of Guido's scales, *e e la*, needed to complete the third *durum* hexachord starting on the highest *G*. *DD la sol* is an odd place to stop, and an asymmetrical one as well.

All through the section on scales, Engelbert seems most concerned with mathematical issues and the inconsistencies in the traditional teaching about music. His discussion centers on the different numbers of notes in various scales, the number of hexachord syllables versus the number of letters for notes, and other questions of that sort. Once again, we see that his focus is *ars, non usus*; he is more concerned with basic issues of number and symmetry than with practical issues.

We see the same bias in Book IV on modes. As we would expect, Engelbert is clearest on modal theory as it relates to the scale, octave species, and relationships between authentic and plagal modes. He searches for logical arguments to support the number of modes, concluding that the existence of eight modes is *sufficiens, congrua,* and *necessaria*.[26] He includes diagrams of each pair of authentic and plagal

modes, pointing out in both text and diagram form the common characteristics of each pair of modes and their distinctive species of fourths,
fifths, and octaves.[27] He explains the relationship between the various
ways of naming the modes, correlating the older system of four modes,
the new ordering of eight modes, and the Greek names. He does not
mention the question of standard phrases for each mode, a practical
question discussed by many theorists, including Guido, who uses *modus
vel tropus* as a compound term for mode, *modus* to mean scale pattern,
and *tropus* to mean the standard phrases peculiar to each mode.[28] The
long tradition of compiling *tonaria* testifies to the importance of this
notion of mode to most medieval writers; Engelbert is silent on this
subject.

In Chapter 3 of Book IV, Engelbert discusses the idea of the ethos
of the modes in great detail and attempts to establish a scientific explanation for the various psychological states traditionally ascribed to the
modes, based on their different species of octave.[29] In this discussion, he
cites his full range of authorities, including Aristotle, Boethius, and
Guido. Once again he opts for faithfulness to his authorities and theoretical concepts, while ignoring practical issues raised by the theory. Here
is one section of his discussion of the ethos of the modes, taken directly
from Boethius.

> . . . Unde multa et mira refert Boetius in prologo musicae de natura harmoniae
> musicalis, qualiter diversitates tonorum musicarum diversas passiones et
> affectiones gaudii et tristitiae et audaciae et desperationis causaverint in
> quibusdam. Et sacra scriptura narrat de David, quod virtute divinorum
> hymnorum et musicae harmoniae immundum spiritum fugaverit a Saule: et per
> ipsam harmoniam ad quosdam prophetas revocatus sit spiritus prophetiae etc.
> Unde Boetius narrat in prologo musicae, quod phrygius tonus, id est, tertius
> in musico instrumento cantatas audiente quodam iuvene proco cuiusdam
> puellae excitavit et provocavit eum in audaciam, ut statim cubiculum puellae
> vim facturus vellet irrumpere: cumque mutatus esset phrygius tonus in
> hypophrygium, id est, tertius in quartum tonum, iuvenis mitigatus lenitate toni
> quievit.[30]

Engelbert cites the two traditional examples of ethos, David's power
to banish an evil spirit from Saul by playing the right music, and the
young man on the brink of sin called back to his senses at the last

moment when the cithara player changed the mode. Note that in the latter story Engelbert specifies the modes in question; the young lady was in danger when the Phrygian mode was sounding, and was saved by the change to the Hypophrygian mode. Compare Engelbert's version to Guido's, as found in Chapter 14 of the *Micrologus*:

Sic enim per fenestras corporis habilium rerum suavitas intrat mirabiliter penetralia cordis. Inde est quod sicut quibusdam saporibus et odoribus vel etiam colorum intuitu salus tam cordis quam corporis vel minuiter vel augescit. Ita quondam legitur phreneticus canente Asclepiade medico ab insania revocatus. Et item alius quidam sonitu citharae in tantam libidinem incitatus, ut cubiculum puellae quaereret effringere dementatus, moxque citharoedo mutante modum voluptatis poenitentia ductum recessisse confusum. Item et David Saul daemonium cithara mitigabat et daemoniacam feritatem huius artis potenti vi ac suavitate frangebat.[31]

Note the differences between the two accounts. Guido put the question of modal ethos in the context of other sense experiences and their ability to affect our health and well-being. More important, Guido did not cite specific modes in the famous story of the youth aroused and then calmed by certain modes. Engelbert repeats Boethius's version just as it is, including the specific modes, and goes on to explain that the Greek modes in the story are the same as the third and fourth chant modes. If Engelbert were concerned with reconciling the tradition of musical lore with current practice, the implications of this story would pose a severe problem for him. Surely all chants of the Phrygian mode, the third church mode, cannot be presumed to have this same effect on the hearer. Engelbert seems unaware that "Phrygian" means something different to the singer of chant than it does to Boethius. We would expect Engelbert to attempt to reconcile this traditional story with chant practice, or at the very least address the obvious question. Engelbert has missed an important point here, and he is much more ready than was Guido to adopt Greek ideas without recognizing the logical problems that result. A further problem arises later in the same chapter, where Engelbert repeats the comments of Boethius about the affective significance of the various *genera* of tetrachord—melodic, enharmonic, and chromatic. The three Greek *genera* have nothing whatsoever to do with the Western scale or the eight chant modes and have no relevance for the singer of chant.

Guido and Engelbert, both relying on Boethius, approach this issue quite differently. Guido based his explanation of the ethos of the modes on the characteristic phrases peculiar to each mode. Note the title of Chapter 14, "Item de tropis et vi musicae"; in his terminology, *tropus* means *mode* in the sense of characteristic phrases. Aware of the problems inherent in this concept and reluctant to provide too many specific details, Guido was deliberately vague. At the end of the chapter he pointed out in a wonderful passage paraphrasing Paul's first letter to the Corinthians that the wondrous power of music to stir the soul is a mystery known fully only to Divine Wisdom; we see these things only darkly: "Quae tamen vis solum divinae sapientiae ad plenum patet, nos vero quae in aenigmate ab inde percepimus."[32] Engelbert, in contrast, attempts to connect the affective connotation of each mode with its mathematical characteristics, particularly the different species of fourth, fifth, and octave. He states his theory more clearly later in the chapter.

> Unde etiam dicit Guido, quod tonus tertius habet saltus fractos, et sic eius cantus est impetuosus. Sextus vero habet saltus lenes, et ita est voluptuosus. Septimus vero est garrulus propter multas et breves reflexiones, quas habet ille cantus. Octavus suavior propter morosos et pauciores reflexus. Et secundum hoc toni ascendentes vel descendentes in istis vel in illis speciebus diatessaron et diapente per consequens sunt asperiores vel leniores et laetiores, vel tristiores auditui, secundum qualitatem suarum proportionum ad diversas complexiones corporum et affectiones animorum audientium.[33]

We admire Engelbert's attempt to develop a scientific explanation for the power of music to move us, an attempt made time and again in the course of the history of music, with varying degrees of success. We should note also that the doctrine of the ethos of the modes caused intellectual problems for Engelbert and other scholastic writers on music that it did not pose for Guido, with his practical bent. Modal ethos, a constant theme in the theoretical tradition, could not be ignored by scholastic writers, but its roots in myth and legend posed problems for them, since they sought to base their teaching on the mathematical and scientific foundations of music. Engelbert's solution is to repeat the teaching of Boethius uncritically, ignoring the question of the difference between the Greek modal system and the eight chant modes, and then seeking for a scientific explanation. He seems not to be bothered by the fact that Guido, his other authority, approached the question in a different way. This passage juxtaposes conflicting traditions rather than reconciling them, and does not address the obvious logical and practical questions raised by the simultaneous consideration of disparate traditions. Again, the practical issues do not concern him; his aim is to pass on the basic scientific teaching from his university background.

Engelbert is at his best when dealing with the mathematical side of music—proportions, species of fourths, fifths, and octaves, the hexachord system and mutation, the relationship between pairs of authentic and plagal modes. In all those areas, his treatment is systematic, orderly, and logical. He also is concerned with the practical side of chant, and later in Book IV he discusses at length how a good chant melody should proceed, including correct starting notes, ways to proceed in the middle of phrases, and fitting cadences.[34] As we have seen, however, he is not so successful when the speculative tradition contradicts chant practice, or when the traditional wisdom raises troublesome practical implications for the singer of chant. He seems not to notice some of the internal contradictions and problems and raises more questions than he answers.

In order to assess fairly the value of this treatise, we need to see it in its context. Engelbert wrote his treatise for the Benedictine monks at Admont, a rural town of the Steiermark, on the Enns river east of Salzburg. They did not have the same educational opportunities that Engelbert had enjoyed; he wanted to share his university learning and his Dominican training with his Benedictine family. He did not write for other university scholars; significantly, the only surviving copy of his treatise has never left the monastic library of Admont. As he says, all he wanted to do was write a *summa* of the basic principles of music, to balance what he viewed as an erroneous tendency to emphasize practice to the detriment of *ars* and *ratio*. He succeeded in his declared aim. Let us quote the couplet that ends his treatise: "Explicit iste labor, cuius sub pondere labor; / Ars ne labatur, qua iam plus usus amatur."[35]

If we judge this treatise by the criterion identified by Carpenter as the primary quality of scholastic works on music, however, viz., the reconciliation of *speculatio* with musical practice, then Engelbert's *De musica* is not typical of musical thought in the age of the universities. His treatise certainly illustrates the special way a university scholar looks at music, but to appreciate the full contribution of the medieval university to musical thought, we still need to look to the *Speculum musicae* of Jacques de Liège, or the works of Prosdocimus de Beldemandis.

Notes

This article is a revised version of a paper presented at a symposium entitled "The Intellectual Climate of the Early University," held at California State University, Northridge, October 20–21, 1988.

1. Jacobi Leodensis, *Speculum musicae*, ed. Roger Bragard, vol. 3 (1955) of Corpus Scriptorum de Musica (hereafter CSM), 7 vols. (Rome: American Institute of Musicology, 1955–69).

2. *Marchetto de Padua, Pomerium*, ed. Giuseppe Vecchi, CSM 6 (1961).

3. Giuseppe Vecchi, *Su la composizione del* Pomerium *di Marchetto da Padova e la* Brevis compilatio (Bologna: n.p., 1957), pp. 153–205.

4. Martin Gerbert, *Scriptores ecclesiastici de musica sacra potissimum*, 3 vols. (St. Blasien: Typis San-Blasianus, 1784; repr. Hildesheim, 1963), 2: 287–369; hereafter cited as G*S*.

5. Nan Cooke Carpenter, *Music in the Medieval and Renaissance Universities* (Norman, Okla.: University of Oklahoma Press, 1958; repr. Da Capo, 1972), p. 73.

6. Klaus Wolfgang Niemöller, "Die Anwendung musiktheoretischer Demonstrationsmodelle auf die Praxis bei Engelbert von Admont," in *Methoden in Wissenschaft und Kunst des Mittelalters*, ed. Albert Zimmermann (Berlin: De Gruyter, 1970), pp. 206–30.

7. General information on Engelbert is found in several standard reference works: Andrew Hughes, "Engelbert of Admont," in *The New Grove Dictionary of Music and Musicians*, 20 vols. (London: Macmillan, 1980), 6: 169; Heinrich Húschen, "Engelbert von Admont," in *Die Musik in Geschichte und Gegenwart: Allgemeine Enzyklopadie der Musik*, 14 vols.

(Kassel and Basel: Barenreiter, 1949; repr. 1986), 3: 1354–55; and B J. Comaskey, "Engelbert of Admont," in *The New Catholic Encyclopedia*, 18 vols. (New York: McGraw-Hill, 1967), 5: 550.

8. For a discussion of courses of study at Padua see Carpenter, *Music in the Medieval and Renaissance Universities*, pp. 37–46.

9. For information about Engelbert's theological writings, as well as the location of published examples, see Comaskey, "Engelbert of Admont."

10. *GS* II, 287 (all translations are the author's): "For the love and pleasure of my friends and (monastic) family, for whom I wish to and should do all that I can, I am now compelled to return to the studies of my youth, which I have put off for a long time, and to present for their edification an introduction, a short and easy sort of *summa* of the art of music, which was explained by Boethius, the first translator, corrector, and amplifier of the science of music from Greek into Latin, and which was also explained in diverse ways by many others after Boethius and constantly renewed by repeated and varied modes of tradition and teaching. I regard this labor of mine as neither superfluous nor pointless, since many teachers and students of music in our time take to heart only those things that pertain to the practice of singing—notes, letters, and *claves*. Once they have attained practical skill, they consider themselves perfect in this art, caring nothing further for those things that pertain to scientific inquiry, distinctions, and judgement, even though true knowledge in any discipline consists of knowing the principles and roots of that art, from which the art itself flows, and on which depend true advancement according to the way and order of reason, both to avoid error and to know the truth in every particular."

11. *GS* II, 288: "Music understood in the general sense is the science of inquiring into and making distinctions according to harmonic proportions, concordance, and consonance between contrary and dissimilar realities joined together and compared."

12. *GS* II, 289: "Leaving out *musica mundana* and *musica humana*, we propose to discuss briefly and in summary a few matters concerning *musica organica*. We promise through our present labor and work not the perfection of this art, which is long, deep, and wide, taking into account the drawing of conclusions from the principles of music, and reducing all conclusions to their first and proper principles, as Boethius attempted in his *De musica*; instead, we promise an introduction to the knowledge of this art. Following his way and outline, after Boethius, our first authority, Guido of Canterbury (?), Odo the monk of Cluny, and Aribo Scholasticus Aurelianensis (?) wrote short books and treatises about music."

13. See the list of manuscripts in Guidonis Aretini, *Micrologus*, ed. Joseph Smits van

Waesberghe, CSM 4 (1955), p. 4.

14. For example, the list at the end of Chapter 3 (*GS* 2: 289).

15. Remigii Antissiodorensis, *Commentum in Martianum Capellam*, ed. Cora Lutz, 2 vols. (Leiden: Brill, 1965).

16. Hucbald of St. Amand, *De harmonica institutione*, GS 1: 104–21; also "Hucbald, Guido, and John on Music," trans. Warren Babb, ed. Claude Palisca, *Music Theory Translation Series* (1978).

17. CSM 4, pp. 4–71.

18. CSM 4, pp. 85–87; or Babb translation, "Hucbald, Guido, and John," p. 58.

19. Coussemaker, Edmond de, ed., *Scriptorum de musica medii aevi,* nova series, 4 vols (Paris 1864–76, repr. Hildesheim Georg Olms, 1963) 2: 293–98, 328–34; hereafter cited as C*S*.

20. C*S* 2: 330, 332.

21. C*S* 2: 293, 321.

22. C*S* 2: 327–28.

23. See Babb translation, "Hucbald, Guido, and John," p. 33.

24. C*S* 2: 332–33.

25. C*S* 2: 322–24.

26. C*S* 2: 338–39.

27. C*S* 2: 343–54.

28. CSM 4, pp. 133, 157, 158.

29. C*S* 2: 339–40.

30. G*S* 2: 339–40: "Boethius, in the prologue to his *De musica*, reports many wondrous things about the nature of musical harmony, how the various musical modes excite

various passions and affections of joy, sadness, bravery, and desperation in certain individuals. Sacred Scripture tells us that David, by the power of divine hymns and harmonious music, drove an unclean spirit out of Saul, and that by this same harmony the spirit of prophecy was summoned back to certain prophets, etc. Boethius tells in the prologue of his *De musica* that the Phrygian mode—that is, the third mode—played on an instrument in the hearing of a certain girl's young suitor, so aroused him and provoked him to boldness that he tried to break into the girl's bedroom by force. When, however, the Phrygian mode was changed to the Hypophrygian—that is, from the third to the fourth mode—the youth calmed down, soothed by the gentleness of the mode."

31. CSM 4, pp. 159–61: "Thus through the windows of the body the sweetness of suitable things enters wondrously into the inmost recesses of the heart. Thus it is that the well-being of both soul and body is either diminished or increased by certain tastes or odors or even by the sight of certain colors. Thus we read that once a madman was called back from his insanity by the singing of Asclepiades the physician. And thus a certain young man was driven to such lust by the sound of the cithara that, in a fit of madness, he tried to break into a maiden's bedchamber, but, as soon as the cithara player changed the mode, repenting his lust, he retreated in confusion. Thus David also calmed Saul's demon with his harp and conquered its demonic fury by the powerful force and sweetness of this art."

32. CSM 4, p. 161: "This power is known clearly only to the divine wisdom, but we perceive these things darkly, from afar."

33. GS II, 340: "Thus Guido says that the third tone has broken leaps, and thus its melody is impetuous. The sixth mode has gentle leaps, and thus is pleasureable. The seventh is garrulous because of the many short turning phrases that characterize its melody. The eighth mode is sweeter because of its fewer and longer turning motives. Accordingly, the modes, ascending or descending through this or that species of fourth and fifth, for that reason are harsher or smoother and happier, or sadder to the ear, according to the way the quality of their proportions relates to the various bodily states and spiritual affections of the hearers."

34. GS 2: 354–69.

35. GS 2: 369: "Now is completed the task under whose weight I have labored / So that art, which nowadays is loved less than practice, should not disappear."

The Understanding
of Aristotle's Natural Philosophy
by the Early Scholastics

Richard C. Dales

*I*n noting Albert the Great's embarrassment over Peter Lombard's claim (*Sent.* 2, d. 1) that Aristotle had said that there were two principles, namely matter and species, and a third called *operatorium*—since, as Albert pointed out, Aristotle's three principles of nature are matter, form, and privation, and the *operatorium* is not to be found in the books that have come down to us[1]—Fr. James Weisheipl remarked: "It is difficult to know what the early scholastic theologians thought of Aristotle."[2] While it is true that even today there are disputes over Aristotle's doctrine on a number of points, the understanding of the Stagyrite's natural philosophy during the twelfth and thirteenth centuries often seems to us to be flawed beyond the normal limits of likely divergent interpretations of his words. The present essay is an introductory attempt to understand some of the reasons for this. We shall not investigate here differences of interpretation that could legitimately arise from ambiguities or inconsistencies in Aristotle's text. Nor shall we investigate meticulously each point on which the scholastics differed from the received modern understanding. Instead we hope to outline some of those factors which might account for the differences between us and them.

Much work has been done during the past three generations on the recovery of the Aristotelian corpus by the Latins, although much remains to be done before we can have any adequate understanding of that process. But several things seem reasonably clear. First, there was a considerable lapse of time between the translations and their systematic

141

employment by Latin authors. And second, during the twelfth century Aristotle was cited much more frequently by way of Arabic intermediaries[3] or Latin authors such as Cicero, Pliny, and Boethius than from the actual texts of his works. Thus William of Conches, deriving his knowledge of Aristotle from Boethius's *De consolatione*, claimed that when Aristotle said that the world did not "ever" begin, he only meant that it began with time (Augustine's position), so that there was no time when the world was not.[4] This interpretation, as we shall notice below, is found in the works of Latin authors through the third quarter of the thirteenth century.

Men who did make direct use of Aristotle from the Latin translations often were ignorant of the philosophical context of his remarks and so would graft a quotation or paraphrase of Aristotle onto their own works, giving it a bizarre twist in the process. Hence an anonymous author of a work on the elements (ca. 1160) quotes *Physica* 2, 1 (192b) on the definition of *physis* and then proceeds to give an atomic account of the cosmos;[5] and he later claims that Aristotle's assertion that the earth is immobile (not a quotation) must be understood as meaning that its minimal parts remain still by their own nature, but no one denies but that the earth may well revolve on its own axis.[6] Clearly, the way in which these men understood Aristotle was conditioned by their expectations. Examples could be multiplied many times over, but these suffice for our purposes.

In addition to the expectations engendered by the standard Latin sources, especially the *Timaeus* with Calcidius's commentary and Boethius's *De consolatione*, the works of Islamic authors added another dimension to the problem. The Aristotelian corpus was available in Arabic long before it was in Latin, and accompanying it were often the commentaries of antiquity, some of which were also translated into Latin at about the same time as the works of Aristotle. From the third through the sixth centuries, Aristotle's writings had been incorporated into the Neoplatonic curriculum, where they were known as the Lesser Mysteries and were studied as a preparation for the Greater Mysteries of Plato. A majority of Platonic commentators believed that Plato and Aristotle were in agreement on most, if not quite all, points, and that it was the responsibility of the commentator to point out the agreement.[7] The resulting skewing of Aristotle's thought became the traditional interpretation, and thus he was understood by most Muslim authors. Consequently, when Aristotle's thought was encountered by the Latins in the works of Arabic authors, it had often already been given a meaning that an objective reading of his bare text would not support, including quite a different meaning of "form," a concept of "active material potency," a separable active intellect, the Intelligences, and a kind of creationism. And when the Aristotelian texts themselves were recovered, they were read in the light of these earlier commentaries, both Greek and Arabic.[8]

Indeed, there seems to have been a notable reluctance to cut loose from the commentatorial tradition even long after Aristotle's natural philosophy was easily available in Latin versions. In his *De anima*, written about 1200, John Blund still leaned heavily on Avicenna, Algazel, and ps.-Alexander of Aphrodisias,[9] even though he had Aristotle's text in front of him. And Alexander Nequam, who like Blund lectured at Paris and Oxford during the late twelfth and early thirteenth centuries, made only the most timid use of the *libri naturales* even in his last work, *Speculum speculationum* (where he also relied on his younger contemporary Blund when using the *libri naturales*), although he displayed an impressive mastery of the "new logic."[10] Both men, and indeed most of their contemporaries,[11] were, in the words of Richard Hunt, "grafting this new learning onto older stock,"[12] thus changing the context and import of the new learning in the process.

As the entire Aristotelian corpus was translated and subjected to more exacting scrutiny in university lectures and disputations, some of the grosser distortions of his meaning disappeared. But the doctrines that were imputed to him still often differed greatly from what seems to us to be the plain meaning of his words.

The most frequently given explanation for this is the faulty Latin translations of Aristotle's writings. This was remarked by Robert Grosseteste in his *Hexaëmeron* in his attempt to understand the Philosopher's teaching on the eternity of the world,[13] and it was repeated by a number of subsequent scholastic authors. I believe, however, that this has been greatly exaggerated, and I do not know of any major misunderstanding of Aristotle's teaching that can be attributed to this cause directly. Indirectly, though, it was put to a perverse use by one of the most perverse of medieval authors, Roger Bacon. He considered that the (unspecified) flaws in the Latin versions of Aristotle gave him license to attribute to Aristotle any doctrine which he felt that the Philosopher must have taught. In his *De viciis contractis in studio theologie* he says that:

> [the philosophers] make clear the creation of the world and its production from nothing . . . , as is clear from Aristotle, since he posits a creator and created things, as has been said, and since he says that there could not be infinite past motion, since the infinite cannot be traversed; but all past motion has been traversed and all past time is finite. And if there were not a first motion, there would not be any subsequent motion, as is clear from the end of *De generatione* and book 3 of the *Physica* and the beginning of the *Metaphysica*; although the world is eternal if one understands "created eternity" for "eternity," as in the second proposition of *De causis*. . . . And understanding "eternity" as the whole extension of time from the beginning of the motion of the sky, which could be made perpetual [i.e., unending] by the divine will, one can posit that the world is eternal because there was not a time in which there was not motion, as he himself argues in book 8 of the *Physica*.[14]

Bacon's justification for this idiosyncratic reading of Aristotle is "because the obscurity of the text of Aristotle and the difficulty of his opinions and the bad translations conceal from many his true teaching on this point,"[15] although he does not specify what flaws in the translations he had in mind or offer any superior reading himself.

One aspect of the above quotation points up another major reason for the differences between the scholastics' understanding of Aristotle and ours. That is the admission into the Aristotelian corpus of the Middle Ages of works not now considered to be authentic.[16] The most important of these are *De mundo*, *De causis*, *De causis proprietatum elementorum* (and another work known simply as *De elementis*), *De plantis*, and to a lesser extent the *Theology of Aristotle*. Of these, the Neoplatonic *De causis* especially distorted the basic standpoint of Aristotle on many matters and contributed to a widespread misunderstanding of his teaching. Thus Aristotle was widely believed to have taught that God was the First Cause of the being of the universe and not just of its motion; that he was a creator at least in the Avicennan sense; and, occasionally, as with Bacon, that he created *de novo* and *ex nihilo*.

A further cause of misunderstanding was the custom, which was intensified by the exigencies of the disputed question, of the oral rather than written transmission of texts, especially of *sententiae* wrenched from their context. This worked to the common detriment of the accurate comprehension of all scholastic *auctoritates*, not just Aristotle. One of the most egregious examples of this is the statement, "Hoc est eternum eterno, quod eviternum eviterno, et tempus temporali," usually attributed to "Aristotle," *De causis*, but sometimes to Augustine, and sometimes given without attribution. I have never found the source of this quotation, but I know that it is not in Augustine or the *Liber de causis*. Still, it was a commonplace in scholastic literature. I have come across it in the works of Philip the Chancellor, John of La Rochelle, an anonymous author of a question on eternity in Douai MS 434, Eustace of Arras, and Alexander of Hales, to which Nicolas Wicki has added Albert the Great, *Comm. in Sent.* 2, d. 9.[17] Interestingly, one anonymous thirteenth-century Parisian theologian took the trouble to check the text of *De causis* and remarked correctly that the alleged text is not there.[18] But all too few of our authors were so conscientious.

Most important, I believe, was a predisposition on the part of the vast majority of early scholastic authors to understand Aristotle in an acceptable way. Much has been made of the series of Parisian condemnations of Aristotle's natural philosophy between 1210 and 1277. But, although there was certainly some feeling of discomfort and even hostility toward the newly acquired works in some quarters, the evidence of the scholastic texts would indicate that we have seriously misunderstood and probably overestimated the degree and nature of the opposition to Aristotle's natural philosophy. Those authors who considered Aristotle dangerous and heretical on certain points, such as Robert Grosseteste and William of Auvergne, were in a small minority and were not much heeded; and both made extensive use of Aristotle themselves.[19] There is very little evidence in the *Sentences* commentaries or the *quaestio* literature that shows any hostility toward Aristotle or fear that his teaching represented a danger to the faith. Most commentators, in fact, appreciated the excellence of his works, and authors of all doctrinal stamps cited him as an authority for their positions.

The Three Parisian theologians, a secular, a Franciscan, and a Dominican, understood Aristotle's natural philosophy in a way which denied that it either did or could conflict with Christian doctrine. So far as I have been able to determine, the originator of this view of Aristotle's natural philosophy was Philip the Chancellor, who, drawing upon both William of Conches and Moses Maimonides, devised the interpretation of Aristotle which would become the majority view until the 1260s and which was revived again in the early fourteenth century. In his *Summa de bono* Philip wrote:

> Concerning this question, one must understand that the arguments which Aristotle gives are only for the purpose of proving that the world is perpetual and not eternal. I call that thing "perpetual" and not "eternal" which is measured by the totality of time and a mobile. For it is [Aristotle's] own meaning, according to the requirements of natural philosophy, that a mobile and motion and time should be shown to be coeval. Nor can these arguments which are taken from the principles of [natural] philosophy be taken further to prove that if the mobile itself were eternal, motion and time would be eternal. But it is not within the realm of that philosophy to investigate the coming forth of the first mobile into act, and then to separate the mobile from the immobile, as in the planets, but that motion is from the immobile. Nor does he determine that the mover is a first cause. But in his comment on *Metaphysica* 9, Averroes establishes that just as the motion of the lesser circular bodies is from an Intelligence, thus the motion of the first body is from the first Intelligence. But according to a theologian, it seems that one ought not to have said *primum mobile*, but that a certain cloudy substance or confused light was moved over the face of the deep.[20]

These ideas were taken over and expanded by Philip's slightly younger colleague, Alexander of Hales:

> It is true that the view is attributed to Aristotle that the world was able to be perpetual and always to have existed. But it should be known that the phrase: "the world always existed" can be understood as meaning that it never had a beginning, and in this sense it is not true; or it can be understood as meaning

that the world is commensurate with the whole of time, and in this sense it is true that the world has always existed; and this is what Aristotle believed. For thus the adverb "always" refers only to the totality of time. And it must also be known that those philosophers who wished to prove that the world always existed proceeded only from the principles of natural philosophy. Therefore they were only speaking about these matters in terms of natural mutation. And therefore, because creation is not a natural mutation but is rather above nature in its principles, their position does not touch upon creation. Therefore they only conclude that things did not first come forth into being through the mediation of change, which is generation—which is true—but rather through the mediation of creation. And because they do not touch upon creation, since it is not a natural mutation, therefore in this way they posit the world to be eternal, but not in an unqualified sense.[21]

And in the other, apparently earlier, version, the argument is presented this way:

We say that motion is neither eternal nor perpetual in an unqualified sense, nor is time, since they have a beginning and an end. But the world may be said to be eternal in the sense that its motion is commensurate with the total duration of time, which has a beginning but not an end, since its existence is only from the will of the Creator. In this way motion can be said to be eternal and always to have existed. And we say that when [the philosophers] offer proofs of its perpetuity, they are only speaking in the way of nature and through natural principles. Therefore, since creation is not a natural beginning but is above nature, it is clear that such things as the motion of the sky and time, which came into being through creation, did not begin by way of nature. And similarly, since the nature of the sky is completely infinite according to nature, motion will not cease, and if not motion, not time either. Therefore, if they cease, they do so by the will of Him who is above all nature. And for this reason, those philosophers who do not transcend nature . . . spoke truly. . . . But when it is objected that the first motion either was made or is eternal, we say that it was made but not by way of nature nor through a motion of nature, but through creation. In creation there is no eduction from potency into act, as eduction takes place in matter, for then that potency would be a potency of matter such as is in a created nature; or if things were made in potency before being made actual, they were not made in the potency of matter, but only of the agent.

Similarly [concerning] the question about whether matter is ungenerable and incorruptible, we say that it is not generable, but of its nature it always exists. For when it is said that it is not generable since generation is accomplished from pre-existing matter, we reply that it did not come into being through a natural mutation, but through a mutation which is above nature, namely creation, and since matter is made to underlie all natural change. And therefore no one speaking as a natural philosopher can do other than posit a matter common to all change.[22]

And Albert the Great confirmed this interpretation in his *Commentary on the Sentences*, composed in the mid-1240s, when he wrote:

Without doubt nothing is more probable even according to reason than that the world began, as Moses says; and this must be held by faith. But it is impossible that it began by motion and generation or that it might end through a motion toward another form or corruption into another matter. And this is all that Aristotle's arguments prove. Therefore they conclude nothing contrary to faith.[23]

This way of understanding the natural philosophy of Aristotle was convenient and may even be justifiable in a way, but it would surely be a mistake to assume that Aristotle himself was aware of the distinction between nature and supernature made by the scholastics. And it was most often invoked to show that Aristotle had not taught the beginninglessness of the world as a demonstrated truth or in a sense inimical to Christianity, an interpretation of Aristotle that most moderns would find very difficult to take seriously.

Of these reasons, some were the result of historical circumstances, such as the tradition of the Neoplatonic commentators or the customs of scholastic disputation. Some were the result of an inadequate knowledge of Aristotle's doctrine, such as one finds in many of the twelfth-century authors. Some were the result of personal perversity, such as Roger Bacon's refusal to take seriously the evidence of the texts available to him. But more important than any of these, I believe, is that the scholastics cared much more passionately than we do what Aristotle had taught. They eagerly studied his natural philosophy and incorporated what they found there into their own thought, attempting in the process to understand him in a manner consistent with the teachings of the church. If we have a more objective view of his doctrine today, it is because it makes less difference to us what that doctrine was.

Notes

1. Albert the Great, *Comm. in Sent.* 2, d. 1, art. 11, *Opera omnia* XXVII, ed. A. Borgnet (Paris: Apud Lodovicum Vives, 1890), p. 30b.

2. James A. Weisheipl, "The Date and Context of Aquinas' *De aeternitate mundi*," in *Graceful Reason: Essays in Ancient and Medieval Philosophy Presented to Joseph Owens*, ed. Lloyd P. Gerson (Toronto: Pontifical Institute of Mediaeval Studies, 1983), pp. 239–71, on p. 261.

3. See especially Richard J. Lemay, *Abu Maʿshar and Latin Aristotelianism in the Twelfth Century: The Recovery of Aristotle's Natural Philosophy through Arabic Astrology* (Beirut: American University of Beirut, 1962).

4. William of Conches, *Glosae super Platonem* 97, ed. Edouard Jeauneau (Paris: J. Vrin, 1965), p. 180, and *In Consolationem philosophiae commentarius*, in *La doctrine de la création dans l'ecole de Chartres. Etudes et Textes*, ed. Joseph M. Parent (Paris and Ottawa: J. Vrin, 1938), pp. 133–35.

5. Richard C. Dales, "Anonymi *De elementis*: From a Twelfth-Century Collection of Scientific Works in British Museum MS Cotton Galba E. IV," *Isis* 56 (1965), 174–89, on p. 181.

6. Dales, "Anonymi *De elementis*," p. 184, lines 95–98.

7. On the Greek commentators see Richard Sorabji, "General Introduction," in *Philoponus. Against Aristotle, on the Eternity of the World*, trans. Christian Wildberg (Ithaca, N.Y.: Cornell University Press, 1987), pp. 1–17.

8. See Sorabji's comment in "General Introduction," p. 2.

9. *Johannes Blund. Tractatus de anima*, ed. Daniel A. Callus and Richard W. Hunt (London: Oxford University Press for the British Academy, 1970), esp. pp. viii–ix and xvii–xviii.

10. *Alexander Nequam. Speculum speculationum*, ed. Rodney M. Thomson (London: Oxford University Press for the British Academy, 1988), esp. pp. xv–xvii.

11. It is tempting to investigate the role of David of Dinant in this connection, but even though much work has recently been done on David by Brian Lawn, M. Kurdzialek, M.-T. d'Alverny, and Enzo Maccagnolo, his authentic doctrine does not seem to me to be

clearly enough established yet to make this a fruitful enterprise. See especially Maccagnolo's chapter on David in *A History of Twelfth-Century Western Philosophy*, ed. Peter Dronke (Cambridge: Cambridge University Press, 1988), pp. 429–42.

12. *Johannes Blund*, ed. Callus and Hunt, p. xvii.

13. *Robert Grosseteste. Hexaëmeron* I, viii, 4, ed. Richard C. Dales and Servus Gieben, O.F.M. Cap. (London: Oxford University Press for the British Academy, 1982), pp. 60–61.

14. *Metaphysica fratris Rogeri: De viciis contractis in studio theologie*, ed. Robert Steele (Oxford: Clarendon, 1909), p. 10.

15. *Metaphysica fratris Rogeri*, ed. Steele, p. 11.

16. In addition to those works falsely attributed to Aristotle which existed in Greek, Charles B. Schmitt and Dilwyn Knox have identified ninety-six pseudo-Aristotelian works that were current in Latin during the Middle Ages. See their *Pseudo-Aristoteles Latinus: A Guide to Latin Works Falsely Attributed to Aristotle before 1500* (London: Warburg Institute, University of London, 1985).

17. *Philippi Cancellarii Parisiensis Summa de bono*, ed. Nikolaus Wicki, 2 vols. (Bern: Francke, 1985), 1: 49.

18. Anonymous, *Utrum deus creaverit vel creare potuerit mundum vel aliquid creatum ab eterno*, Florence MS Laurentian Plut. 17, sin. 7, fol. 154ra: "Item, dicit Philosophus in libro *De causis*, ut allegatur, licet ibi non inveniatur, quod hoc est eternum eterno, quod est eviternum eviterno, et tempus temporali."

19. Grosseteste's Aristotelian studies require no comment. On William of Auvergne see Steven P. Marrone, *William of Auvergne and Robert Grosseteste: New Ideas of Truth in the Early Thirteenth Century* (Princeton: Princeton University Press, 1983).

20. *Philippi Cancellarii*, ed. Wicki, 1: 53.

21. *Alexandri de Hales. Quaestiones "De eternitate, evo, et tempore" et "De duratione mundi,"* ed. Donald Nathanson (Ph.D. diss., University of Southern California, 1986), pp. 80–81.

22. Alexander of Hales, *De duratione mundi*, Paris, Bibl. nat. MS lat. 15272, fol. 149va.

23. Albert the Great, *Comm. in sent.* 2, d. 1, art. 10. *Opera omnia*, XXVII, 29a.

The Condemnations of 1277 and the Intellectual Climate of the Medieval University

Leland Edward Wilshire

*J*n 1277, the intellectual life of the universities of Paris and Oxford reverberated with the slamming of two ideological doors. On March 7, 1277, Stephen Tempier, bishop of Paris, published at and for the University of Paris a condemnation of 219 propositions. Three weeks later, Robert Kilwardby, archbishop of Canterbury, published a prohibition of thirty theses at and for the University of Oxford. Any study of the intellectual climate of the medieval university must face and interact with these two events. Yet one cannot treat these two occurrences as if they were past and completed actions. The issues of academic freedom, the relationship of the Christian faith and philosophical inquiry, and the intertwining of the two continue to the present day. Even dealing with the modern scholarship surrounding the two medieval condemnations, one realizes that the apologetic and the invective triggered by these two events continues to be carried on within this secondary literature. This present study finds that it, too, cannot be completely dispassionate, as the author exists in contemporary academia where these concerns continue to swirl and eddy.

Our inquiry into the Condemnations of 1277 will begin by looking at the debate over whether Thomas Aquinas, the most well-known of the thirteenth-century figures, is the main focus of the two condemnations. Out of this study of popular interest emerges the issue of finding those persons and events behind the condemnations. This larger question opens up a further area of inquiry, one that modern scholars are just beginning to explore. Should not the real question be the condemnations themselves? Why are they framed the way they are? What do the condemnations project as the objects of its wrath? How do they react to this projection? Why do they rely upon distortion in their response? It is these new questions that relate, even more than the others, to the relationship of the condemnations to the intellectual climate of the medieval universities.

It has been commonplace to see either or both of the Paris and Oxford Condemnations as directed against Thomas Aquinas. In regard to the Paris Condemnations, the contemporary scholar John Wippel comments, "a number of the propositions prohibited at Paris were surely aimed at Aquinas and were so understood by contemporaries."[1] The problem is in the number. Etienne Gilson, for instance, finds twenty of the Paris Condemnations directed against Thomas, although he is aware that "the list of Thomistic propositions involved in the condemnations is longer, or shorter, according as it is compiled by a Franciscan or a Dominican" and continues, "The list could be made shorter, or longer, because these propositions cannot always be found literally in Thomas Aquinas, at least not without important qualifications, while others could just as well be added, with the same reservation."[2]

Other scholars see a more limited number of Thomistic theses condemned at Paris but acknowledge that they hide behind identical ones promulgated by the Arts faculty. Theodore Crowley, for instance, isolates nine propositions that are common to Thomas and also to the masters of the Arts faculty.[3] A minimalist standpoint is found in the massive study by Roland Hissette, who tried to find exact references for each of the 219 propositions of the Paris Condemnations. After a detailed study of both the condemnations and the extant works from this period, Hissette can find only one reference found exclusively in a work of Aquinas, and this one centering on a minor and happenstance statement taken from Thomas's *Sententia libri Ethicorum* (#213-Mandonnet: "That death is the end of all terrors.—This statement is erroneous if it excludes the terror of hell, which is the last").[4]

Along with the shrinking number of references that modern scholars have found in common between the Paris Condemnations and the works of Aquinas, there is the historical situation that would seem to point

away from Thomas being the main or predominant target of the condemnations. Aquinas had been dead for three years before the Paris Condemnations of 1277, and although he was to have followers, they seem to be
little in evidence by 1277. Also, Aquinas was a theologian. The Paris
Condemnations were directed against the Arts faculty, those "studying
in Arts at Paris and overstepping the limits of their own Faculty."[5] In a
papal letter of January 1277, Pope John XXI had called the attention of
Etienne Tempier, the bishop of Paris, to the teaching of those who had
revived old errors and brought confusion to the minds of both masters
and students.[6] In a second letter, dated April 28, 1277, and after the
condemnations themselves, Pope John XXI commended the 1277 Paris
Condemnations as dealing with the Arts faculty and asked, upon explicit
instructions, that a further inquiry be made into suspect theologians.[7]
Because of a papal interregnum, according to the later remarks of John
Pecham, the curia intervened and asked that the matter be laid to rest.[8]
No further action is known to have been taken. Thomas would have
come under the classification of theologian, not Master of Arts.

During his second regency at the University of Paris, Aquinas was
looked upon as one of the theologians who countered the views of the
"radicals" in the Arts faculty. It would again be strange to consider that
the theological establishment, who had looked upon him as one of their
champions over an extended period of time, would now turn and
consider him a part of the "radical" element, whose views had to be
countered by the Paris Condemnations of 1277.

There were disputes among the theologians, but the theological
faculty had regular ways to deal with their own divergent thinkers. They
would be invited into a closed gathering of the theologians, where they
would be asked to explain their views. If their views were found to be
suspect after the examination by their fellow theologians, they would
modify them until a satisfactory conclusion could be reached. As later
reported by John Pecham, this is what Thomas Aquinas himself did in
regard to his views on plurality and unity of form.[9] To Roger Marston,
who was present at this gathering, the Thomist opinion on unity of form
was condemned as contrary to the doctrines of the Fathers and especially
Augustine and Anselm.[10] Although the theologians who differed from

Thomas may have looked upon their involvement in the compiling of the 219 propositions for the bishop of Paris as an opportunity to censure Thomas, they still considered him part of the theological faculty and wanted to deal with him within that faculty's own private methods of discipline. The one direct reference, as noted by Hissette, seems an aberration. The theological ranks, when dealing with the radical arts faculty, should look solid and not appear to be contentious and divided (however they may be so in reality).

If there was one doctrine unique to Thomas and one that piqued the ire of certain theologians it was Thomas's doctrine of "unity of substantial form," yet this is not found in any form in the Paris Condemnations of 1277. It is possible that the theological faculty had already heard Thomas's explanation and were satisfied or that this major issue was not included in the Paris Condemnations because it was looked upon as primarily a theological issue and not one raised by the provocative teachings of the Arts faculty. In an unpublished doctoral dissertation, Henry Nardone labels eight propositions relating to Thomas's *Summa Theologia* or his *De aeternitate mundi*, including four dealing with angels, one dealing with the sophistical nature of Aristotle's belief in the eternal motion of the heaven, two dealing with the principles of material things, and one concerning the human will.[11] The exact wording cannot be located in the citations, and the condemnations have little relevance to Thomas's own argumentations, although the jibe in one proposition that "it is surprising that men of profound intellect do not see this" could be a veiled reference to Thomas. The Paris Condemnations, even if these are admitted, show little interest in Thomas Aquinas.

On March 18, 1277, some three weeks after the Paris Condemnations, the archbishop of Canterbury, Robert Kilwardby, in the office of "visitor" or Patron of Merton College, condemned thirty errors in grammar, logic, and natural philosophy. This was done with the full assent of the Oxford faculty. Thomas Aquinas has also been seen as the object of these condemnations. In the words of John Wippel, "a number of the theses condemned at Oxford seem to presuppose (or touch on) the doctrine of unicity of substantial form in man, a position closely associated with the name of Thomas Aquinas."[12] Daniel A. Callus, in his study of the Oxford Condemnations, finds eleven of the sixteen propositions on natural philosophy relating directly or indirectly to Thomas's thesis on the unicity of substantial form.[13]

In regard to the specific content of the Oxford propositions, Kilwardby's list made no mention of Aquinas or his followers, nor did it mention the technical terms of any specific Thomistic formulation. In the first two parts of the Oxford Condemnations—the sections on grammar and logic—Kilwardby dealt with such issues as whether the noun agrees with the verb and the correct way to form syllogistic arguments. All of this seems superfluous if Kilwardby was trying to counter the sophisticated theology of Thomas. The works of Thomas do not suffer from simple grammatical or logical errors. In the final section on Natural Philosophy, the archbishop did raise both the hotly debated issue of the "rationes seminales" in man and the problem of whether the human soul is either simple or composite. Yet these issues had been part of the general debate raging over these points at the medieval universities over a fifty year period, particularly at Oxford, and were peculiar neither to Kilwardby nor to Aquinas.

The issue of whether Kilwardby was dealing with the unique formulation of Thomas's "unicity of substantial form" is be found in the correspondence carried on after the Oxford Condemnation of 1277 between Kilwardby and Peter of Conflans, archbishop of Corinth and a Dominican then residing in Paris. Conflans was an emerging young disciple of Thomas. In his correspondence to Kilwardby, which is not extant, Conflans seemed to have raised seven points arising directly or indirectly out of the Oxford Condemnations. In his response, which is extant, Kilwardby defended the Oxford Condemnations as a matter of orthodoxy against heresy, true philosophy against that which is manifestly false, and the Christian faith against that which is repugnant to it. There was no mention of Aquinas, and Kilwardby buttressed his remarks with appeals to Augustine, Aristotle, and Averroes.[14]

In his side of the correspondence, Peter of Conflans raised the issue of the specific Thomistic theory of "unity of substantial form." Kilwardby replied to this issue in the famous "seventh point" of the letter, that "by these words, such an article was not condemned at

Oxford nor do I remember hearing of it. Why it is called 'positio de unitate formarum' I do not sufficiently understand."[15] These are the words not of a person who has directly opposed Thomas in the Oxford Condemnations (indeed, he had indicated that this was not done) but of a person who had just learned about this unique view in this later correspondence with the young Dominican scholar. Kilwardby, from what he had understood from Conflans, came out against the theory, but that is posterior to the Oxford Condemnations themselves.

Other scholars have seen historical events as showing that Thomas was really the target of the Oxford Condemnations. Could it be that the Oxford speech of Kilwardby set up such an agitation in the intellectual world that the General Chapter of the Dominicans in 1278 sent delegates to England to investigate those who disparaged "the writings of the venerated Friar Thomas Aquinas?"[16] In answer, one can find no disparaging of the writings of Thomas in any of the known works of Kilwardby, and Kilwardby himself had been promoted to the cardinalate one month before the Dominican chapter meeting. Either as archbishop or cardinal, he would seem to be beyond such a petty investigation.

Still other scholars have seen a strong reaction in favor of Thomism at Oxford in the writings of a certain Richard Knapwell, which reaction, it has been argued, was the immediate cause of the 1277 Condemnations. Scholars have also asserted that Kilwardby was promoted to the cardinalate to "save the old prelate from serious difficulties."[17] The young scholar Knapwell, however, did not incept until 1280, and his provocative writings come after that date. The promotion of Kilwardby to the cardinalate was probably more in the opposite direction of strengthening the "conservative" element in the curia, with John Pecham, a more strident individual, being elevated to the archbishopric of Canterbury.

John Wippel, in a scholarly exchange to an earlier study of mine, raised the issue of the inclusion, in a 1310 text of Henry of Harclay, of the statement that the prohibitions of both Kilwardby and Pecham were directed against Thomas's thesis of the unicity of substantial form.[18] It is true that Henry of Harclay does contain two propositions, in paraphrase form, from the 1277 Oxford Condemnations, but reference to Kilwardby's prohibitions had been standard practice for polemical

Franciscan writers ever since the days of John Pecham.[19] We also find references in the fourteenth-century author Walter Catton.[20] To turn a Dominican against a Dominican was an opportunity just too good for a Franciscan to pass up. Harclay's use of the two propositions gives us insight into fourteenth-century polemics, but it carries little weight in contrast to Kilwardby's own words on the subject.

If Thomas Aquinas was not the target of either the Paris or the Oxford Condemnations, toward whom or what issues were the condemnations directed? In his analysis of the Paris Condemnations, Roland Hissette has given us the following complex formula: thirty treatises dealing directly with assertions of Siger of Brabant; fourteen probably dealing with Siger of Brabant; thirteen propositions directly against the views of Boethius of Dacia; three possibly against Boethius of Dacia; four condemnations directly taken from an anonymous work edited by Ph. Delhaye, with three probable condemnations, five sentences directly taken from an anonymous work edited by A. Zimmermann, and five statements taken directly from an anonymous work edited by M. Giele. There is then the one Thomistic reference, as we have noted, that Hissette finds taken from his *Sententia libri Ethicorum*. Hissette finds seventy-two propositions for which he can give no hypothesis, either because they cannot be found in any extant text or because they are common statements found in a multiplicity of authors. He ends this analysis by stating that he finds sixty-eight propositions that remain unidentifiable.[21] The large number of specific articles relating to Siger of Brabant and Boethius of Dacia seems to bear up the titles that later medieval editors gave to the Paris Condemnations indicating that they were compiled specifically against these two individuals; "Against the heretics Siger and Boethius" and "The main defender of these articles was a certain cleric named Boethius."[22] A collection of the works of Raymond Lull labels his manuscript on the Paris Condemnations as "Book against the errors of Boethius and Siger."[23]

Who were these two individuals, Siger of Brabant and Boethius of Dacia? Siger was born in the Duchy of Brabant around 1240. He studied at the Arts Faculty of the University of Paris sometime between 1255 and 1260 and became Master of Arts between 1260 and 1265. His name first appears in a university document concerning a university quarrel in 1266. Of his writings we have fourteen authentic works and six probable commentaries on the *Metaphysics* and *Physics* of Aristotle. His most important works include *Quaestiones in Metaphysicam*, *Impossibilia* (six exercises in sophistry), *Quaestiones super librum De causis*, *Quaestiones in tertium De Anima*, and *Tractatus de anima intellectiva*. His teachings created an intellectual agitation and were challenged by Bonaventure and Thomas Aquinas. Statements from his works relating to Aristotle are found in the Paris Condemnations of 1270 and later, as we have already indicated, in the Paris Condemnations of 1277. On November 23, 1276, the inquisitor of France summoned Siger of Brabant, Goswin of the Chapel, and Berneir of Nivelles to appear before his tribunal. The three fled to Italy and probably appealed to the tribunal of the papal curia. Siger stayed at the curia in the company of a cleric. Although there is some reference to his "leading a long life," the story told by those at the time was that he was stabbed by this cleric, who had gone mad, and thus was murdered before November 10, 1274, during the pontificate of Martin IV.

We know little about the life of Boethius of Dacia. The dates of his birth and death remain unknown, but we do know that by 1270 he was a member of the Arts Faculty at the University of Paris. His writings included a series of commentaries on Aristotle (in the form of questions), various works on logic and speculative grammar, some questions on ethical topics, and a *Metaphysics* commentary, along with three treatises that have been discovered by modern scholarship: *On the Supreme Good* (*De summo bono*); *On the eternity of the world* (*De aeternitate mundi*); and *On Dreams* (*De somniis*). He was not cited to appear before the inquisitor in 1276, and it has been suggested that perhaps by 1272–73 he had concluded his teaching career at the University of Paris. A fourteenth-century Dominican catalogue states that he became a member of that order after 1272/73. Statements from his works regarding Aristotle appear, as have been indicated, in the Paris Condemnations of 1277, and the influence of his works on grammar and logic has been seen as being behind those particular sections of the Oxford Condemnations of 1277.

Let us take the best known of these two, Siger of Brabant, and see what it was about him that led to his being a main suspect for the strictures of the Paris Condemnations of 1277. Modern scholars have given this thinker various descriptive titles. He has been called an "anti-clerical free thinker,"[24] a "founder of Western Rationalism,"[25] a "Latin Averroist,"[26] a "radical or heterodox Aristotelian,"[27] or an "Aristotelian."[28] Instead of giving him a title, let us take an alternate route of seeking to understand Siger of Brabant as he is found in six areas of university life, as modern as they are medieval: 1) the person and personality of the teacher; 2) the method and technique of teaching; 3) the interaction of scholarly peers; 4) the instructor in faculty/student relations; 5) the identification and interaction with the subject matter of the master's expertise; and 6) the individual's role in the university's institutional politics.

First there is the issue of the personal characteristics of the instructor. Could it be that Siger had an abrasive or combative personality and it was because of personal traits that he became known as a troublemaker? Fernand van Steenberghen writes:

> We know that Siger was of a fiery temperament, impetuous and easily led to excess. We find in his works that strong and peremptory tone, that pugnacious attitude, that hatred for compromise, which the canon of Brabant manifests in the management of the affairs of his Faculty.[29]

Although the anonymity and objective character of the primary material makes verification of van Steenberghen's picture difficult, there is enough in the records of the university to make the assertive personality of this particular university master at least a factor in his later difficulties.

Second, Siger as a university master was involved in the act of education. The method and techniques of teaching have always been arenas of contention in university life, especially in the thirteenth century. The Irish scholar Alfred J. Rahilly suggests that it was Siger's teaching method of critical inquiry that got him into trouble. Rahilly quotes from the *Tractatus de anima intellectiva*, where Siger states that his object was to stimulate his students to think for themselves. Rahilly continues:

If my contention be right, there is no essential difference between the Aristotelianism of Albert and Siger and that of Thomas. The differences are purely extrinsic and have really nothing to do with philosophy. The dispute merely turns on the question whether the young clerics of Paris University were or were not sufficiently advanced to be given a course of lectures on the history of philosophy.[30]

This is not to say that Siger used modern methods of critical inquiry, but the lecture and disputation method of teaching in the Middle Ages offers its own type of challenge to student creative thought.

Third, Siger was a part of an intellectual community. The medieval university was, above all, a community of scholars. In this community, one experienced the collegiality of learning, the interaction of one's peers, and the intellectual stimulation of other scholars. Siger seemed to have found this interaction with Thomas Aquinas. Aquinas wrote *De unitate intellectus* against what he had heard about Siger. Siger replied to Aquinas in his later works *De intellectu* and *Tractatus de anima intellectiva*. In this scholarly interaction, Siger seemed to have modified his views on the intellective soul and spoke of it later as a form rather than as a mover. The impression is that Siger welcomed this interaction, especially with a brilliant fellow scholar who could challenge his use of Aristotle and his commentators, and possibly modified his views. Edward P. Mahoney writes:

The various arguments and authorities which Thomas had presented forced him (Siger) to reconsider over a period of years both his interpretation of Aristotle and also what he himself thought human reason must conclude regarding the nature of the intellective soul.[31]

In the medieval university, this community of scholars with its intellectual challenge by one's peers was of primal essence, and Siger took part in the freedom of this scholarly interaction. To those wishing to find suspected faculty members, however, the discussion of certain dangerous issues in this interaction offered open targets of accusation.

Fourth, there is the relation to the persons being taught, that is, the students. There is a tendency to think of the medieval university as devoid of students. This is not true. A university primarily is and has been

an institution organized for the purpose of teaching students. In the medieval undergraduate school of Liberal Arts, where Siger taught, he dealt with teenagers, students fourteen to seventeen years of age. Some of these students, one would assume, were quiet vocationally minded students who were taking liberal arts to quickly go on into the graduate schools of theology, law, or medicine. Others seemingly had other interests. The records of the University of Paris portray a turbulent time. In 1269, the authorities of the university condemned students who were armed and committed crimes.[32] In 1276, students were excommunicated for public indecency and rowdy behavior.[33] The Paris Condemnations of 1277 speak of prohibiting the reading of *De amore*, books on geomancy, necromancy, experiments in fortune telling, invocations of devils, and incantations. These actions were probably extracurricular student activities or seen by a concerned bishop as student activities.

An area not yet entirely understood is what role the students played in the difficulties of Siger of Brabant. If Siger as a teacher was drawing fine distinctions in the interaction between Aristotelian philosophy and Christian theology, the students were taking down in their notes what they understood and what they were interested in especially if it gave credence to their own skepticisms, life styles, and student campus ferment. It seems that Aquinas got what he knew about Siger, garbled as it was, from student notes (*reportationes*). Thomas complains that his opponent should "not speak in corners, nor in the presence of boys who do not know to judge about such difficult matters."[34] The Paris Condemnations of 1277 may portray not so much the teaching of the Arts masters but, rather, what the Arts students understood, what they took down in their notes, and what they altered to meet their own interests and enjoyments. Siger may have gotten into trouble because the student perceptions of his lectures as they filtered through their own agendas were different from his own tightly drawn intellectual distinctions of faith and non-faith. Siger may have drawn fine inferences of the primacy of Christian truths over those of Aristotle, but it was probably the student recasting of bits of Siger's lectures into their radical formulations that caught the eyes of the authorities and the conservative theologians of the university.

Fifth, the subject matter being taught entered into the troubles of Siger. As a member in the Arts faculty, Siger taught Aristotle and his commentators. The Arts school had gone through the restrictions on the use of Aristotle in the edicts of 1210 and 1215 along with the papal letter of 1228, setting up a commission to look into what could be used of Aristotle's works on nature. Some time between 1230 and 1260, however, the university had turned itself into a philosophical school with both the availability and perceived freedom to teach the natural works of Aristotle. A list of courses and books dated 1255 shows how far this freedom had been taken. Siger was enraptured by Aristotle and all that he meant to a fuller understanding of the natural world. In his enthusiasm, however, Siger always qualified his comments with his own allegiances to the Christian faith. There is not a single known work of Siger in which he says that necessary philosophical conclusions were true when they contradicted the Christian faith. Siger always maintained that truth was on the side of faith. Armand Mauer, in his recent study "Siger of Brabant and Theology," writes:

> It is certain that he (Siger) accepted not only the absolute truth of Christian revelation, even though he thought the conclusions of philosophy are sometimes contrary to it, but also the science of theology as a rational and scientific development of the data of revelation. For him, moreover, this theology is not only a science; it is wisdom itself, whose teachings have greater certainty than those of metaphysics.[35]

If this is an accurate analysis of Siger's theology, why did he become the object of condemnations? Insight may be gained by comments in the last section of Thomas Aquinas's work "On the Unity of the Intellect Against the Averroists" written around 1270. It is commonly thought to be directed against Siger, although no direct quotes from Siger's known writings can be found. A frustrated Thomas writes, "It is deserving of even greater wonder and even of indignation that someone who professes that he is a Christian, should presume to speak so irreverently about the Christian faith." He then offers a quote that seems to be a garbled paraphrase of Siger, "I necessarily conclude through reason that the intellect is one in number but I firmly hold the opposite through faith." Thomas answers that if a statement is true ("concluded necessar-ily"), the opposite would be false and impossible and thus that "faith would be concerned with something false and impossible that not even God could effect. This the faithful cannot bear to hear."[36]

Thomas P. Bukowski has recently pursued Siger further in this anti-Christian direction. He believes that Siger showed an "antipathy towards theology," that Siger wished to keep theologians from interfering with philosophy, and wanted to protect faith by isolating it from philos-ophy and demonstrative reasoning.[37] There are, however, no direct statements from his writings that these were his aims. Recently Armand Maurer has called our attention to the one place in Siger's *Quaestiones in Metaphysicam* where Siger gives six differences between "sacred the-ology" (or "sacra scriptura") and "theology that is part of philosophy." Maurer summarizes Siger's list as: 1) different modes of procedure be-tween them with sacred theology being based on divine revelation; 2) the restriction of philosophic theology to that which can be known by human reason; 3) the universal science of sacred doctrine as it includes the con-clusions of all the particular sciences; 4) the greater certitude of sacred Scripture; 5) the greater usage of sacred theology as it is both practical and theoretical; and 6) the greater claim to wisdom of sacred theology over that of philosophical theology. Siger assents in each instance to the primacy of the Christian faith, and Maurer ends his study by com-menting that Siger "shared with the great Christian theologians of the thirteenth century, a respect for, and an appreciation of, theology as the Queen of the sciences."[38]

Finally, Siger became the focus of conflict because he was in the nexus of university politics. The thirteenth-century university, as with its modern extension, was replete with "turf wars." There were the issues of papal versus royal control and of chancellor versus the faculty, along with the conflict among various factions of the liberal arts faculty over who would be their proctor. In 1276, in a celebrated instance, Siger was himself the candidate of a minority of the liberal arts faculty to be the proctor. One of the longest documents in the records of the medieval university of Paris compels Siger and his faction to submit to the new proctor.[39] Because of Siger's active involvement in the issues of university governance, it would not be surprising if it was university politics that played a major role in the citation to appear before the inquisition and his flight that brought an end of his teaching career.

When we move from the Paris Condemnations of 1277 to the Oxford Condemnations of 1277, we are faced with interpretations that lead in two directions. One direction is to see the Oxford Condemnations as a hastily drawn addendum to the Paris Condemnations. That is, both Stephen Tempier and Robert Kilwardby have been asked to search out errors; and the two critics are seen working in tandem. A series of radical beliefs is enumerated in the Paris Condemnations; but the conflict over unity/plurality of form is neglected. Kilwardby, noticing that that error is absent from the Paris Condemnations, makes it the focus of the Oxford Condemnations, and, thus, the whole range of condemned doctrines is covered.

Another direction of interpretation is to see the differences and independent nature of the two condemnations. There may have been papal bulls to both of these churchmen from the pope, although no document has ever been found instructing Kilwardby to inquire into errors at Oxford. There are some notable differences between the situations and content of the two condemnations, which would point to the independence of their issuance. First, the conflict between the faculties of Arts and Theology in the Paris Condemnations is not present in the Oxford Condemnations. This is noted in the later titles of the manuscripts of the Oxford Condemnations, "These are the errors condemned by Father R. Kilwardby Archbishop of Canterbury, on the consensus of all magistrates both regent and non regents."[40] In his later correspondence to Peter Conflans, Kilwardby reiterates that his series of prohibitions were issued with the full assent of all faculty, regent and non regent, the faculty from both theology and philosophy (i.e., Arts).[41]

Second, we find in this later correspondence to Conflans that the Oxford list is not a list of heretical doctrines that would end in excommunication but, rather, a list of propositions that would end in the person being asked to relinquish his teaching responsibilities. In his letter to Peter of Conflans, Kilwardby makes the point that his 1277 Oxford Condemnations were a different type of prohibition. He repudiates categorically that he had condemned any thesis. His was not a condemnation in the canonical sense of the word in the manner in which heresies were usually censured, but a mere prohibition to teach, or to maintain certain tenets with "pertinacity" in the schools, that is, at the university.[42]

The form of the Oxford Condemnations is also different, as it is divided into the three sections of grammar, logic, and natural philosophy. The early sections on grammar and logic have usually been bypassed in the haste to get to the propositions on Natural Philosophy. Examples of these grammatical and logical prohibitions would be the third error in grammar, "That a verb deprived of all of its accidents can still remain a verb," and the second logical prohibition, "That the syllogism which is materially defective is not a syllogism."[43]

The late scholar P. Osmund Lewry was intrigued with these early sections and noted that the "referential aspects of language are clearly a central issue for Kilwardby." He then tried to analyze them in the light of a comparison with the Oxford grammatical and logical works from the second half of the thirteenth century. Although he could find no direct references, he believed that there were hints of the influence of the teachings of Boethius of Dacia on certain scholars at Oxford and that a work by John de Secceheville (1265), an Oxford master heavily influenced by Averroes, may also lie behind some of these prohibitions.[44] Other scholars, however, make the point that Kilwardby "seems less concerned with the nature of rational thinking than with the importance of thinking soundly" and that Kilwardby is more interested in "unskilled reasoning" than on countering specific Modalist works.[45]

The third section on "Natural Philosophy" has usually been the area of attention. It contains such statements as prohibition three, "That no active potency is in matter," prohibition ten, "That Aristotle did not originate the statement that the intellectual principle remains after the point of death," and prohibition sixteen, "That the intellective principle is united to prime matter in such a way that all preceding forms are destroyed."[46] The main philosophical issue behind the Natural Philosophy prohibitions of Oxford Condemnations of 1277 was the issue of whether the human soul was simple or composite, the issue of "unity of form" in its formulation by Aristotle and his commentators.

It is difficult to find the persons and events behind these statements. Daniel A. Callus calls our attention to an anonymous commentary on Aristotle's *Metaphysics*, written by a secular master in Arts at Oxford sometime before 1250, which concludes that the vegetative, the sensitive, and the rational principles are in man not three substances but one and the same substance.[47] There may have been other works at Oxford supporting unity of form, either hidden under the cloak of anonymity or not extant today, that lie behind Kilwardby's prohibitions.

Although some of the conclusions of the Oxford Condemnations are to found in Aquinas (# 7, 13, and 16 in Natural Philosophy), Thomas had already responded to others (#2 in Natural Philosophy), and it would seem strange that they be brought up again.[48] This lack of familiarity has led D. E. Sharp to respond that "St. Thomas seems to be the only contemporary whose speculations interested him, but even here he displays no detailed first-hand knowledge, such as might be reasonably expected of one who assumed the role of censor."[49] Later, as we shall see, John Pecham, Kilwardby's successor as archbishop of Canterbury, will add to the list a condemnation dealing specifically with the doctrine of the "unity of substantial form."

The Oxford Condemnations of 1277 seem to be not so much a response to particular opponents as they are a reiteration of Kilwardby's own interpretation of Aristotle. A study of Kilwardby's earlier works—such as the *De ortu scientiarum* (1230–40), his commentaries on the *Sentences* (1254), and his correspondence with Peter of Conflans that came after the 1277 Condemnations—shows that Kilwardby knew his Aristotle and quoted him hundreds of times but used him mainly as a source for supplying the deficiencies of Augustine. Kilwardby took Aristotle's concept of the active principle and infused it with the Augustinian doctrine of the seminal reasons or "rationes seminales" that would be necessary for the explanation of becoming in the natural world. Although in his *De ortu scientiarum* Kilwardby made the distinction between theological knowledge and philosophical knowledge ("Scienciarum alia est divine, alia humana"), he believed that all knowledge resided in the divine light and that thus an Augustinian view of the nature of man could be made to fit Aristotle. Kilwardby was not trying to find anti-Christian views of Aristotle; if he had, he would have brought in the issue of the numerical unity of human souls or the issue of the eternity of the world. He was trying to state in the condemnations that Aristotle, rightly interpreted through Augustinian doctrine, could be usable. The Aristotelian theory of potency and act became a justification of his own belief. The Oxford Condemnations were in many respects an attempt to rescue Aristotle for the Christian cause rather than an attempt to curtail study of this thinker. That this attempt at interpretation was obsolete and out of date by 1277 did not occur to Kilwardby. There is much to bear out Trivet's observation that after Kilwardby succeeded Fishacre in the chair of theology at Oxford (1248), he devoted himself entirely to theology and the study of the Scriptures and the Fathers.[50]

We now enter the newly opened inquiry promised at the beginning of this study. Should not the real question be the condemnations themselves rather than seeking who or what lies beyond the condemnations? The Paris Condemnations of 1277 state in their preface that there were specific reasons behind their publication. These must be given serious consideration. To begin with, Bishop Tempier proclaimed that the faculty of the school of Arts were going beyond their expertise and discussing theological issues. He writes:

> We have received frequent reports, inspired by zeal for the faith, on the part of important and serious persons to the effect that some students of the arts in Paris are exceeding the boundaries of their own faculty and presuming to treat and discuss, as if they were debatable in the schools, certain obvious and loathsome errors, or rather "vanities and lying follies" [Ps. 39: 5], which are contained in the roll joined to this letter. These students are not hearkening to the admonition of Gregory, "Let him who would speak wisely exercise great care, lest by his speech he disrupt the unity of his listeners," particularly when in support of the aforesaid errors they adduce pagan writings that—shame on their ignorance—they assert to be so convincing that they do not know how to answer them. . . .[51]

Before we get to an analysis of the statements from the preface to the Paris Condemnations of 1277, it is interesting to compare its approach with the simple preface to the Paris Condemnations of 1270. Seven years earlier, the preface had only stated, "These are the errors which Stephen . . . condemned and excommunicated along with all who shall have taught or asserted them knowingly," followed by thirteen statements beginning with the first article, "That the intellect of all men is numerically one and the same."[52] The weakness of this earlier approach and the reason why it possibly did not slow the intellectual ferment was that no one admitted to teaching or asserting them "knowingly." No one in the Arts faculty would declare himself as "knowingly" a pagan or atheist or non believer.

Coming now to a detailed analysis of the preface to the 1277 Paris Condemnations, we learn the following things. First, there was an agenda set by certain people who prompted this action. Tempier could be referring to the pope and his letter to the bishop requesting an examination, but the specific concern over the faculty of Arts exceeding their own area of inquiry was not in the papal letter. It seems to have come from a group of concerned theologians at the University of Paris.

Second, we learn that the perpetrators have "exceeded the boundaries of their own faculty." This would be a reassertion of a public restriction, dated 1272, that the Arts faculty should not teach theology. The basic concern was a theological one. One is reminded of a brief treatise Albert the Great wrote in 1256 when commanded by Pope Alexander IV to refute the errors of Averroes concerning the agent intellect. In this work, *De unitate intellectus contra Averroem*, Albert constructs the imaginary literary figure of "the young professor" and shows how his teaching of such statements as the eternity of the world and monopsychism comes out of the assertion that Aristotle says so and "Aristotle is always right." Albert then goes on to show how these conclusions lead, in the "young professor," to doctrinally heretical conclusions.[53]

Third, we learn that the issue is not "the search for truth" or academic inquiry but that there were certain "errors" or "vanities" that disturb the faithful. Whether the faithful are faculty, students, or the non-academic clergy and laity, Tempier does not spell out. Possibly all of these are assumed within the term. Bonaventure had earlier, in his *In Hexaemeron,* made this same point when he stated the concern for the effect that such truths were having upon the faithful. He wrote:

> It is more prudent to say that Aristotle did not think that the world was eternal, whether he himself thought so or not, because he was so great that all would follow him and affirm that he said so. All the light spread from what preceded would be extinguished. Let us follow him in the truth he said, not in those things in which he was obscure, which he did not know or which he concealed.[54]

Fourth, the preface informs us that, in support of the errors, pagan writers were adduced (as specific writers are not mentioned by name within the 219 propositions, the issue would seem to be the thought of the pagan writers). For example, theological errors are found in philosophic statements. Furthermore, the opponents were asserting them, and in such a convincing manner that the authors themselves were carried away and did not know how to answer them. They were putting forth propositions without counter arguments. The opposing theological truth was not set out in detail.

Stephen Tempier continues:

> . . . So as not to appear to be asserting what they thus insinuate, however, they conceal their answers in such a way that, while wishing to avoid Scylla, they fall into Charybdis. For they say that these things are true according to philosophy but not according to the Catholic faith, as if there were two contrary truths and as if the truth of Sacred Scripture were contradicted by the truth in the sayings of the accursed pagans.[55]

The issue was becoming complex. It was not an issue of overt teachings, it was one of concealed answers. The bishop proclaims that a conscious deception was going on. In attempting to avoid the Scylla of avoiding a theological argument thinkers were relegating intellectual items to the realm of philosophy. To Tempier, these thinkers were falling into the opposite danger of stating that a proposition has truth in philosophy but not truth in the Christian faith. The argument that it was pagan philosophers hiding as Christians who were the danger rather than self-declared Averroists can be found in Bonaventure's earlier 1273 work, *In Hexameron*, where he states that it was written not just against Averroes but also against Christians who maintain in the name of philosophy positions contrary to faith.[56] We have seen that Siger of Brabant and Boethius of Dacia both used these qualifications.

Roland Hissette found sixty-four examples in the Paris Condemnations of 1277 where the compilers of the condemnations ascribed to an author a doctrine taught only by that person as a philosophical truth and did not take under consideration the restrictions of the original thinker who labeled such assertion as "natural philosophy" (*philosophus naturalis*) or that the truth was developed according to the "intention of the philosophers" (*secundum intentionem philosophorum*). In some cases a truth is rejected entirely by the original proponent, but the person compiling the condemnation has not seen fit to mention this rejection. Thirty of the sixty-four are linked, in some way, to Siger of Brabant, eight to Boethius of Dacia, ten to both Siger and Boethius, and fifteen from other works. The one quote from Thomas Aquinas is found in this grouping, where even his restrictions were not taken under consideration.[57]

More than taking a proposition out of context, there are instances of intentional distortion. Roland Hissette finds nine examples of propositions in which the thought of the author was hardened beyond what the author intended. Hissette finds an additional ten times in which the nuances introduced by the original author, which rendered the proposition incompatible with Christianity, were neglected in the condemnation. In one of these instances, the passage was made more heterodox than the author intended and thus was made to defend Averroistic monophysism. Of the ten instances, six are from Boethius of Dacia and four are from Siger of Brabant. Whether it was intentional or not, Hissette finds sixteen times when the text was misunderstood. Of the sixteen examples of textual misunderstanding, fourteen are related to Siger of Brabant, ranging from direct quotation to possible inference; one is from an unknown source; and one is a direct quote from Boethius of Dacia.[58]

Armand Maurer has recently called our attention to the two Paris condemnations that deal with "falsehood and fables" in the Christian religion: "That there are fables and falsehoods (*fabulae et falsa*) in the Christian law just as in others" and "That the teachings of the theologian are based on fables" (#181, #183-Mandonnet classification).[59] These two statements are not found, in this exact formulation, in Siger, although the linking of the two terms "fabulosa et falsa" is found three times in one manuscript of his *Commentary on the Metaphysics*. Indeed, in his commentary Siger made it quite clear that far from reducing theology to a legendary or a mythical account of the truth, he was praising it as a higher kind of wisdom than metaphysics. He went on to comment that theology, because it is based on sacred Scripture, is more certain than metaphysics and, unlike human reason, cannot err. When discussing Aristotle's specific treatment of "fables and falsehoods," however, Siger does not mention the Christian religion or exempt it from contamination by childish tales or errors, and he goes on to state that "authority" may make a falsehood appear as a truth. This led the modern scholar Maurer to state:

> in the troubled atmosphere of the 1270's in Paris the separation (and not only
> the distinction) of reason and faith practiced by Siger and his circle made them
> an object of suspicion to the ecclesiastical authorities and open to misunder-
> standing and misrepresentation.[60]

Along with the works of Siger of Brabant, those of Boethius of Dacia also suffer from selective or intentional confusion in the Paris Condemnations of 1277. In his treatise *On the Supreme Good*, Boethius of Dacia makes the distinction between the happy life on this earth which, by the taking up of philosophy, is knowing truth, doing good, and taking delight in both and "that happiness which we expect in the life to come on the authority of faith."[61] Again there is a proposition from the Condemnations of 1277 (#1-Mandonnet): "There is no more excellent kind of life than to give oneself to philosophy," which takes up the argument without taking into effect the qualification of the original author.

There are two instances in which propositions taken from Boethius of Dacia's tractate *On the eternity of the world* were changed by adding one word. Boethius, in this tractate, tried to bring into harmony the views of the Christian faith concerning the eternity of the world and the position held by Aristotle and other philosophers. His argument was that creation is a concept that cannot be understood by natural philosophy. Therefore it cannot be denied by natural philosophers. A Christian speaks the truth when he says the world became to be; there was a first man, . . . and the same man will return.   The passage ends with: "whether enjoying a position of dignity or not, if one cannot understand such difficult matters, then let him obey the wise man and let him believe in the Christian law."[62] As it was found in the Paris Condemnations, the article was "That only philosophers were and are the wise men of the earth" (#2-Mandonnet). The word "only" does not appear in Boethius, and the omission changes the meaning of the proposition into an unacceptable statement.

Again, one proposition shows an addition that changes the meaning of an argument of Boethius of Dacia. It reads, "That the natural philosopher has to deny absolutely the newness of the world because he bases himself on natural causes and natural reasons, whereas the faithful can deny the eternity of the world because he bases himself on supernatural causes. (#191-Mandonnet). The word "absolutely" (*simpliciter*, "without qualification") is not found in Boethius. Boethius always made the point that a natural philosopher should deny the world according to natural causes only in a qualified sense (*secundum quid*). There is also a series of condemnations where Boethius would have refused to admit to own them in an unqualified sense (#214, 215, 216-Mandonnet).

In raising these propositions from the Paris Condemnations of 1277 that show editorial inductions, as analyzed by Roland Hissette in regard to Siger of Brabant and other scholars in regard to Boethius of Dacia, we are still left with over half of the condemnations that have not been shown to have been either intentionally altered or misunderstood. The conclusion should not be reached that the Paris Condemnations are completely stilted. There are two areas where, by and large, there are few altered statements: the section on unicity of the human intellect and the section on personal ethical issues. Yet even here there are still questions of inclusion.

The assertion of the unicity of the human intellect, a teaching of Averroes, was a belief that Siger of Brabant had stated quite boldly in his earlier work, the *Quaestiones in librum tertium De Anima* (1265–70). Later, in his work *De intellectu* (1270; lost but recovered in summarized form by the Renaissance philosopher Augustino Nifo), Siger still maintained that the union of the possible intellect with the human race was more essential than the union with the individual human beings. It was these bold assertions that prompted the works against "Averroists" by Albert and Thomas along with the earlier condemnation of 1270.

In 1272 or 1274, Siger of Brabant wrote an additional work, the *Tractatus de anima intellectiva*, where he modified and qualified his thinking on this matter. He now offered the qualification that the truth about the soul can only be achieved through Christian revelation and not by natural reason. He reiterated his method of seeking only the intention of the philosophers, especially Aristotle, who, having no experience of a true soul, did not teach that souls existed as separate entities. In this work he attacked both Albert and Thomas by name and argued that according to Aristotle the intellective soul was separate in existence from the body and united with the body in only an operational mode, as a sailor and a ship. In the 1277 Paris Condemnations we will have a prohibition such as article #123, "That the intellect is not the form of the body, except in the manner in which a helmsman is the form a ship, and that it is not an essential perfection of man."

Yet in this 1272–74 work, Siger will begin to stress the other side of the intellect and body relationship in answer to objections raised by Thomas. The intellect is somehow united by its very nature to the body and is somehow a "form" that operates as an internal agent in matter. After a long discussion of what he believed Aristotle and his commentators taught on the matter, Siger confesses that he had long been in a state of "doubt" as to what natural reason held on this issue and what Aristotle believed on this question. He ended his treatise by stating that he accepted the multiplicity of the intellect on the basis of religious faith.[63] If he is the author of a later work, the *Liber de causes* (1274–76), he now considered the unity of the intellect not only heretical but also irrational and offered a series of philosophical arguments supporting his acceptance of the plurality of intellect. This later work is so much a blanket repudiation of his earlier works, however, that one is hesitant in ascribing it to Siger unless the threat of the inquisition caused a radical reversal of his views. Whether his *Tractatus de anima intellectiva* or the *Liber de causes* is his last work on this subject, the Paris Condemnations still single out unity of the possible intellect in a series of condemned articles, and there were plenty of earlier statements of Siger that openly state such a position. Here would be a case of later qualifications either not believed or not considered.

Another area of statements not analyzed by Roland Hissette because he can find no related texts is a series of condemnations relating to personal ethics, as, for example, "That one should not pray" (#202-Mandonnet) or "That simple fornication, namely that of an unmarried man with an unmarried woman, is not a sin" (#205-Mandonnet) or "That one should not confess except for the sake of appearances" (#203-Mandonnet). These statements are so extreme that no master would seriously propose them. They look like satirical student utterances that would go along with the reading of the book *De Amore*, which Bishop Tempier had prohibited in the preface to the Paris Condemnations.

When we move from an analysis of the Paris Condemnations to an analysis of the Oxford Condemnations, we are impressed with the academic nature of the prohibited items. We have seen that Archbishop Kilwardby framed the Oxford Condemnations of 1277 in such a way that they were grammatical, logical, and philosophical statements. We do not have the situation, as in the Paris Condemnations, where the issue was one of Christians hiding under the cloak of their faith. We have seen in his letter to Peter of Conflans how Kilwardby stated that he had framed his statements as propositions rather than as condemnations and had repudiated categorically that he had condemned any thesis. He had instead issued a mere prohibition to teach, or to maintain certain tenets with "pertinacity" in the schools.[64]

The academic quality of Kilwardby's presentation, however, did not continue in the further controversy. In October of 1284, John Pecham, now archbishop of Canterbury upon the death of Kilwardby, summoned the masters of Oxford to the abbey of Osney, where he verbally renewed Kilwardby's Oxford Condemnations along with an additional condemnation against the Unity of Form.[65] The Dominicans at Oxford resented Pecham's action at Osney as specifically directed against them, and their prior made a formal protest. In response to this action, Pecham, in a letter dated November 10, 1284, asked the chancellor of Oxford to investigate the full list of propositions prohibited by Kilwardby, the penalties prescribed, and the names of those who had been compelled to recant and of those who defended them or dared still to defend them or any of them.[66] The propositions were to be re-examined by a panel of theologians.

Pecham's comments on penalties and finding the names of those compelled to recant shows that he had no direct familiarity with Kilwardby's 1277 Condemnations, as this is not the form in which they were issued. It is interesting that Pecham not only felt obliged to add an additional statement on the unity of substantial form in this renewal of Kilwardby's articles but also that he listed two theological arguments against unity of form: 1) that Christ's body was not one and the same before and after death; and 2) that the relics of the saints venerated in Rome and all Christendom do not in reality appertain to their own natural bodies.

What we learn from later documents is that Pecham did not have Kilwardby's prohibitions in his possession, nor did he know exactly what was in them. He tried to make up for this omission with letters, dated November 14, 1284, to the chancellor of the University of Oxford and Master Fleckham of the school of theology, asking them if they would "carefully but quietly and without raising the alarm" find him what errors Kilwardby had condemned and the penalties prescribed by him for continuing to uphold them, whether any proceedings had been taken against anyone for defending them, and whether anyone was still maintaining them in defiance of his own decree.[67] A full report was to be back to Pecham by St. Nicholas's feast. Alas, no report was forthcoming. On December 7, 1284, the archbishop sent additional letters to the chancellor and to Master Fleckham censuring them for their neglect of his letters of November tenth and November fourteenth.[68] In a letter about his meeting with the Dominican prior, Pecham spoke of the "childish disputations" at Oxford that his predecessor had censured.[69] This comment may show that Pecham may have had Kilwardby's prohibitions but could not believe they were actually the condemnations he had heard about.

This situation continued for three years, into the year 1287. Pecham still had not laid his hands on what he believed to be Kilwardby's Oxford Condemnations of 1277. In March of that year, Pecham sent an urgent letter to the bishop of Lincoln, demanding information in regard to Kilwardby's prohibitions and any penal measures that had resulted from them.[70] There was a papal mandate to him asking him to send to the curia a copy of Kilwardby's 1277 Condemnations, and Pecham did not believe he had one. Pecham acknowledged in this letter to the bishop of Lincoln that he acted negligently in omitting to see the much-needed information during his visitation at Oxford. This omission, however, had not hindered him, in the previous year, from including references to Kilwardby's prohibitions in his excommunication of Richard Knapwell (Clapwell) as found in the Annals of Dunstable.[71] If Siger of Brabant and Boethius of Dacia were the targets of the Paris Condemnations, Richard Knapwell became the target of Pecham's crusade against the Thomistic doctrine of "unity of substantial form."

Knapwell, when challenged by Pecham, appealed to the academic nature of Kilwardby's concept of prohibitions rather than condemnations and to Kilwardby's statement that punishment should only be given if a view was held with pertinacity. In his *Quaestiones Ordinariae*, Knapwell distinguished between a condemnation and a prohibition and strongly denied that the thesis of Unity of Form, argued by him, had ever been condemned as heretical.[72] He made the additional point that all the masters of the University of Oxford, regents and non-regents, who were in town at the time of Kilwardby's proclamation and took part at the General Congregation assembled for this purpose, bore witness that this opinion was not condemned. Knapwell argued that he was just exercising his undoubted right as a master to discuss the issue in a cautious fashion as allowed by the restriction, and he ended his work with the words:

> All this is said without pertinacity and without injury or detriment to a better opinion, lest we ascribe to the human nature united to the Word something not belonging to it, or do not attribute something which belongs to it, and thus be found false witnesses of the Word incarnate of the Virgin.[73]

This appeal to free academic discussion, with its "pertinacity" caveat, did not save Knapwell. On April 30, 1286, Archbishop Pecham with his suffragans, selected eight theses taken from the writings of Knapwell, including a statement of the thesis of Unity of Form, and excommunicated all those who maintained them.[74] Included among the accusations was an additional alarming statement suggesting that Knapwell had rejected the Church Fathers and had appealed only to the Bible and direct experience. One feels that this additional charge brought the issue into a radical configuration, somewhat similar to the distortions of the Paris Condemnations. Knapwell gave repeated public denials of this particular radical accusation and set out for the papal court to defend his case in person. When Knapwell arrived in Rome he found that a new pope, however, was on the papal throne, Nicholas IV, a former Franciscan minister general and an old friend of Pecham. Knapwell was ordered never again to discuss the subject of Unity of Form and was sent to or left on his own for a house of his order in Bologna.

What conclusions can be drawn in regard to the two condemnations of 1277? First, the condemnations have little to do directly with Thomas Aquinas. Whether eight references or one, the total is insignificant. This position is argued in full knowledge that in 1325, Stephen de Bourret, a later bishop of Paris, will annul the actions of the Paris Condemnations to the extent that they attacked the theses of Thomas Aquinas.[75] The bishop does not indicate the specific numeration of the annulled articles. In regard to the Oxford Condemnations, Archbishop Kilwardby expressly indicates that the Thomistic doctrine of unity of substantial form is not raised in his articles.

It would seem that Siger of Brabant, Boethius of Dacia, and possibly a handful of the Arts faculty were the ones against whom the Paris Condemnations were directed. Giles of Rome, one of the commission set up by Bishop Tempier, stated that it was only the stubbornness of a few masters that lay behind the propositions.[76] With the Oxford Condemnations, the issue of against whom the condemnations were directed is more difficult. The condemnations could have been a continuation of the controversy concerning the interpretation of Aristotle, or specific works could have triggered Kilwardby's actions. The possibility was also suggested in the present study that the Oxford Condemnations may be an expression, in negative terms, of Kilwardby's own interpretation of Aristotle on the issues of unity and plurality of form.

In relation to the condemnations themselves, we have found a difference between the Paris and Oxford articles. The preface of the Paris document stated that it was seeking those hiding their radical beliefs, fostered by the natural philosophy of Aristotle, within the cloak of Christianity. It thus distorted the views of various scholars in this process of exposure. It was John Pecham who appropriated Kilwardby's Oxford Condemnations for his own use in the controversy with Richard Knapwell. Even though he complains through the whole encounter that he does not have a copy of the 1277 prohibitions, it will be his own added condemnation on the unity of substantial form that will be used to excommunicate Knapwell.

The condemnations of 1277 played a role in the silencing of various scholars. Siger of Brabant, threatened by the inquisition, never returned to teaching. Boethius of Dacia disappeared from the academic scene. Richard Knapwell lost his appeal at the papal curia. Yet within twenty years the Paris scholar Godfrey of Fontaines will comment that at the University of Paris, the Paris Condemnations of 1277 were ignored completely or interpreted in a way entirely contrary to the intentions of their framer. He goes on to say that they were of interest only to "simple minded" masters or those wishing to get a rival into trouble by denouncing him to the chancellor or the bishop as breaking one of the condemnations (Godfrey of Fontaines, *Quod.* xxii, q. 5: "Whether the bishop of Paris sins by failing to correct certain articles condemned by his predecessor").[77] In regard to the Oxford Condemnations, William of Ockham, writing some fifty years later, will raise the issue that some thought Kilwardby had assumed rights of regulating university teaching not entitled by his position, and others wondered that he had dared to include in his condemnations doctrines that were held by many as established truths.

Although the philosophical issues raised by these two condemnations, especially those dealing with the absolute power of God, will continue to be a part of the academic debate over the next century they failed to dominate the intellectual climate of the medieval universities.[78] Ideological doors were slammed but not locked; they swung back to an open position. The actions of the threat of the inquisition and the use of excommunications could not be used on a massive scale with the faculty of the medieval universities who used their hard-won liberty to freely inquire and teach. A sense of academic freedom within the medieval universities ultimately prevailed, a climate that is challenged but staunchly defended even in modern academia.

Appendix
Examples of Editorial Inductions from the
Paris Condemnations of 1277

(As listed in Roland Hissette, *Enquête sur les 219 article condamnés à Paris le 7 mars 1277*, Louvain and Paris: Publications Universitaires, 1977, pp. 316–17. Classification from Pierre Mandonnet, *Siger de Brabant et l'averroisme latin au XIIIme siècle*, vol. 2, *Textes inédits*, 2nd ed., Louvain: Institut Supérior de philosophie de l'Université, 1911, pp. 175–91. English translation by Ernst L. Fortin and Peter D. O'Neill, "Condemnation of 219 Propositions," *Medieval Political Philosophy: A Sourcebook*, ed. Ralph Lerner and Muhsin Mahdi, New York: Free Press, 1963, pp. 337–54.)

A. *Sixteen examples of propositions in which the texts were misunderstood.*

1. Article 8: That our intellect by its own natural power can attain to a knowledge of the first cause.—This does not sound well and is erroneous if what is meant is immediate knowledge.

2. Article 63: That the higher intelligences impress things on the lower, just as one soul impresses things on another and even on a sensitive soul, and that through such an impression a spellbinder is able to cast a camel into a pitfall just by looking at it.

3. Article 93: That some things can take place by chance with respect to the first cause, and that it is false that all things are preordained by the first cause, because then they would come about by necessity.

4. Article 98: That, among the efficient causes, the secondary cause has an action that it did not receive from the first cause.

5. Article 99: That there is more than one mover.

6. Article 109: That a form that has to exist and come to be in matter cannot be produced by an agent that does not produce it from matter.

7. Article 134: That the rational soul, when it departs from an animal, still remains a living animal.

8. Article 151: That the soul wills nothing unless it is moved by another. Hence the following proposition is false: the soul wills by itself.—This is erroneous if what

is meant is that the soul is moved by another, namely by something desirable or an object in such a way that the desirable thing or object is the whole reason for the movement of the will itself.

9. Article 152: That all voluntary movements are reduced to the first mover.—This is erroneous unless one is speaking of the simply first, uncreated mover and of movement according to its substance, not according to its deformity.

10. Article 153: That the will and the intellect are not moved in act by themselves but by an eternal cause, namely the heavenly bodies.

11. Article 157: That when two goods are proposed, the stronger moves more strongly.—This is erroneous unless one is speaking from the standpoint of the good that moves.

12. Article 160: That it is impossible for the will not to will when it is in the disposition in which it is natural for it to be moved and when that which by nature moves remains so disposed.

13. Article 188: That it is not true that something comes from nothing or was made in the first creation.

14. Article 191: That the natural philosopher has to deny absolutely the newness of the world because he bases himself on natural causes and natural reasons, whereas the faithful can deny the eternity of the world because he bases himself on supernatural causes.

15. Article 194: That material things cannot be created.

16. Article 210: That perfect abstinence from the act of the flesh corrupts virtue and the species.

B. *Nine examples of propositions in which the thought of the author was hardened beyond what the author intended.*

1. Article 1: That there is no more excellent state than to study philosophy.

2. Article 46: That the separated substances are the same as their essences because in them that by which they are and that which they are, is the same.

3. Article 49: That the separated substances are infinite in act; for infinity is not impossible except in material things.

4. Article 66: That God could not move the heaven in a straight line, the reason being that He would then leave a vacuum.

5. Article 80: That the reasoning of the Philosopher proving that the motion of the heaven is eternal is not sophistic, and that it is surprising that profound men do not perceive this.

6. Article 86: That eternity and time have no existence in reality but only in the mind.

7. Article 116: That individuals of the same species differ solely by the position of matter, like Socrates and Plato, and that since the human form existing in each is numerically the same, it is not surprising that the same being numerically is in different places.

8. Article 170: That all the good that is possible to man consists in the intellectual virtues.

9. Article 171: That a man who is ordered as to his intellect and his affections, in the manner in which this can be sufficiently accomplished by means of the intellectual and moral virtues of which the philosopher speaks in the *Ethics*, is sufficiently disposed for eternal happiness.

C. *Ten examples of propositions in which those who compiled the condemnations isolated a phrase from its context and stretched its meaning beyond that intended by the author.*

1. Article 2: That the only wise men in the world are the philosophers.

2. Article 6: That there is no rationally disputable question that the philosopher ought not to dispute and determine, because reasons are derived from things. It belongs to philosophy under one or other of its parts to consider all things.

3. Article 13: That God does not know things other than himself.

4. Article 141: That the possible intellect is nothing in act before it understands, because in the case of an intelligible nature to be something in act is to be actually understanding.

5. Article 177: That raptures and visions are caused only by nature.

6. Article 211: That humility, in the degree to which one does not show what he has but depreciates and lowers himself, is not a virtue.—This is erroneous if what is meant is: neither a virtue nor a virtuous act.

7. Article 214: That God cannot grant perpetuity to a changeable and corruptible thing.

8. Article 215: That it does not happen that a corrupted body recurs numerically the same, and it will not rise numerically the same.

9. Article 216: That a philosopher must not concede the resurrection to come, because it cannot be investigated by reason.—This is erroneous because even a philosopher must "bring his mind into captivity to the obedience of Christ."

10. Article 218: That nothing can be known about the intellect after its separation.

D. *Examples in which the compilers of the condemnations ascribed to an author a doctrine taught only from a limited point of view and did not take under consideration such restrictions as "natural philosophy" or developed according to the "intention of the philosophers" (secundum intentionem philosophorum) or rejected entirely by the Master.*

1. Article 3: That in order to have some certitude about any conclusion, man must base himself on self-evident principles.—The statement is erroneous because it refers in a general way both to the certitude of apprehension and to that of adherence.

2. Article 4: That one should not hold anything unless it is self-evident or can be manifested from self evident principles.

3. Article 5: That man should not be content with authority to have certitude about any question.

4. Article 7: That, beside the philosophic disciplines, all the sciences are necessary but that they are necessary only on account of human custom.

5. Article 16: That the first cause is the most remote cause of all things.—This is erroneous if so understood as to mean that it is not the most proximate.

6. Article 18: That what is self-determined, like God, either always acts or never acts, and that many things are eternal.

7. Article 20: That God of necessity makes whatever comes immediately from Him.—This is erroneous whether we are speaking of the necessity of coercion, which destroys liberty, or of the necessity of immutability, which implies the inability to do otherwise.

8. Article 21: That from a previous act of the will nothing new can proceed unless it is preceded by a change.

9. Article 22: That God cannot be the cause of a newly made thing and cannot produce anything new.

10. Article 23: That God cannot move anything irregularly, that is, in a manner other than that in which He does, because there is no diversity of will in Him.

11. Article 24: That God is eternal in acting and moving, just as He is eternal in existing; otherwise He would be determined by some other thing that would be prior to Him.

12. Article 26: That God has infinite power in duration, not in action, since there is no such infinity except in an infinite body, if there were such a thing.

13. Article 27: That the first cause cannot make more than one world.

14. Article 28: That from the first agent there cannot proceed a multiplicity of effects.

15. Article 33: That the immediate effect of the first being has to be one only and most like unto the first being.

16. Article 34: That God is the necessary cause of the first intelligence, which cause being posited, the effect is also posited, and both are equal in duration.

17. Article 35: That God never created an intelligence more than He now creates it.

18. Article 36: That the absolutely first unmoved being does not move save through the mediation of something moved, and that such a unmoved mover is a part of that which is moved of itself.

19. Article 37: That the first principle is not the proper cause of eternal beings except metaphorically, in so far as it conserves them, for unless it was, they would not be.

20. Article 38: That the intelligences, or separated substances, which they say are eternal, do not have an efficient cause properly speaking, but only metaphorically, in so far as they have a cause conserving them in existence; but they were not newly made, because then they would be mutable.

21. Article 39: That all the separated substances are coeternal with the first principle.

22. Article 40: That everything that does not have matter is eternal, because that which was not made through a change in matter did not exist previously; therefore it is eternal.

23. Article 41: That the separated substances, having no matter through which they would be in potency before being in act and being from a cause that always exists in the same manner, are therefore eternal.

24. Article 44: That no change is possible in the separated substances, nor are they in potency to anything because they are eternal and free from matter.

25. Article 45: That the intelligence is made by God in eternity because it is totally immutable; the soul of the heaven, however, is not.

26. Article 56: That the separated substances by means of their intellect create things.

27. Article 57: That an intelligence receives its existence from God through mediating intelligences.

30. Article 59: That an angel is not in potency to opposite acts immediately but only through the mediating agency of something else, such as a sphere.

31. Article 61: That since an intelligence is full of forms, it impresses those forms on matter by using the heavenly bodies as instruments.

32. Article 62: That external matter obeys the spiritual substance.—This is erroneous if understood absolutely and according to every mode of change.

33. Article 64: That God is the necessary cause of the motion of the higher bodies and of the union and separation occurring in the stars.

34. Article 67: That the first principle cannot produce generable things immediately because they are new effects and a new effect requires an immediate cause that is capable of being otherwise.

35. Article 68: That the first principle cannot be the cause of diverse products here below without the mediation of other causes, inasmuch as nothing that transforms, transforms in diverse ways without being itself transformed.

36. Article 70: That God is able to produce contraries, that is, through the medium of a heavenly body which occupies diverse places.

37. Article 71: That the nature that is the principle of motion in the heavenly bodies is a moving intelligence.—This is erroneous if what is meant is the intrinsic nature, which is act or form.

38. Article 72: That the heavenly bodies have of themselves eternity of substance but not eternity of motion.

39. Article 73: That the heavenly bodies are moved by an intrinsic principle, which is the soul, and that they are moved by a soul and an appetitive power, like an animal. For just as an animal is moved by desiring, so also is the heaven.

40. Article 78: That there would be nothing new if the heaven were not varied with respect to the matter of generable things.

41. Article 81: That a sphere is the immediate efficient cause of all forms.

42. Article 82: That if in some humor by the power of the stars such a proportion could be achieved as is found in the seed of the parents, a man could be generated from that humor; and thus a man could be adequately generated from putrefaction.

43. Article 83: That the world, although it was made from nothing, was not newly made, and, although it passed from non-being to being, the non-being did not precede being in duration but only in nature.

44. Article 85: That the world is eternal as regards all the species contained in it, and that time, motion, matter, agent, and receiver are eternal, because the world

comes from the infinite power of God and it is impossible that there be something new in the effect without there being something new in the cause.

45. Article 88: That time is infinite as regards both extremes, for although it is impossible for an infinity to be passed through when one of its parts had to be passed through, it is not impossible for an infinity to be passed through when one of its parts had to be passed through.

46. Article 89: That it is impossible to refute the arguments of the Philosopher concerning the eternity of the world unless we say that the will of the first being embraces incompatibles.

47. Article 92: That with all the heavenly bodies coming back to the same point after a period of thirty-six thousand years, the same effects as now exist will reappear.

48. Article 94: That fate, which is the disposition of the universe, proceeds from divine providence, not immediately, but mediately through the motion of the higher bodies, and that this fate does not impose necessity upon the lower beings, since they have contrariety, but upon the higher.

49. Article 95: That for all the effects to be necessary with respect to the first cause, it does not suffice that the first cause itself be not impedible, but it is also necessary that the intermediary causes be not impedible.—This is erroneous because then God could not produce a necessary effect without posterior causes.

50. Article 96: That beings depart from the order of the first cause considered in itself, although not in relation to the other causes operating in the universe.—This is erroneous because the order of beings to the first cause is more essential and more inseparable than their order to the lower causes.

51. Article 101: That no agent is in potency to one or the other of two things; on the contrary, it is determined.

52. Article 102: That nothing happens by chance, but everything comes about by necessity, and that all the things that will exist in the future will exist by necessity, and those that will not exist are impossible, and that nothing occurs contingently if all causes are considered.—This is erroneous because the concurrence of causes is included in the definition of chance, as Boethius says in his book *On Consolation*.

53. Article 107: That God was not able to make prime matter save through the mediation of a heavenly body.

54. Article 108: That, just as nothing can come from matter without an agent, so also nothing can come from an agent without matter, and that God is not an efficient cause except with respect to that which has its existence in the potency of matter.

55. Article 111: That the elements were produced from chaos by an antecedent generation, but they are eternal.

56. Article 112: That the elements are eternal. They were nevertheless newly produced in the disposition that they now possess.

57. Article 115: That God could not make several numerically different souls.

58. Article 150: That that which by its nature is not determined to being or nonbeing is not determined except by something that is necessary with respect to itself.

59. Article 176: That God or the intelligence does not infuse science into the human soul during sleep except through the mediation of a heavenly body.

60. Article 189: That creation is not possible, even though the contrary must be held according to the faith.

61. Article 190: That he who generates the world in its totality posits a vacuum, because place necessarily precedes that which is generated in it; and so before the generation of the world there would have been a place with nothing in it, which is a vacuum.

62. Article 196: That to make an accident exist without a subject has the nature of an impossibility implying contradiction.

63. Article 197: That God cannot make an accident exist without a subject or make more than one dimension exist simultaneously.

64. Article 198: That an accident existing without a subject is not an accident except in an equivocal sense, and that it is impossible for quantity or dimension to exist by itself, for this would make it a substance.

65. Article 199: That since God is not related to beings as a material or formal cause, he does not make an accident exist without a subject, inasmuch as it is of the nature of an accident to exist actually in a subject.

66. Article 213: That death is the end of all terrors.—This statement is erroneous if it excludes the terror of hell, which is the last.

Notes

My thanks to Biola University for a faculty research grant that aided in the completion of this study. Those sections dealing with the Oxford condemnations are developed from an earlier version read at the "Symposium on the Early University" at California State University–Northridge, October, 1988, and at the Medieval Congress, Medieval Institute, Western Michigan University, May, 1989, under the title "The Oxford Condemnations of 1277 and the Intellectual Climate of the Medieval University." The Medieval Congress paper along an English translation of the Oxford Condemnations of 1277 are now published in *Aspectus et Affectus*, Festschrift for Richard C. Dales, New York: AMS Press, 1992, pp. 129–42. An earlier version of portions of this paper dealing with the Paris Condemnations of 1277 was delivered at the Biennial Convention of Phi Alpha Theta, the International History Honor Society, St. Louis, Mo., December, 1989, under the title "Siger of Brabant in Paradise?: Radicalism and Structure in the Medieval University." A later version of this paper was read for the conference "Universities and their Contexts of Power: Cases Medieval and Modern," History Guild of Southern California, April 2, 1992.

1. John F. Wippel, "The Condemnations of 1270 and 1277 in Paris," *The Journal of Medieval and Renaissance Studies* 7 (1977), 169–201.

2. Etienne Gilson, *History of Christian Philosophy in the Middle Ages* (New York: Random House, 1955), p. 728, n. 52.

3. Theodore Crowley, "John Peckham, O.F.M., Archbishop of Canterbury versus the New Aristotelianism," *Bulletin of the John Rylands Library* 33 (1950–51), 242–55.

4. Roland Hissette, *Enquête sur les 219 articles condamnés à Paris le 7 mars 1277* (Louvain and Paris: Publications universitaires, 1977), p. 314.

5. *Chartularium Universitatis Parisiensis* (hereafter *CUP*), ed. Heinrich Denifle and Emile Chatelain, 4 vols. (Paris: Ex Typis Fratrum Delalain, 1889), 1: 543.

6. *CUP*, 1: 541.

7. A. Callebaut, "Jean Pecham, O.F.M. et L'Augustinisme. Aperçus Historiques (1263–1285)," *Archivum Franciscanum Historicum* 18 (1925), 459–60.

8. *Registrum epistolarum fratris Johannis Peckham, archiepiscopi cantuariensis*, ed. Charles T. Martin, 3 vols. (London: Longman, 1882–85), 3: 866.

9. *Registrum . . . Peckham*, ed. Martin, 3: 866, 871.

10. Maurice de Wulf, *Histoire de la philosophie médiévale*, 6th ed., vol. 2 (Louvain: Institut Supérieur de Philosophie/Vrin, 1936), p. 256.

11. Henry F. Nardone, "St. Thomas and the Condemnation of 1277" (diss., The Catholic University of America, 1963), pp. 63–68.

12. Wippel, "The Condemnations of 1270 and 1277 in Paris," p. 170.

13. Daniel A. Callus, *The Condemnation of St. Thomas at Oxford*, 2nd ed. (London: Aquin Press, 1955).

14. Franz Ehrle, "Der Augustinismus und der Aristotelismus in der Scholastik gegen Ende des 13. Jahrhunderts, Beiträge zur Geschichte der mittelalterlichen Scholastik II," *Archiv für Literatur- und Kirchengeschichte des Mittelalters* 5 (1889), 614–32; and Aleksander Birkenmajer, "Der Brief Robert Kilwardbys an Peter von Conflans und die Streitschrift des Agidius von Lessines," *Vermischte Untersuchungen zur Geschichte der Mittelalterlichen Philosophie* (Münster: Aschendorff, 1922), pp. 46–69.

15. Birkenmajer, "Der Brief Robert Kilwardbys," p. 60.

16. Maur Burbach, "Early Dominican and Franciscan Legislation Regarding St. Thomas," *Medieval Studies* 4 (1942), 139–58.

17. Ellen M. F. Sommer-Seckendorff, *Studies in the Life of Robert Kilwardby, O.P.* (Rome: Istituto Storico Domenicano, 1937), p. 129.

18. Wippel, "The Condemnations of 1270 and 1277 in Paris," p. 170; and Leland E. Wilshire, "Were the Oxford Condemnations Directed Against Aquinas?" *New Scholasticism* 48 (1974), 125–32.

19. Armand Maurer, "Henry of Harclay's Disputed Question on the Plurality of Forms,"

in *Essays in Honour of Anton Charles Pegis*, ed. J. Reginald O'Donnell (Toronto: Pontifical Institute of Mediaeval Studies, 1974), pp. 125–60.

20. Jeremiah O'Callaghan, "The Second Question of the Prologue to Walter Catton's Commentary of the Sentences, on Intuitive and Abstractive Knowledge," in *Nine Medieval Thinkers: A Collection of Hitherto Unedited Texts*, ed. J. Reginald O'Donnell (Toronto: Pontifical Institute of Mediaeval Studies, 1955), pp. 233–61.

21. Hissette, *Enquête sur les 219 articles condamnés à Paris,* p. 314.

22. MS Paris, Bibl. Nat. lat. 4391, fol. 68; and MS Paris. Bibl, Nat. lat. 16533, fol. 60.

23. MS Paris, Bibl. Nat. lat. 15.450. fol. 80.

24. B. E. Bykhovskii, "Siger of Brabant—A Beacon of Light in the Darkness of Scholasticism," *Soviet Studies in Philosophy* 17 (1978), 80–98.

25. Eric Voegelin, "Siger of Brabant," *Philosophy and Phenomenological Research* 4 (1943–44), 507–25.

26. Pierre Mandonnet, *Siger de Brabant et l'averroisme latin au XIIIme siècle*, vol. 2, *Textes inédits*, 2nd ed. (1908; Louvain: Institut Superior de philosophie de l'Universite, 1911).

27. Fernand van Steenberghen, "Siger of Brabant," *The Modern Schoolman* 29 (1951–52), 11–27.

28. Stuart Mac Clintock, "An Approach to the Problem of Latin Averroism," *The Review of Metaphysics* 8 (1954–55), 176–99, 342–56, 526–45.

29. Steenberghen, "Siger of Brabant," p. 17.

30. Alfred J. Rahilly, "Averroism and Scholasticism," *Studies, An Irish Quarterly Review of Letters, Philosophy and Science* 2 (1913), 322.

31. Edward P. Mahoney, "Saint Thomas and Siger of Brabant Revisited," *The Review of Metaphysics* 27 (1973–74), 550.

32. *CUP*, 1: 481.

33. *CUP*, 1: 540–41.

34. Thomas Aquinas, *On the Unity of the Intellect against the Averroists*, trans. Beatrice H. Zedler (Milwaukee, Wis.: Marquette University Press, 1968), p. 75.

35. Armand Mauer, "Siger of Brabant and Theology," *Mediaeval Studies* 50 (1988), 273.

36. *On the Unity of the Intellect,* trans. Zedler, p. 74.

37. Thomas P. Bukowski, "Siger of Brabant vs. Thomas Aquinas on Theology," *New Scholasticism* 61 (1987), 30–31.

38. Mauer, "Siger of Brabant and Theology," p. 274.

39. *CUP*, 1: 521–30.

40. *CUP*, 1: 558–560.

41. Ehrle, "Der Augustinismus und der Aristotelismus in der Scholastik," p. 614.

42. Ehrle, "Der Augustinismus und der Aristotelismus in der Scholastik," p. 614.

43. *CUP*, 1: 558–59; and Leland E. Wilshire, "The Oxford Condemnations of 1277 and the Intellectual Climate of the Medieval University," in *Aspectus et Affectus: Essays and Editions in Grosseteste and Medieval Intellectual Life in Honor of Richard C. Dales*, ed. Gunar Freibergs (New York: AMS, 1993), pp. 129–42.

44. P. Osmund Lewry, "The Oxford Condemnations of 1277 in Grammar and Logic," in *English Logic and Semantics from the End of the Twelfth Century to the Time of Ockham and Burleigh*, ed. H. A. G. Braakhuis, C . H. Kneepkens, and Lambertus M. de Rijk (Nijmegen: Ingenium, 1981), pp. 235–78.

45. Dorothea E. Sharp, "The *De Ortu Scientiarum* of Robert Kilwardby," *New Scholasticism* 8 (1934), 23.1–30.

46. *CUP*, 1: 559; and Wilshire, "The Oxford Condemnations of 1277," pp. 129–42.

47. Daniel A. Callus, "The Function of the Philosopher in Thirteenth-Century Oxford," *Beiträge zum Berufbewusstsein des mittelalterlichen Menschen, Miscellanea Mediaevalia* 3 (1964), 160–61; for edited text, see Gedeon Gàl, "Commentarius in 'Metaphysicam' Aristotelis cod. Vat. lat. 4538 fons doctrinae Richardi Rufi," *Archivum Franciscanum Historicum* 43 (1950), 209–42.

48. Dorothea E. Sharp, "The 1277 Condemnation by Kilwardby," *New Scholasticism* 8 (1934), 308.

49. Dorothea E. Sharp, "Further Philosophical Doctrines of Kilwardby, *New Scholasticism* 9 (1935), 55.

50. Sharp, "Further Philosophical Doctrines," p. 55.

51. "Condemnations of 219 Propositions," trans. Ernst L. Fortin and Peter D. O'Niell, in *Medieval Political Philosophy: A Sourcebook*, ed. Ralph Lerner and Muhsin Mahdi (New York: Free Press, 1963), pp. 337–38.

52. "The Parisian Condemnations of 1270," in *Medieval Philosophy from St. Augustine to Nicholas of Cusa*, trans. and ed. J. Wippel and Allan Wolter (New York: Free Press, 1969), p. 366.

53. Fernand van Steenberghen, *Aristotle in the West: The Origins of Latin Aristotelianism*, trans. L. Johnson (Louvain: Nauwelaerts, 1955), pp. 172–73.

54. Bonaventure, *In Hexaemeron,* quoted in Gilson, *History of Christian Philosophy in the Middle Ages*, p. 727.

55. "Condemnations of 219 Propositions," trans. Fortin and O'Niell, pp. 337–38.

56. Gilson, *History of Christian Philosophy*, p. 404.

57. Hissette, *Enquête sur les 219 articles*, pp. 316–17; for the complete list see the appendix to this study, "Examples of Editorial Inductions from the Paris Condemnations of 1277."

58. Hissette, *Enquête sur les 219 articles,* pp. 316–17; see also appendix to this study.

59. Armand Maurer, "Siger of Brabant on Fables and Falsehoods in Religion," *Mediaeval Studies* 43 (1981), 515–30.

60. Maurer, "Siger of Brabant on Fables and Falsehoods," p. 526.

61. Boethius of Dacia, *On the Supreme Good, On the Eternity of the World, On Dreams,* trans. John F. Wippel (Toronto: Pontifical Institute of Medieval Studies, 1987), p. 6.

62. Wippel, *A Translation of Boethius of Dacia*, p. 17.

63. Mahoney, "Saint Thomas and Siger of Brabant Revisited," pp. 531–53.

64. Ehrle, "Der Augustinismus und der Aristotelismus in der Scholastik," p. 614.

65. *Annales de Oseneia*, vol. 4 of *Annales Monastici*, ed. Henry R. Luard (London: Longman, Roberts, and Green, 1869), pp. 297–99.

66. *Memorandum, Registrum Johannis de Pontissara, Episcopi Wyntoniensis* A.D. *MCCLXXXII–MCCLV*, ed. Cecil Deedes, vol. 1 (London: Canturbury and York Society, 1915), pp. 307–08; and *Registrum . . . Peckham*, ed. Martin, 3: 840–43.

67. *Registrum . . . Peckham*, 3: 852–53.

68. *Registrum . . . Peckham*, 3: 862–63.

69. *Registrum . . . Peckham*, 3: 866.

70. *Registrum . . . Peckham*, 3: 944–45.

71. *Annales Prioratus de Dunstaplia,* vol. 3 of *Annales Monastici*, p. 325.

72. MS Bologna, Biblioteca Universitaria, 1539, 51r–54v.

73. MS Bologna, Biblioteca Universitaria, 1539, 54v.

74. *Registrum . . . Peckham*, 3: 921–23.

75. *CUP*, 2: 281.

76. Mandonnet, *Siger de Brabant*, 1: 231.

77. Marie-Hyacinthe Laurent, "Godefroid de Fontaines et la Condamnation de 1277," *Revue Thomiste* 35 (1930), 275–81.

78. Edward Grant, "The Condemnation of 1277, God's Absolute Power, and Physical Thought in the Late Middle Ages," *Viator* 10 (1979), 211–44.

The Schoolmen

Allan B. Wolter, O.F.M.

*L*et me begin by explaining the title of this essay. "The schoolmen" refers to the university-trained professionals of the Middle Ages. "Scholasticism" is the corresponding educational movement that bred them. A view of scholasticism is that it began in the twelfth century, climaxed around the middle of the thirteenth century, and continued into the first part of the fourteenth century. Scholasticism waned when the "black plague" or bubonic fever struck Europe between 1347 and 1350, destroying between a quarter and a third of the European population.

During the preceding "dark ages," when the barbarians overran Europe and gradually crumbled the Roman Empire, it was the monasteries that preserved the classics of ancient learning. Monks copied these works down in precious illuminated manuscripts. From monastic scriptoria missionaries set out not only to convert but also to educate the barbarians. In 800, when Charlemagne became the first Holy Roman Emperor, he sought out teachers to educate his children and those of his knights and nobles.[1] In his own palace he set up a school like those in the more famous abbeys. As the great cathedrals were built in the larger cities, the canons who daily recited the Divine Office there also set up schools: cathedral schools. When at the time of St. Francis a new form of religious life, the mendicant orders, came into existence, these orders too built study houses near other schools so that qualified religious among them could study theology. These clusters of schools became known as "universities" because the papal bulls encouraging their growth and bestowing on them special privileges always began with the phrase "Universitas vestra"—which can be translated as "all of you" or "you-all."

As for the curriculum, the undergraduate program was that of the seven liberal arts: the trivium (grammar, rhetoric, and logic or dialectics) and the quadrivium (arithmetic, geometry, astronomy, and music), leading to graduate studies in one of three areas—medicine, civil and canon law, or theology—and, respectively, the degree of Doctor of Medicine, Doctor of Laws, or Master of Theology.[2]

As I recall, my seminary textbook attributed the great interest in studies that reached its climax or golden age in the mid-thirteenth century to three factors: 1) the creation of universities; 2) the introduction of Aristotle's systematic philosophy; and 3) the existence of the new mendicant orders, particularly the Dominicans and Franciscans.[3] To what I have already said about the universities, let me add a word about the methodology of the schoolmen before turning to Aristotle's philosophy and the mendicant orders.

The scholastic method grew out of Abelard's famous work *Sic et non*. Up to his time it was customary to teach theology by citing various scriptural passages with comments from the Fathers of the Church. Abelard gathered a collection of these passages and comments showing that on any given subject one could find opposing views. "Sic" (it is so) refers to texts in favor of something; "non" means this is not so. Take "peace," for example. Lk. 1: 78–79 promises the Messiah as the "day-spring" who "has visited us . . . to guide our feet into the way of peace." And when Jesus is about to leave this earth he assures his disciples: "Peace is my farewell gift to you, my peace is my gift to you" (Jn. 14: 27). Yet in Matt. 10: 4–36 Christ says the very opposite: "Do not suppose that my mission on earth is to spread peace. My mission is to spread not peace but division. I have come to set a man at odds with his father, a daughter with her mother, a daughter-in-law with her mother-in-law; in short to make a man's enemies those of his own household" (see also Lk. 12: 51–53). As with the Scriptures so too with the Fathers of the Church. In their works one can find statements for and against almost every important topic. In his *Sic et non* Abelard's idea was not to discredit the authority of the Bible or the Fathers but to show that some rational analysis was required in interpreting them, thus giving rise to a rational or philosophical analysis of theological truths. Peter

Lombard, for the benefit of the theological student whose poverty prevented him from owning a library that contained the works of the Fathers of the Church, drew up a four-volume collection of opinions or "sentences," in which he cited the most important texts from the Fathers on just about every important theological topic. Book I deals with God as one and triune; Book II with creation, the Fall, the angels, and the sin of our first parents; Book III with the Incarnation, redemption, virtues, and the ten commandments; and Book IV with the sacraments and the four last things, namely, death, judgement, hell, and heaven. This collection, through the influence of the great Franciscan theologian Alexander of Hales, became the university textbook of theology. Bachelors of theology gave a course based on all four books of these sentences of Peter Lombard, in which they gave arguments both for (*sic*) and against (*non*) their personal views on any theological topic. Only when they had covered the whole field with their own "Commentary on the Sentences" were they eligible to become Masters of Theology.

What of Aristotelianism? Aristotle had dealt with all the topics of curriculum in a systematic way in what came to be called "Philosophy" (which means "Love of Wisdom," the wise man being one who knows the causes or reasons for anything). His philosophy gradually replaced the liberal arts undergraduate program.[4] It comprised, first, logic as a systematic tool of reasoning; then three branches of theoretical philosophy (physics, the Greek term for all the natural sciences; mathematics; and metaphysics or natural theology); and, finally, three branches of practical philosophy (ethics, politics, and economics) together with poetic philosophy (which corresponds to our version of literature). Because theologians were always trying to justify their beliefs by showing their reasonableness, they turned eagerly to Aristotle's philosophy to explain and support their theological opinions.[5] Earlier, St. Augustine, one of the most influential of the Fathers of the Church, had said "I believe in order that I may understand" ("Credo ut intelligam"). St. Anselm of Canterbury, the Father of scholasticism, gave this movement its slogan or motto in a work entitled "Faith Seeking Understanding," later called *Proslogion*. When Aristotle's works were introduced into their undergraduate program, it was natural for Masters of the Arts who were continuing on for graduate theology to apply Aristotle's ideas as the rational basis for their theological views.

It was at this juncture that the third ingredient of scholasticism enters the university scene, namely, the mendicant orders of Franciscans and Dominicans. Both orders were concerned in a special way with preaching sound Christian doctrine to refute heretical movements in thirteenth-century Europe. As a matter of fact, Francis's was the first religious rule to introduce the ministry of preaching as an integral part of a perfect life according to the Gospel.[6] St. Dominic went even further, expressly naming his followers the "Order of Preachers." One cannot preach effectively, however, without some training in the Scriptures and systematic and moral theology. Hence, the Dominican and Franciscan friars set up study houses in the university cities. No sooner had the friars invaded the university campuses than their religious fervor and piety influenced theological students and masters of good will to join their ranks, and so many were the trained theologians among them that the Franciscans and Dominicans were referred to as the two "study orders" to distinguish them from the older monastic orders.[7]

Some, particularly the so-called "spirituals" among the Franciscans, opposed this intellectual and educational trend and argued that Francis was opposed to studies, because of his insistence in chapter 10 of the Rule that "those who are ignorant of letters should not be anxious to learn." However, this argument overlooked the fact that Francis was referring in chapter 10 to lay brothers who in his day were, by and large, unable to read. Clerics, in contrast, were encouraged by Francis to study, especially theology, and Francis himself appointed St. Anthony as their first lector or teacher. Among Francis's letters we have this: "To Brother Anthony, my bishop, Brother Francis sends greetings. It is agreeable to me that you should teach the friars sacred theology, so long as they do not extinguish the spirit of prayer and devotedness over this study, as is contained in the Rule. Farewell."[8] (Note: Bartholomew of Pisa says Francis called Anthony his "bishop" because of the great love and reverence he had for him, just as he called the Cardinal Protector of his order his "pope" or father.[9]) Bartholomew also wrote: "The purpose of study for a Friar Minor is to understand the sacred page, that from it he may know how to defend the faith and instruct the people."[10] He goes on to say that the learned men of the order have always been true to this purpose and that the people they ministered to were flooded with instructive and encouraging writings by the friars. Though the friars were primarily interested in theology, other knowledge (especially philosophy) was necessary as a preparation for theological studies. Furthermore, even studies of profane subjects were useful to their work. J. S. Brewer, a Protestant scholar, writes: "The care which the Franciscans took of the sick and of the lepers itself led them to the study of the natural sciences. The first systematic studies in medicine and in natural philosophy came from the friars. Experimental physics began with them."[11]

The first Franciscan study house was that set up at the university center of Bologna by Pope Gregory IX (formerly Cardinal Hugolinus, Francis's friend and protector). At that time Bologna was the most famous school of law but had no theological faculty. But so famous was this Franciscan theological house that even seculars came to study there, and in 1360 by papal decree it became the university faculty of theology.[12]

The second Franciscan center of learning was at Paris, famed for its arts program and theological faculty. Among the many admirers among the Parisian masters who themselves joined the Franciscan order was Alexander of Hales,[13] perhaps the greatest theologian of the time. He was already in his fifties and held a chair at the university when he entered the order, thus giving the Franciscans a university chair of theology.

The third most important Franciscan study house was at Oxford. Agnellus of Pisa brought the first Franciscans to England in 1228. Four years later, encouraged by their great friend Robert Grosseteste, chancellor of the University of Oxford, Agnellus erected a house of studies there and engaged Grosseteste to teach theology to his friars. Master Robert was also known for his studies in science, so that the Franciscan school at Oxford was well acquainted not only with theology but also with the science of its day. As chancellor of the university and later bishop of Lincoln (the diocese in which Oxford was located), Robert Grosseteste, though he never joined the order himself, so admired the friars that he left them as his deathbed legacy his valuable library.

Because of its many trained teachers, the English province became and remained a model to the entire order. The Minister General, John of Parma, whom the "spirituals" regarded as one of their own, when he visited England exclaimed: "Would that such a province were placed in the middle of the earth that it might serve as an example to all the churches!"[14]

Alexander of Hales

Of these three university centers, however, that of Paris was the most prestigious, and almost all of the most famous Franciscan schoolmen studied or taught there at some time or other. Also, all the provinces of the order sought to get teachers trained in Paris for their study houses. The list of notables began with Alexander of Hales, who gave Franciscans their first chair of theology. He was soon joined by Master John of La Rochelle (Rupella), who gave Franciscans a second teaching chair, followed by Eudes Rigaud (Odo Rigaldus), later archbishop of Rouen. (In a day when no seminaries existed for adequately training candidates for the priesthood, the popes continually looked to university graduates and former professors for worthy candidates for the episcopate and as effective leaders who would foster religious life and maintain a zealous and fervent clergy in their dioceses.)

Apart from the tasks entrusted to him by the pope and his reform of the educational system of his day, Alexander left a rich legacy of theological writings, written both before and after he became a friar. He also made the first literal commentary on Peter Lombard's *Sentences*, dividing it into appropriate distinctions so that it might be used more effectively as the basic textbook for bachelors of theology as a guideline for their lectures. This use of the *Sentences* was quickly adopted at the other important universities. Alexander was also responsible for initiating the creation of the first "Summa of Theology." It served as a research source book or theological encyclopedia for the Franciscan students as well as for the many secular students who flocked to their schools. Based largely on his own magisterial questions and those of Rupella and Odo Rigaldus, the *Summa fratris Alexandri*, as Alexander's summa came to be called, contained the latest opinions on the whole of theology,

arranged in a more systematic and practical way than distinctions of
Peter Lombard's *Sentences*. Though it was incomplete when he and
Rupella died in 1245, the pope himself thought it so important that he
commanded the fourth Franciscan master of theology, William of
Melitona, to bring it to completion, something the papacy has never done
for any other "Summa," even that of St. Thomas. So large was this work
that Roger Bacon described it as "pondus unius equi" (the weight of one
horse). Historians were never sure whether this described the *Summa*
itself or indicated that one horse was required to carry it.

St. Bonaventure

The most famous of the Franciscan theologians of Paris was John of
Fidanza, who, on entering the order, took the name Bonaventure. No
name could have been more appropriate. Alexander of Hales is reputed
to have said. "In him Adam never sinned." Bonaventure's splendid
natural gifts, his beauty of soul, and his manly external appearance
brought under his spell everyone who came in contact with him. Not
only was Bonaventure a profound thinker and an outstanding Scripture
scholar but also he had one of the most beautiful and mellifluous Latin
styles. Literally it sings to you. As a university preacher he must have
been as famous as Fulton Sheen in his day. Had he remained in studies
his output would have surpassed that of the most famous Dominican
teacher, St. Thomas Aquinas. But when the pope requested that John of
Parma, the Minister General of the Franciscans, resign—because of the
accusations of Joachimism against him—John called a general chapter
of the order at which he declared to the assembled friars that there was
no more worthy individual in the entire order who should succeed him
than Bonaventure.

Let me digress for a moment on the menace of Joachimism, which
threatened to split and destroy the Franciscan order at this time. Joachim
of Fiore (d. 1202) circulated mystical ideas on the basis of a questionable historical theology; he held, for instance, that the unity of the
separate divine persons in the Trinity was one of collaboration or
cooperation rather than that of possessing one individual divine nature.
Each person had its own historical age: the Father represented the Old

Testament and the aged; the Son the New Testament and the young; the Holy Spirit the yet unborn and the age to come (approximately around the year 1260). In this new age all the structural organization of the Church would be dissolved. It would be replaced by a spiritual unity; the written gospels would be replaced by an unwritten "eternal gospel"; and a special religious order would arise that went back to the simplicity of the gospel. Those dissatisfied with the Franciscan intellectual movement that led to the building of large convents for students and the gathering of books into big libraries, like that of Assisi, claimed that the ideals of poverty and simplicity of Francis's early followers were being destroyed. As the poet Jacopone da Todi put it: "Paris is destroying Assisi!" Such as these welcomed the ideas of Joachim. This was especially true of Gerard of Borgo San Donnino, who wrote an anonymous work entitled "Introduction to the Eternal Gospel," in which he claimed that Franciscans represented the special religious order Joachim referred to in his prophecy. This aroused the ire of the secular masters at Paris, who were warring with the friars at the moment, a conflict to be explained as follows.

The festive celebrations before the beginning of Lent (the Mardi Gras) were often marked by "town and gown" disputes. On two notable occasions these celebrations even caused the university to go on strike. One occurred in 1229 and was instrumental in the development of medieval Aristotelianism. Though Aristotle's works might be studied privately by the masters of arts, the Church had forbidden the University of Paris to use these works as classroom textbooks until certain errors in them were corrected. Among the objectionable doctrines was Aristotle's contention that the world was eternal, not created in time; another was that the planetary movements somehow deterministically controlled even the human will. When the university shut down during the 1229 strike and masters and students left for other cities, however, they were no longer bound by this restriction, and the masters welcomed the opportunity to read Aristotle's works openly in their classroom lectures. As for the cause of the 1229 Mardi Gras strike, it began with a tavern dispute about a drinking bill. The keeper had his "bouncer" beat up the delinquent student; on the next day the students came back in force and tore up the tavern, set the spigots of wine flowing, and created general havoc; the innkeeper retaliated by appealing to Queen Blanche, who called in the gendarmes. They attacked and killed some innocent picnicking students who had nothing to do with the affair. The university masters protested this outrage, since it violated the privilege that university students could be arrested or tried in civil courts only by Church authorities. They suspended classes in protest and left the city for other university centers, taking their students with them. Since the prohibitions against using Aristotle as a teaching text were limited exclusively to Paris, other universities, such as that of Toulouse, used the occasion to advertise to prospective students: "Come to our university and read Aristotle." The strike did not end until 1231, by the papal bull "Parens scientiarum." Called the "Magna Charta" of the university, this bull gave the masters the right to suspend lectures for an outrage not remedied within fifteen days and the right to make their own statutes and punish any breach thereof by excluding the offenders from the university. Another result of the strike was that the Masters of the Arts could teach Aristotle openly.

It was during this first dispersion that the beginning of the conflict between the secular and religious masters began. The friars who were not free to pick up their books and leave Paris for other campuses not only continued to teach but also threw open their schools to those secular students who could not afford to leave with their masters. After the strike was settled, the religious houses continued to keep their classes open to secular students. Though the more famous secular masters did not object at first and academic relations between seculars and friars were amicable, friction eventually developed. Generally speaking, the mendicant masters were more conscientious and diligent in preparing their lectures, and students came to prefer to study under them, thus creating financial difficulties for the secular masters, who depended on teaching fees for their livelihood. Secular masters' envy and ill-feeling towards the Franciscans and Dominicans came to a head in 1250 at the time of the second great strike. This second strike occurred during Bonaventure's graduate student days as a bachelor of theology. It was also occasioned by the death of a student in a tavern brawl in connection with the pre-Lenten carnival. The university decreed a "Cessation of Lectures," which the two Dominican doctors and the one Franciscan refused to obey. Since the cessation proved ineffectual, the university asked the masters to take an oath to insist on obtaining justice. Because an oath bound the oath taker under mortal sin and could be dispensed with only by papal power, the mendicant masters considered it unwarranted in this case, if not against the gospel exhortation to avoid oaths entirely. When they refused to take the oath, they were expelled from the masters' guild or consortium.

To prevent such occurrences in the future, the university passed a statute in April 1253 demanding that no master of any faculty be admitted to the College of Masters or fellowship of the university unless he took an oath to observe the university statutes, keep its secrets, and observe any strike it ordered. When the friars refused to honor the statute, since it had not yet been finally sealed, they were expelled and proclaimed excommunicate as having disobeyed statutes to which papal authority had been annexed. The mendicants promptly procured papal bulls requiring that they be reinstated, and the two bishops entrusted to execute the statutes without a hearing had the whole body of masters and scholars suspended from their office. The university protested, arguing that the masters' guild was a voluntary society and could therefore determine who should and who should not become a member.

The Joachimite development among the Franciscans, mentioned above, also fueled the conflict, for Gerard of Borgo San Donnino, who had written the offensive "Introduction to the Eternal Gospel," was a lector of theology in the Franciscan friary of Paris. And William of St. Amour, the leading spirit of the secular masters, violently attacked the entire mendicant movement. His work, entitled "The Perils of the Last times," portrayed the friars as the "ungodly men" whose advent the Apostle had foretold as an immediate sign of the coming of the Antichrist and the end of the world. Both Bonaventure and Aquinas had to write special treatises justifying religious poverty. Bonaventure's work, *Apologia pauperum*, is translated under the title "Defense of the Mendicants." It was Bonaventure's masterful personality and administrative ability that held the order together during this time and eventually healed the rift between the seculars and the Franciscans. As a result, he is rightly regarded as the second founder of the Franciscan order.

More than once the popes sought to use Bonaventure's talents as bishop of an important diocese, but he begged off because of his responsibilities as Minister General. However, cardinals and prelates sought his advice, and when they could not decide upon the election of a suitable pope, Bonaventure helped them choose Gregory X as a worthy successor of St. Peter. The pope upon his election sought to heal the rift between the Greek Church and the see of Rome. He decided to convene the Second Ecumenical Council of Lyons, asked for Bonaventure's help in organizing it, and commanded him under his vow of obedience to accept the position as Cardinal Bishop of Albano. Bonaventure was instrumental in getting the Greeks to attend the Council, and he preached twice at the Council, once when the ambassadors of the Greek church first came to Lyons and again when their official delegation arrived. Already in poor health, however, Bonaventure became fatally ill during the Council, and according to the "Brevis notitia" about his death, we find the following remark: "At his funeral there was much sorrow and tears, for the Lord gave this grace that all who saw him were filled with an immense love for him." His solemn obsequies were attended by the pope and the entire body of delegates, and the pope requested every priest in Christendom to say a mass for the repose of his soul.[15]

Bonaventurian Themes in Raphael's *Disupta* and *School of Athens*

Pope Julius II commissioned young Raphael to do the frescoes on the four walls of the Vatican's *Stanza della Segnatura*, so called because the most important papal documents were signed there. The four walls, as the medallions on the ceiling above them indicate, are dedicated to Theology, Justice, Philosophy, and Poetry. As the art critic Harry B. Gutman has pointed out:

Like the great cathedrals of the thirteenth century the *Stanza della Segnatura* was intended to be a *speculum mundi* and to represent the whole idea of the moral and mental world. The "Disputa," *divinarum rerum notitia*, reveals the climax of wisdom and goodness in the representation of the Beatific Vision. It shows the outpouring of the Holy Spirit according to the writings of Bonaventura. The "School of Athens," *causarum cognitio*, symbolizes human thought, the "Mount Parnassus" poetry as divine inspiration, while Justice (*jus suum cuique tribuit*) is illustrated by the transmission of the pandects and decretals, and demonstrates the two great medieval powers, the Empire and the Papacy. . . .

The predominance of Franciscan ideas in the *Stanza della Segnatura* is not at all accidental. In the time of Julius II the Franciscan philosophy had the dominant influence. The first member of the della Rovere family who became Pope, Sixtus IV, the uncle of Julius II, had been Franciscan General and a distinguished Franciscan theologian before having been elected to the papal throne. Under his reign, Julius, who fervently admired and loved his uncle, had become priest, got his Cardinalate, and had become, later on, Cardinal-Protector of the Franciscan order. The most distinguished Franciscan philosopher, Bonaventura, was sainted in 1482 during the reign of Sixtus IV. The leading Franciscan theologian of Raphael's days was the Cardinal Marco Vigerio, also of the della Rovere family, a close friend of Julius II, to whom he devoted his chief work *Decachordum Christianum* in 1507. It is possible that he gave his advice as to the decoration of the *Stanza della Segnatura*, inasmuch as he had to do with the papal residential buildings. The important rôle played by the Franciscans, especially under the two Popes named, is also shown by the number of contemporary Franciscans who were, later on, sainted.[16]

The two most striking frescoes, where the illusion of depth of a great hall is created, are the *Disupta* (representing theology) and the *School of Athens* (representing philosophy). Though both illustrate Bonaventure's ideas, his thought is especially evident in the *Disputa*.

The overriding concept in Bonaventure's *Itinerarium mentis in Deum* is that no one comes to wisdom, except through scientific knowledge, justice and grace. If the purpose of theology is to help us attain justice and grace, then scientific knowledge or philosophy in the broad sense that Aristotle understood this term is the natural basis upon which revealed knowledge builds. In his *Breviloquium* or summary of theology Bonaventure pointed out that philosophy is an integral part of theology, and in his *De reductione artium ad theologiam* he made the important point that both the manual and the liberal arts (which includes philosophy) lead step by step to theology. Ideas from all these works are apparent in the *Disputa*. Furthermore, Bonaventure himself occupies a noteworthy place on the right side of the fresco. Note that the central "rock" (or altar) in the painting, representing the Church, bears the name of Pope Julius II. The outstanding figure in the lower right side is the portrait of Julius's esteemed uncle, the Franciscan Pope Sixtus IV, who canonized St. Bonaventure, the striking figure with the brown robes and cardinal's hat beside him.

As Boehner has pointed out in his supplement to Gutman's article,[17] the entire composition of the fresco is dominated by Bonaventure's notions of theology and how it relates to philosophy and the arts and sciences. As Bonaventure's famous university sermon to the Parisian students and masters, "Christ, the One Teacher of All," made clear, Christ as the Word and Wisdom of the Father is central to all knowledge but especially to the science of theology. Bonaventure, we recall, was the only great schoolman who regarded theology's subject to be Christ, and he came under criticism from many theologians for this view. The *Disupta* clearly reflects this Christocentrism. To begin with, we see Christ at the very center of the painting, enthroned in glory, with Mary and John the Baptist on either side. But Christ is central also to the three hierarchies composing the *Disputa*. Bonaventure spelled out his conception of Christocentric theology in his *Breviloquium*. The prologue reminds us that the sublimity of Sacred Scripture, which is called Theology, layers its description of the three hierarchies symbolized in the fresco: the terrestrial or ecclesiastical hierarchy at the bottom; the celestial hierarchy in the middle; and the supercelestial hierarchy hidden at the invisible point at which the rays at the top culminate. These three hierarchies, Bonaventure tells us, are also arranged like steps leading from the lowest or most accessible to the highest, which is lost, as it were, at the very peak of the picture. But Christ is the central figure, the "medium" who brings the three internally and externally together. As *verbum increatum* he is the middle person in the supercelestial hierarchy of the divine Trinity. As *verbum incarnatum* on his throne beneath the Father he is the central figure in the celestial hierarchy. Through the Holy Ghost whom he sends into our midst to explain what he has taught, Christ is the *verbum inspiratum*.

One of Bonaventure's most characteristic doctrines was his interpretation of the Augustinian theory of illumination, in which he pointed out that divine influence from the ideas of eternal reasons in the mind of

God is essentially involved in any true form of knowledge. In almost all his important works Bonaventure connected this famous illumination theory with the epistle of St. James: "Every best gift, and every perfect gift, is from above, coming down from the Father of lights" (James 1: 17). In fact, this text forms the opening line of Bonaventure's *De reductione artium ad theologiam*. In the *Disputa* this divine illumination streams downward from the invisible Godhead, symbolized by the rays that originate in an imaginary point above the picture. It passes through the celestial hierarchy on its way to the ecclesiastical hierarchy; or, if we may borrow the triple designation Bonaventure used so often to express the manifestations of the one Word in God, this light from the uncreated word or *verbum increatum* creates the golden glow at the apex of the picture. It surrounds the incarnate word (*verbum incarnatum*) enthroned at the center of the celestial hierarchy; and through the Holy Spirit (note the position beneath, not above him) as *verbum inspiratum* he inspires the four Evangelists (four cherubic angels hold the open gospel books). The light then descends to the "symbol of faith," the Holy Eucharist in the midst of the terrestrial hierarchy. Counterbalancing this downward "emanation," as Bonaventure called it, is "reductio," or return of all human knowledge to God through theology. This was the theme of his special work *De reductione artium ad theologiam*, where he showed how, scattered though it be in the various arts and sciences, all knowledge is reunited and directed back to God through theology and leads man while still on earth to mystical union with God. In the fresco this upward trend begins with the philosophers and poets in the foreground on each side of the *Disputa* and with architecture symbolized probably by the cathedral under construction in the background of the scene. From the "arts," the return movement passes to the center of the ecclesiastical hierarchy, Christ in the Eucharist. From there it moves upward to Christ in heaven, whose hands point above to the Father, from whom all light originates. The movement ends in the golden light surrounding the invisible Godhead where all creation attains its ultimate goal.

As for the figures in the celestial hierarchy, we see the prophet Ezechiel partially concealed behind the Blessed Virgin. Bonaventure explained his vision of a wheel within a wheel as applying to the conformity between the Old and New Testaments containing the word of God. On the far left is St. Peter, head of the Church, and St. Paul, his counterpart, is on the far right; beside Peter is Adam, father of the human race; beside Paul, Apostle of the Gentiles, is Abraham, bearer of the first promises of God. All the figures in the celestial hierarchy either have been inspired by or have personally experienced the presence of God. Next to Adam is St. John, towards whom the angel with his gospel at the center is directing his gaze. Next to John is David, followed by St. Francis and the less clear figure of Ezechiel with a turbaned head; on the right, after Paul and Abraham, comes the familiar figure of St. James, whose Epistle provided the light-theme that dominates the *Disputa*. Beside James is Moses with the two tables of the law, followed by St. Stephen with his palm of martyrdom, who had seen this vision of the heavens opened to him at the time of his death. And next to him is the warrior Joshua, partially concealed like Ezechiel on the opposite side. Gutman sees Stephen and his counterpart Francis playing a symbolic role: Stephen looks upward to the ceiling of the Stanza where the fresco of Apollo and Marsyas, symbolizing martyrdom as a road to revelation, is depicted; Francis is identified by the stigmata on his left hand, symbol of his love that leads to God, and with his right hand he points downward to the fair youth guiding mankind to the Eucharist as symbol of faith, resting on the rock (with Julius' name) as the symbol of the Church.

The terrestrial hierarchy consisting of laymen, clergymen, monks, bishops, and popes is organized into three main clusters. The central group around the Eucharist is dominated by the four Fathers of the Church, each reflecting a different mode of arriving at the truth. On the left is Pope Gregory the Great, identified by the book of moral sermons at his feet and looking upward for his inspiration for what he writes. Next to him is Jerome with his translation of the Bible at his feet, absorbed by what he finds in the original text of the Scriptures in his hands. On the right side St. Ambrose in his white bishop's miter seems lost in ecstasy, enthralled with the vision of heaven; whereas St. Augustine, in possession of knowledge, is dictating to the scribe sitting before St. Bonaventure. Two other striking figures are at the immediate right and left of the rock symbol of the Church. The former, draped in ancient garb, is pointing upward to Christ in heaven; the latter, dressed as a priest, is pointing to Christ in the Eucharist. As teachers of the Fathers of the Church, they have been identified as Justin Martyr (on the right) and St. Ignatius of Antioch (on the left). Both were the apologists most closely associated with the Eucharist. Ignatius, who first used that term, held the foreground of interest in Raphael's day, because the genuineness of his letters, defended by the Church, were doubted by a group who eventually embraced Calvinism. Justin Martyr, in his first Apology (I, xvi, 2), formulated the doctrine of the real presence in the following words: "In the same way that through the power of God Jesus Christ our Savior took flesh and blood for our salvation, so the nourishment consummated by the prayer formed of the words of Christ . . . is the flesh and blood of this incarnate Jesus." The Franciscan friar kneeling before St. Jerome is Nicholas of Lyra, successor to St. Jerome as a commentator on the Scriptures. His "Postillae perpetuae in universe biblie" was the authoritative commentary in Raphael's day. Between Ignatius and St. Ambrose is the head of a friar, whom Vasari hints is the Subtle Doctor, John Duns Scotus, since it shows some resemblance to other representations of him.

The group on the right side is dominated by the central figure of Pope Sixtus IV, referred to above. On his left is another papal figure, which Gutman identifies as Sixtus I, patron of Sixtus IV. Sixtus I is flanked by St. Thomas, the figure in black on his right (the Dominicans because of their outer cloak were known as the "blackfriars"), and St. Bonaventure on his left. Behind Sixtus IV is the poet with the crown of laurel, usually identified as Dante. And the blackfriar with the white locks is the Dominican Savonarola. An ideal figure in blue and gold calls attention to Sixtus IV with one hand and looks back to the builder. Gutman sees the latter as

associated with the architectonical structure in the background, which is contrasted, on the left side, by the friendly landscape of a green hill and trees, cultivated by industrious people. We see there a small house, and another building, not much larger, in the process of construction. On the right side, however, the building under construction reveals powerful forms. From the

square stones, which are already in evidence in the group of theologians of the
School of Athens, a temple of God is to be built, the temple of the Church, the
terrestrial Jerusalem, a work of knowledge and wisdom. We may not be wrong
if we see here an allusion to the already planned erection of St. Peter's.[18]

Gutman describes the third group as follows:

On the left side, mankind is guided to knowledge and truth. A tall figure, in
antique raiment, with books at his feet, forms the pivot of the whole assembly.
He represents a sage and writer of antiquity calling attention to the books
before the altar. If we wish to identify him we should think of a personality
such as Boethius. Behind him a group of young men prostrate themselves before the altar. In the background groups of monks and clergy are visible. The
only group which seems to be really engaged in a dispute is that of the laymen
at the extreme left side. The youthful guide refers them to the altar as the final
answer.[19]

The Dominican in black at the extreme left has been identified as Fra
Angelico. The figure with the book is Bramante, and the ideal figure of
the youthful guide is Francesco Maria della Rovere, who is also painted
as St. John in the *School of Athens*.

Let us turn now to the other great fresco in the *Stanza della
Segnatura*. As Gutman has pointed out:

Few works of art have been so differently interpreted by their commentators
as Raphael's "School of Athens." Since the seventeenth century the famous
fresco has usually been considered to be a triumphant representation of worldly
science and philosophy, strictly separated from theology, represented in the
opposite fresco of the "Disputa. . . ."

According to Vasari the picture shows "theologians engaged in the reconciliation of Philosophy and Astrology with Theology. In the work all the sages
of the world are depicted, arranged in different groups, and occupied with various disputations. There are certain astrologers standing apart who have made
figures and characters of geomancy and astrology, on tablets which they send
by beautiful angels to the evangelists who explain them. . . . St. Matthew is
copying the characters from the tablet which an angel holds before him, and
setting them down in a book."[20]

Gutman goes on to show that with the exception of Borghini[21] almost all the later interpreters ignored Vasari's report, to their own confusion, and he goes on to prove that Vasari, who was nine years old when Raphael died in 1520, is the only commentator who can be considered a contemporary and who had the opportunity to meet friends and pupils of the master for information. Not only should he be accepted, therefore, as a relatively trustworthy source but also his interpretation alone makes sense of this composition.[22]

The two central figures in the *School of Athens* are Plato, the older man on the left pointing upward to the heavens, and Aristotle, his younger pupil on the right pointing downwards to the world about him. We find the explanation of these two in Bonaventure's university sermon to the Parisian students and Masters: "Christ, the One Teacher of All." There he points out that Plato looked above, relating all certain knowledge to his archetypal Ideas (i.e., the ideal world with its eternal laws), and for this way of wisdom he was justly praised by Augustine. But "he destroyed the way of science which proceeds according to created reasons. Aristotle, in contrast, provided a firm foundation for the way of science while neglecting the world above. "It seems, therefore, that among the philosophers, the word of wisdom is to be granted to Plato and the word of science to Aristotle. For the former looked above all at the higher realities, while the latter looked principally to the lower things." It was only Augustine, depicted in the *Disputa*, who had been given "through the Holy Spirit . . . both the word of science and that of wisdom as an outstanding expositor of the whole of Scripture."

Gutman points out that Bellori made the mistake of identifying the man who sits in the left foreground, Vasari's St. Matthew, with Pythagoras, because he recognized the signs on the tablet before him as Pythagorean. However, Nicholas of Cusa, whose writings were highly regarded in Raphael's time, had shown that the foundations of all knowledge and wisdom were symbolized by the three quarternari: sense knowledge by $100 + 200 + 300 + 400$; lower reason (which is science of the world) by $10 + 20 + 30 + 40$; and higher or theological reason by $1 + 2 + 3 + 4 = 10$, the sign on Matthew's tablet. The true Pythagoras is the tall stately bearded figure on the right, who points down to the globe of the heavens held by Zoroaster and that of the earth held by

Ptolemy. Pythagoras, as well as Zoroaster and Ptolemy, enjoyed in Raphael's time the reputation of an astrologer, and thus we can understand why Vasari speaks of geomancers and astrologers. Pythagoras is looking over in the direction of St. Matthew on the opposite side, to whom he has sent his tablet to be interpreted. Peering over Matthew's left shoulder is the turbaned figure of Averroes, the great Muslim philosopher and commentator on Aristotle, and looking over the other shoulder is the Jewish philosopher Maimonides. The standing figure in white on Matthew's left is the portrait of Francesco Maria Della Rovere, representing St. John, with Mark holding his gospel, and Luke sitting down writing (the latter has the features of Michelangelo).

Having identified the group on the left as evangelists, Gutman finds it easy to interpret the other groups of the painting.

> Raphael follows exactly the doctrines of the medieval Franciscan philosophy. He differentiates between the natural and the rational sciences quite in the sense of the Franciscans. Their classification issued from Bonaventura who subdivided the natural sciences into Mathematics, Physics, and Metaphysics, and the rational sciences into Grammar, Logic, and Rhetoric.[23] We see, accordingly, at the right side Euclid and his group as representatives of Mathematics, Ptolemy and Zoroaster with their globes as representatives of Physics, and, on the higher level, the metaphysicians. The high and lonely figure [of Pythagoras] under the statue of Athena is of special compositional importance. . . . He connects the lower with the higher groups by the gesture of his hand pointing at the globe in the hands of Zoroaster. But he is also connected with the group of theologians by the direction of his gaze. . . . It is possible to recognize other metaphysicians too, for instance, Empedocles, the old priestlike man with the walking staff.
>
> On the left side we see, on the higher level, the logicians and rhetoricians. Among others we see Socrates (one of the few figures of the painting that can be derived from older representations of this thinker) explaining something to his attentive listeners, among whom the martial figure of Alcibiades (or Xenophon?) is conspicuous."[24]

Other figures that Vasari has identified include Diogenes, the half naked figure sitting on the steps below Aristotle, and the self-portrait of Raphael and Sodoma at the extreme lower right of the fresco.

Conclusion

In this essay I have only touched on a few of the first famous schoolmen among the Franciscans and said nothing of Adam Marsh, Matthew of Aquasparta, John Peckham, Roger Bacon, Richard of Mediavilla, Peter Olivi, Vital du Four, or William of Ware, or even of outstanding and independent thinkers of the fourteenth century such as John Duns Scotus, William of Ockham, Peter Aurioli, and Adam Wodam. The reason for devoting so much attention to Bonaventure, however, should be apparent. Not only is he justly considered the second founder of the Franciscan order but also, as a Doctor of the Universal Church, he ranks with St. Thomas Aquinas, the great Dominican schooman, as several popes have pointed out.[25]

Several of the lecturers in the series on Franciscanism from which this essay developed alluded to the fact that while the followers of Francis in general may have possessed certain features in common, by and large they were individuals, each with merits of their own. In a famous and oft-cited incident—recorded only in the *Mirror of Perfection*—Francis was asked to describe the perfect friar. He went on to say that the perfect friar should have the faith and poverty of Br. Bernard, the simplicity and purity of Br. Leo, the courtesy of Br. Angelo, the good sense of Br. Masseo, the mind upraised to God of Br. Giles, the prayer of Br. Rufino, the patience of Br. Juniper, etc.

We might say the same of the Franciscan schoolmen. By and large they were individuals with their own ideas. Rather than attempting to characterize the Franciscan intellectual movement by any set of particular doctrines, it might be better to designate it, as Boehner has in his "The Spirit of Franciscan Philosophy,"[26] as being "critical, scientific and progressive." While the great Franciscan thinkers respected and often shared ideas in common, they were not loath to criticize or differ from those notions of their predecessors which they did not find true. As Maurice O'Fihely (Mauritius à Portu) explained, what prompted William of Ockham's criticism of John Duns Scotus, whom he obviously admired and from whom he borrowed so many of his doctrines, was not as much an attempt to disparage the Subtle Doctor as it was the rigorous quest for truth that spared no one.[27]

Part of this individuality, characteristic of Franciscans generally, stems from the fact that Francis never had any preconceived ideas of establishing an order to begin with (as he put it: "The Lord gave me brothers . . ."), much less a specific type of order geared to a particular ministry. When it became evident to him that he needed a rule of sorts he gave his brothers the Gospel, which is as broad as Christianity itself. Bonaventure noted this fact in his famous letter to an unknown Parisian Master of Arts explaining why the friars came to be known as a "study order":

> You should not be disturbed over the fact that in the beginning the Friars were simple and unlettered. This ought rather to strengthen the more your faith in the Order. I confess before God, that this is what has made me love so deeply the life of the Blessed Francis, that it is like the beginning and perfection of the Church, which first began with simple fishermen and afterwards progressed to such brilliant and learned doctors.
>
> You will find the same thing in the religion of the Blessed Francis, that God may show thereby that is was not effected through the prudence of men but through Christ. And as the works of Christ do not become less but grow, this work is proved to be of God, since learned men have not disdained to join themselves to the company of simple men but have heeded the Apostle: "If any one of you thinks himself wise, let him become a fool that he may come to be wise."[28]

Notes

This essay was originally delivered as one of the lectures sponsored by the Santa Barbara Mission Archive-Library to commemorate the 7th centenary of the birth of St. Francis.

1. John F. Wippel and Allan B. Wolter, *Medieval Philosophy: From St. Augustine to Nicholas of Cusa* (New York: Free Press, 1969), p. 6.

2. Hastings Rashdall, *The Universities of Europe in the Middle Ages*, ed. Frederick M. Powicke and Alfred B. Emden, 3 vols. (1936; Oxford: Oxford University Press, 1942).

3. William Turner, *History of Philosophy* (Boston: Ginn and Co., 1929), p. 319: "There were three events which more than any others influenced the development of Christian

thought at the beginning of the thirteenth century: the introduction of the works of Aristotle, the rise of the universities and the foundation of the mendicant orders."

4. Fernand van Steenberghen, *The Philosophical Movement in the Thirteenth Century* (Edinburgh: Nelson, 1955).

5. Fernand van Steenberghen, *Aristotle in the West: The Origins of Latin Aristotelianism* (Louvain: E. Nauwelaerts, 1955).

6. See chapter 9 of the Rule of 1223 in *St. Francis of Assissi: Writings and Early Biographies: English Omnibus of the Sources for the Life of St. Francis*, ed. Marion A. Habig (Chicago: Franciscan Herald Press, 1973), p. 63.

7. Philotheus Boehner in one of his summer courses given at the Franciscan Institute of St. Bonaventure University was wont to stress that the Franciscan order had become an *ordo studens* or "order devoted to studies" by force of a development within the order and in the Church and by the express wish of the popes. Together with the Dominicans, the Friars Minor were destined to be a stronghold of the Church at the center of studies in Paris. Hence Bonaventure obeyed his own vocation, as a Franciscan and a Doctor, answering the needs not only of his own personality but also of the order and the Church. By so doing he did not sacrifice anything worthwhile but saved the order. In one of Bonaventure's evening conferences on the "Six Days of Creation," said Boehner, the saint set forth, in a few lines impregnated with his seraphic spirit, a clear definition not only of his own task as a university professor but also that of the order as *ordo studens* in distinction to the Dominican order, the other *ordo studens*. The Dominicans and the Franciscans, Bonaventure declares, hold in the earthly or ecclesiastical hierarchy the place corresponding to the cherubim in the ecclesiastical hierarchy. Both have learning or intellectual speculation as their special task. The difference, however, between the two orders lies in that the Dominicans emphasize more speculation than unction; the Franciscans emphasize more unction than "deep spiritual feeling." Bonaventure wrote: "The second way in which an order tends [to contemplate God] is by means of intellectual contemplation, that is, the speculative way. Such are those who engage in examination of Scripture, which only purified minds understand. For you cannot grasp the words of Paul unless you have the spirit of Paul: wherefore it is necessary that you be sequestered with Moses in the desert and climb the mountain. To these, the Cherubim correspond. These are the Preachers and the Minors.   The first strive mainly for speculation—from which they receive their name—and afterwards for unction. The second strive mainly for unction and then for speculation. And would that this love or unction be no less than that of the Cherubim. . . . Blessed Francis said he wanted his friars to study, so long as they first practiced what they preached. For of what use is learning if

you do not taste it"; St. Bonaventure, *Collationes in Hexaemeron*, ed. Ferdinandus Delorme, 22.21; *Opera omnia*, 15 vols. (Quaracchi: Ad Claras Aquas, 1934), 5: 440.

8. "It was Francis's first biographer, Thomas of Celano, who made mention of a letter that Francis wrote to St. Anthony which began, 'To Brother Anthony, my bishop.' . . . That Francis wrote a letter to St. Anthony, therefore is certain. But the authenticity of the text of the letter as it has been handed down is often called in to question"; *St. Francis of Assisi: Writings and Early Biographies*, pp. 163–64. For the Latin version in the *Chronica XXIV Generalium* see Analecta Franciscana 3 (Quaracchi: Typographia Collegii S. Bonaventurae, 1897), p. 132.

9. "Fuit etiam beatus Antonius a beato Francisco plurimum dilectus; unde sanctus Franciscus eum episcopum suum vocabat propter reverentiam magnam, quam ad eum habebat"; *De conformitate vitae beati Francisci ad vitam Domini Jesu*, I, fructus 8, pars 2, Analecta Franciscana 4 (Quaracchi: Typographia Collegii S. Bonaventurae, 1906), p. 270.

10. "Nam finis studii fratris Minoris est studere in sacra pagina, ut de ipsa fidem defensare et populum sciat informare"; *De conformitate*, I, fr. 9, pars 2, Analecta Franciscana 4, p. 560.

11. *Monumenta Franciscana*, ed. J. S. Brewer, I, xliii; quoted by Heribert Holzapfel, *The History of the Franciscan Order*, trans. Antonine Tibesar and Gervase Brinkmann (Teutopolis, Ill.: St. Joseph Seminary, 1948), p. 216.

12. Hilarin Felder, *Geschichte der wissenschaftlichen Studien im Franziskanerorden bis um die Mitte des 13. Jahrhunderts* (Freiburg im Breisgau: Herder, 1904), p. 123.

13. Aquilinus Emmen, "Alexander of Hales" in *New Catholic Encyclopedia*, 18 vols. (New York: McGraw-Hill, 1967), 1: 296–97.

14. Felder, *Geschichte*, p. 254; for a list of the Franciscan lectors at Oxford see Analecta Franciscana 4, p. 270.

15. For a summary of Bonaventure's philosophy see my article "Bonaventure" in *The Encyclopedia of Philosophy*, ed. Paul Edwards, 8 vols. (New York: Macmillan, 1967), 1: 339–44; for a good historical account see Ignatius Brady, "Bonaventure, St." in the *New Catholic Encyclopedia*, 2: 658–64.

16. Harry B. Gutman, "The Medieval Content of Raphael's 'School of Athens'," *Journal of the History of Ideas* 2 (1941), 420–29, here 427–29.

17. Harry B. Gutman, "Raphael's Disputa," *Franciscan Studies* 2/1 (1942), 35–43, with Boehner's additional remarks pp. 44–48.

18. Gutman, "Raphael's Disputa," pp. 42–43.

19. Gutman, "Raphael's Disputa," p. 42.

20. Gutman, "The Medieval Content of Raphael's 'School of Athens'," p. 420.

21. *Il Riposo* (Florence, 1584) (quoted by Gutman, "The Medieval Content," p. 420).

22. Gutman, "The Medieval Content"; see also his "Franciscan Interpretation of Raphael's 'School of Athens'," *Archivum Franciscanum Historicum* 34 (1941), 3–12.

23. This is a reference to St. Bonaventura, *De Reductione Artium ad Theologiam*, ed. Collegium a S. Bonaventura ad Claras Aquas, 1882–1902, vol. 5, pp. 319–25.

24. Gutman, "The Medieval Content of Raphael's 'School of Athens'," pp. 424–25.

25. Pope Sixtus V said of these two doctors: "By the Divine gift of him, who alone gives the spirit of knowledge and wisdom and understanding, and who, through the ages, according to her needs enriches his Church with new gifts, surrounds her with new safeguards, our ancestors, being men exceedingly wise, developed the study of scholastic theology. There were especially two glorious doctors, teachers of this famous science, that is, the angelic St. Thomas and the seraphic St. Bonaventure. With surpassing abilities, with ceaseless study, with laborious toil and long watchings, they worked it out and adorned it. They arranged it in the very best way, unfolded it brilliantly in many methods and then handed it on to their successors"; quoted by Leo XIII in his encyclical *Aeterni patris*.

26. Boehner, "The Spirit of Franciscan Philosophy," *Franciscan Studies* 2 (1942), 217–37.

27. "Forte etiam non in vituperium Doctoris, quem suum et religionis et subtilem plerumque nominat, scripsit, sed rigore Minorum qui nemini parcunt, synteresi et conscientia sibi appropriatis, moti cunctos ingenii elevatione et indagine, salve pace aliorum dixerim, transcendentes, usus est. Sed quomodocumque fecerit, aurum purgavit quoties in fornace examinans rigorosi verba Scotica commovit"; "Annotationes," in ch. 3 of *De primo rerum principio*, ed. Vivès, t. IV (Paris, 1891), p. 762.

28. See my article in *The Cord: A Franciscan Spiritual Review* 5 (1955), 224–35.

Contributors

Richard C. Dales, Department of History,
  University of California,
  Los Angeles, CA 90087

Nancy Van Deusen, Faculty of Music,
  The Claremont Graduate School,
  Claremont, CA 91711

Barnabas B. Hughes, O.F.M., School of Education,
  California State University, Northridge,
  Northridge, CA 91330

Gary Macy, Department of Religious Studies,
  University of San Diego, Alcala Park,
  San Diego, CA 92110

Nancy Spatz, Department of History,
  University of Northern Colorado,
  Greeley, CO 80639

Leland Wilshire, Department of History,
  Biola University, 13600 Biola Avenue,
  La Mirada, CA 90039

Richard C. Wingell, School of Music,
  University of Southern California,
  Los Angeles, CA 90089

Allan B. Wolter, O.F.M., Old Mission,
  Santa Barbara, CA 93105